MW00444171

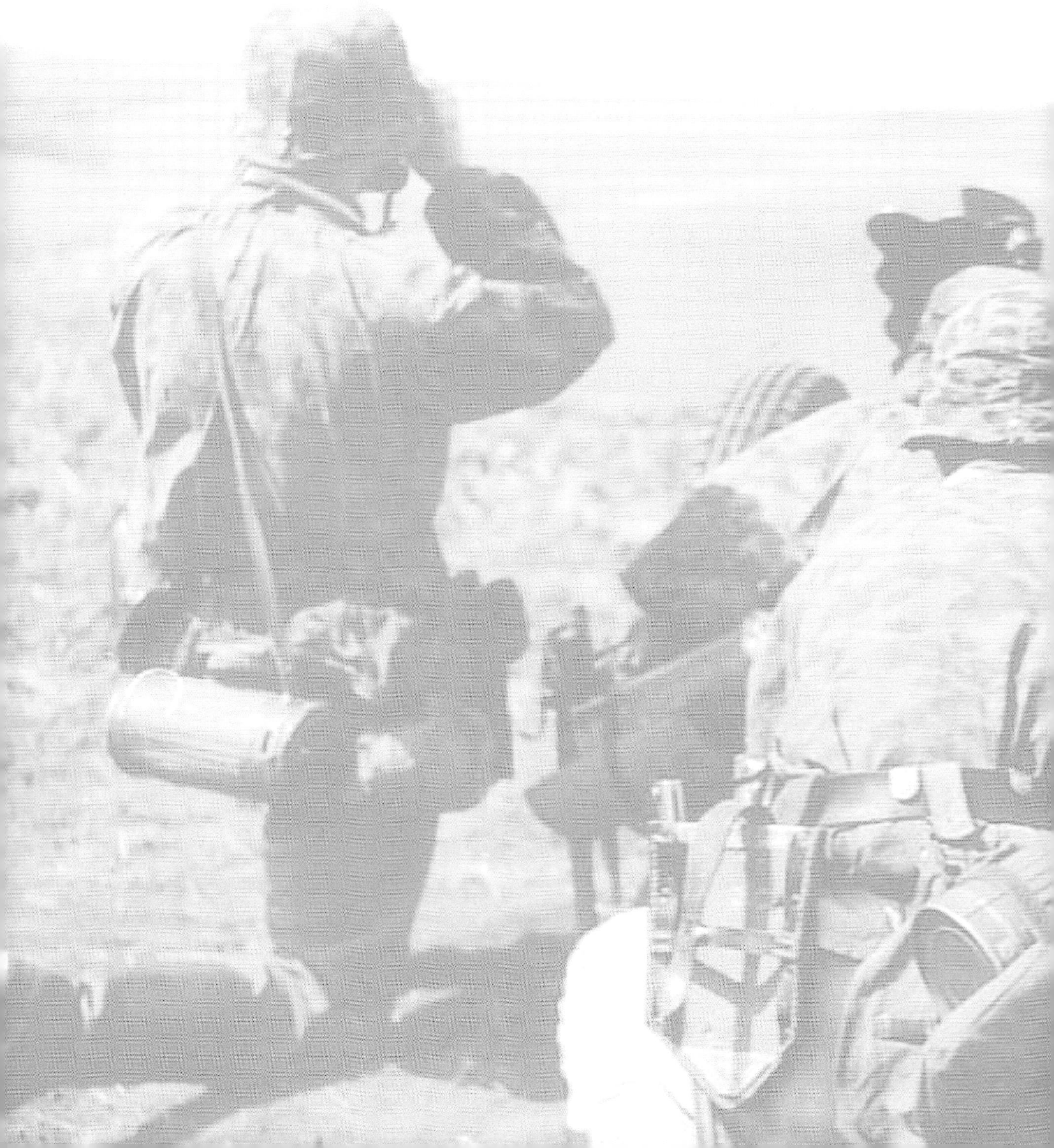

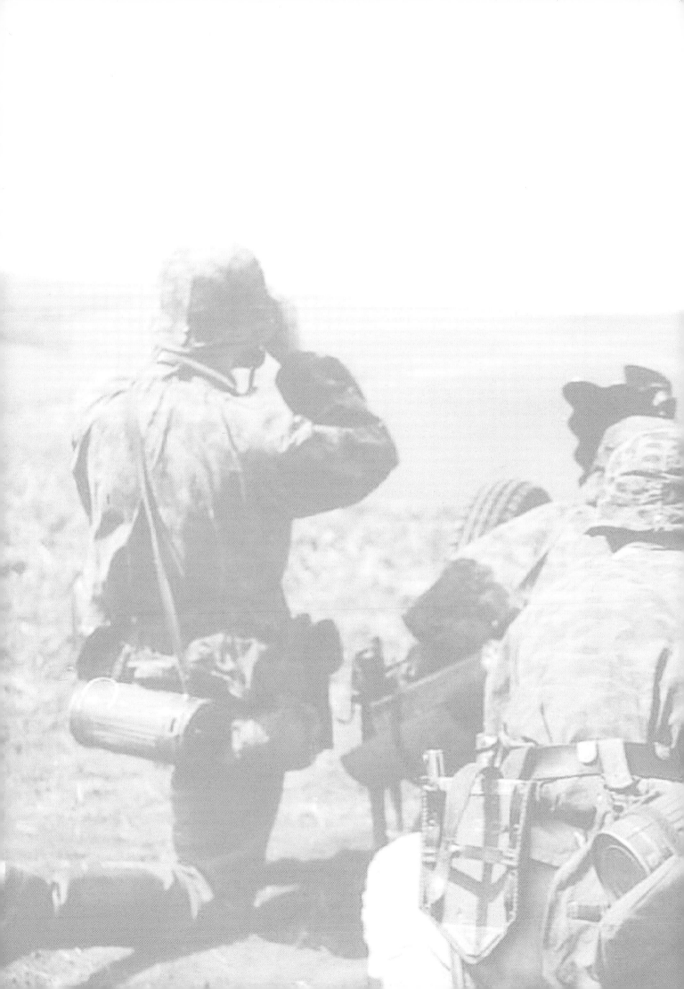

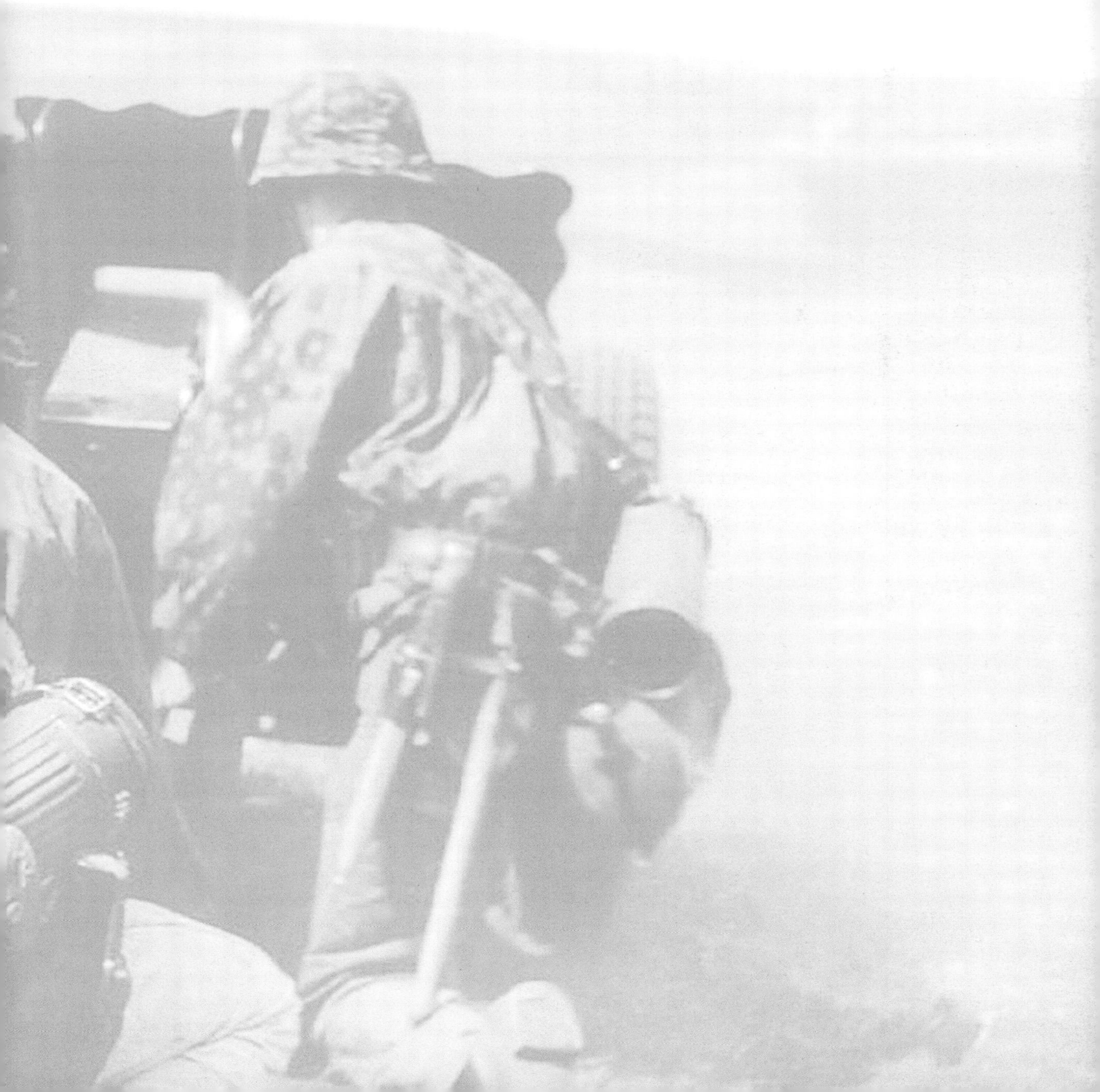

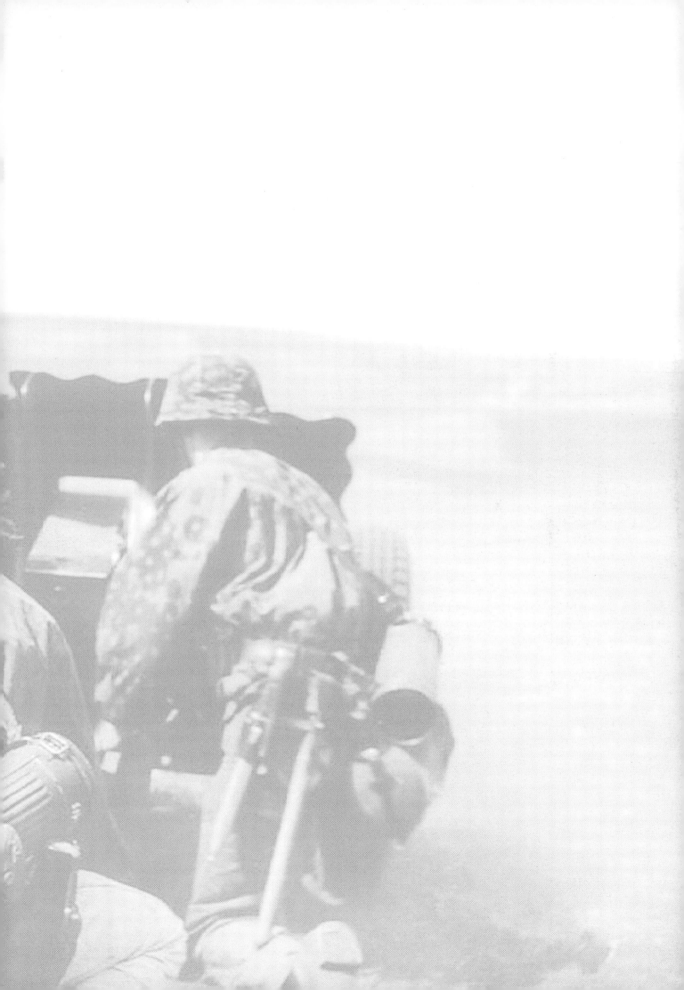

WAFFEN-SS
HANDBOOK
1933–1945

WAFFEN-SS
HANDBOOK
1933–1945

GORDON WILLIAMSON

SUTTON PUBLISHING

First published in the United Kingdom in 2003 by
Sutton Publishing Limited · Phoenix Mill
Thrupp · Stroud · Gloucestershire · GL5 2BU

Copyright © Gordon Williamson, 2003

Paperback edition first published in 2005

All rights reserved. No part of this publication may be reproduced, stored in a retrieval system, or transmitted, in any form or by any means, electronic, mechanical, photocopying, recording or otherwise, without the prior permission of the publisher and copyright holder.

Gordon Williamson has asserted the moral right to be identified as the author of this work.

British Library Cataloguing in Publication Data
A catalogue record for this book is available from the British Library.

ISBN 0 7509 3911 7

Endpapers, front: *Waffen-SS* artillerymen with the 7.5 cm *Leichte Infanterie Geschütze*. *Back*: A *Waffen-SS* panzer unit bury their dead.

Typeset in 10/13 pt New Baskerville.
Typesetting and origination by
Sutton Publishing Limited.
Printed in Great Britain by
J.H. Haynes & Co. Ltd, Sparkford.

CONTENTS

INTRODUCTION AND ACKNOWLEDGEMENTS

Few military forces in history have generated as much interest as Germany's *Waffen-SS*. Whether that interest is expressed in the form of admiration for its military accomplishments or opprobrium for the atrocities committed by it, feelings still run high almost sixty years after its last few soldiers, their *Führer* dead and his 'Thousand-Year Reich' reduced to ashes, laid down their arms and surrendered to the victorious Allies.

In the years since the end of the First World War, countless books have been written on the subject of the *Waffen-SS*. These have ranged from extremely negative works concentrating almost exclusively on atrocities, both alleged and real, committed by *Waffen-SS* soldiers, and the corrupt and evil nature of the regime they served, to unabashed 'whitewashes' which would have the reader believe that no *Waffen-SS* man would ever have been so ignoble as to have even considered committing the sort of crimes of which they were accused.

As is inevitably the case with such emotive subjects, the truth lies somewhere in between these two diametrically opposed viewpoints. Certainly, many heinous war crimes were committed by those wearing the uniform of the *Waffen-SS*, and even though many of these atrocities were committed in the heat of battle (and anyone wishing to carry out the research will soon find ample evidence of battlefield atrocities carried out

by *all* of the combatant nations in the Second World War), this can only in some small way *explain*, but in no way *excuse*, them. It must also be said, however, that if many *Waffen-SS* soldiers may be rightly accused of unacceptable behaviour, then just as many must be recognised as acting with incredible bravery and self-sacrifice on the field of battle. Towards the end of the war, the majority of even the most hard-bitten *Waffen-SS* men in the so-called 'classic' SS divisions had lost their faith in Hitler and National Socialism, yet continued to fight on with determination when all around them were surrendering or fleeing. By then, most were fighting out of loyalty, not to their political masters, but to their comrades in arms, and from the intense pride they felt for their individual units, which had invariably earned enviable reputations for gallantry and dependability even in the face of overwhelming odds.

The *Waffen-SS* will probably always remain somewhat of an enigma, reviled for its many cruelties and for the regime it represented, yet possessed of many values (comradeship, loyalty, gallantry, dependability) which, though they may have been perverted by being exercised in the service of an evil regime, are still attributes to which many would aspire.

This book is intended as a general handbook on the subject of the *Waffen-SS*, and as such will restrict itself to factual information. For those who wish to study the sociological aspects of this organisation, there is no shortage of in-depth study material available. It would take a large multi-volume set to cover every aspect of the *Waffen-SS*, and countless books already exist which study it from almost every conceivable viewpoint. This work will therefore restrict itself to providing an overview of some of the most important points relating to the purely military function of Hitler's 'Praetorian Guard'. For those who wish to study the subject further, some of the most useful references available are listed in the Bibliography.

Similarly, because of constraints on space, it would be impossible to provide extensive and detailed coverage of the very many individual battles in which troops of the *Waffen-SS* were involved.

Once again, countless existing works cover this information in considerable detail; a selection of these is listed in the Bibliography.

I should particularly like to thank the following for their kind contributions of both information and photographic material: Herr Robert Noss, the owner of a huge collection of original wartime photographic material, a selection of which may be viewed at his excellent web-site http://www.photosammler.de; and Gary Wood, noted English collector of military ephemera and photographic material.

Wartime photographs and photographs of surviving original militaria used in this work have been sourced from Robert Noss, Gary Wood, Josef Charita, Jamie Cross, S. Nielsen, Mark Miller, H. Schumann, Bernie Brule and the author's collection.

CHAPTER ONE

GENERAL HISTORICAL BACKGROUND

The origins of the SS lie right back at the genesis of the Nazi movement in Germany in 1923. These were turbulent times, and few then would have been willing to bet on the outcome of the struggle for domination of Germany between the Nazis and the Communists. The two sides often battled violently in the streets, and injuries and deaths were far from uncommon. It was clear that some form of bodyguard element was required to protect those who spoke at Nazi outdoor meetings. The SA Stormtroopers, the *Sturmabteilung*, or 'Brownshirts', were little more than an unruly rabble, most of them unemployed thugs with no real loyalty to Hitler, but useful for meeting the opposing Communists head on in countless violent street fights while, in the main, being by no means trustworthy or disciplined enough to provide reliable bodyguards for the Party leadership.

Hitler, however, had been impressed by the performance of at least some of his 'minders', and in March 1923 he decided to form an elite, dedicated bodyguard unit from a number of such dependable comrades. The task of forming this trusted band was delegated to his faithful chauffeur, Julius Schreck, and another trusted follower, Josef Berchtold. To begin with, this group was simply a small detachment within the SA, and was known as the *Stabswache*, or Headquarter Guard. Within a few weeks it had been expanded and took on the name *Stosstrupp Adolf Hitler*. This so-called 'Shock Troop' took part in the abortive Munich Putsch of 9 November 1923, providing personal protection for Hitler. On Hitler's release from Landsberg Prison following the abortive Putsch, he decided to re-form his bodyguard, and once again turned to Julius Schreck to create this new unit. Initially, it consisted of just eight chosen men, and thanks to Hermann Göring was given the title of *Schutz Staffel*, or 'Protection Squad'. This was a reference to Göring's highly successful career as a fighter pilot during the First World War, when this title was used for aircraft allocated to flying escort duties.

It was intended that the *Schutz Staffel*, which rapidly became known by its abbreviated form 'SS', would not exceed ten men plus one officer in each district, the exception to this being the Reich's capital city, Berlin, where the SS detachment was to be double the normal size.

The elite status of the SS was enhanced by the extremely high standards of physical fitness and general appearance of those

An enlisted *SS-Mann* from *SS-Standarte Deutschland*, wearing the black pre-war service dress also worn by the *Allgemeine-SS*. Note the '1' alongside the SS runes on the collar tab. No *Allgemeine-SS* units wore the SS runes. The helmet being worn is of First World War vintage, with large runic symbols within a circular border on the right side. A brown shirt is worn with black tie.

recruited to its ranks, but most importantly, by the fact that its owed its allegiance, not to the Party, but to the person of Adolf Hitler himself.

In April 1926, Schreck relinquished command of the SS to another of Hitler's most loyal followers, Josef Berchtold, who had by this time recovered from wounds he had received marching by Hitler's side during the Munich Putsch. The general ranks of the brownshirt army, the SA, were highly suspicious and resentful of this new elite unit which appeared in their midst, the

SS still at this time being subordinate to the SA. This resentment grew when Hitler entrusted the care of the so-called *'Blutfahne'*, a Nazi flag splattered with the blood of those marchers killed or wounded during the Putsch, and which had, to the Nazis, acquired the status almost of a holy relic, to the SS. The SA had previously cared for the *Blutfahne*.

The situation was far from ideal, with the SA's resentment matched by the SS's rancour by reason of its subordination to the SA. SS units in any area were eventually restricted to a maximum of 10 per cent of the size of the SA contingent, and this only when the SA unit to which it was subordinated actually reached its full, allocated strength. The SA therefore found it easy to manipulate the size of SS units over which it had control, many SA units also taking great delight in allocating the most menial task to their SS contingents.

Resentful of the restrictions placed on the development of the SS, Berchtold resigned, command passing to his deputy, Erhardt Heiden. Heiden, unfortunately, had no more success than Berchtold in circumventing the spiteful machinations of the SA, and he too lasted for only a short time as commander of the SS before he resigned. The SA no doubt took great pleasure in this, and anticipated just as easily manipulating his successor. In this they were to be greatly mistaken. Heiden's successor was another veteran of the Munich Putsch, one Heinrich Himmler. Though his appearance was far from impressive, with his pince-nez spectacles and rather weedy turnout, Himmler was a superb organiser and was fired with enthusiasm for, and dedication to, the success of the SS. In 1928 he was appointed *Reichsführer-SS*.

By 1929 Himmler had persuaded Hitler to approve a recruitment plan for the SS, and within a year it had grown in strength to around one thousand men, although still subordinated to the SA. In 1931 there occurred an incident which was to greatly enhance the status of the SS in the eyes of Hitler. The Berlin SA had been growing resentful of what it saw as Hitler's favouritism towards the Bavarian SA, based in Munich, which was of course the 'spiritual home' of Nazism. On 1 April, the SS in Berlin alerted Hitler to the fact that the SA leader, *Oberführer* Walther Stennes, had revolted and occupied the premises of the Nazi newspaper *Der Angriff*, published by the *Gauleiter* of Berlin, Josef Goebbels, and had evicted the Nazi propaganda chief. In the event, however, the revolt quickly fizzled out through lack of support, and the rebel SA members were quickly purged. Hitler was greatly appreciative that the SS had remained loyal during this potentially dangerous episode and publicly congratulated them. Himmler's reward was to be appointed as Head of Party Security. From this position of power, Himmler set about expanding his nascent SS empire, so that by the end of 1932 it had grown in strength to some 50,000 men.

By this time, life in Germany had deteriorated into a situation of near total anarchy, with armed Nazis and Communists battling in the streets. Hitler's promises of full employment and a return of law and order swung the votes in the 1933 elections in his favour, and on 30 January *Reichspräsident* von Hindenburg appointed Hitler to the office of Chancellor. Within a month, the Reichstag building was gutted in an arson attack, for which the Communists were blamed, and Hitler lost no time in issuing a proclamation granting police powers to the SA and the SS. This resulted in over 15,000 SS men being sworn in as police 'auxiliaries', and the round-up of political opponents began.

The original SS was required to provide security for the Party hierarchy in general, but at this point Hitler decided to form a special armed bodyguard unit from within the ranks of the SS whose purpose would be to provide him personally with a protective escort. The task of raising this 'elite within an elite' was given to one of his most trusted friends, the Bavarian *SS-Gruppenführer*, Josef 'Sepp' Dietrich. Dietrich, a decorated combat veteran of the First World War, set to work immediately, and by March 1933 had established a guard unit of some 120 hand-picked men which was to become known as the *SS-Stabswache Berlin*. In late April, this guard unit moved into the old Officer Cadet Institute at Berlin-Lichterfelde. Within just two months it was undergoing expansion, and the enlarged unit was renamed as the *SS-Sonderkommando Zossen*.

A further special guard element known as *SS-Sonderkommando Jüterbog* was formed in May, interestingly, with a number of attached Army officers to assist with training, and in September both were brought together to form the *Adolf Hitler Standarte*, each member of the unit being issued with a cuffband bearing Hitler's name. From July to October of 1933, these elite SS guards provided security at Hitler's retreat at the Obersalzberg, near Berchtesgaden in Bavaria.

On 9 November 1933, on the tenth anniversary of the Munich Putsch, this regiment took a personal oath of fealty to Adolf Hitler and had its name amended to *Leibstandarte SS Adolf Hitler*, once again emphasising its unique elite status. (The *Leib-Hussaren*, *Leib-Standarte*, of Imperial Germany were the direct equivalent of the 'Life Guards' in other nations such as Great Britain, traditionally entrusted with the safety of the monarch or head of State.)

The wording of the oath was as follows:

I swear to you, Adolf Hitler, as leader and Chancellor of the German nation, loyalty and courage. I vow to you and to the superiors appointed to you, obedience unto death, so help me God.

The similarities between the Praetorian Guard of Roman times and Hitler's new SS Elite Guard are too obvious to be coincidental.

Pre-war officer's black service dress. Note the aluminium chin cords worn by officer ranks and the officer's circular belt buckle. Just visible on the right sleeve is the so-called 'Alte Kämpfer' chevron, worn by those who joined the SS prior to 30 January 1933.

The recruitment criteria for this unit were extremely selective. Applicants had to be between seventeen and twenty-two years of age, a minimum of 5 ft 11 in tall, later raised to 6 ft ¼ in, and in perfect physical health.

Shortly thereafter, the unit terminology of the *Allgemeine-SS*, the *Schar*, *Sturm* and *Sturmbann*, began to be replaced by the equivalent military terms, such as *Zug* (Platoon), *Kompanie* (Company) and *Bataillon* (Battalion) as used in the *Wehrmacht*, further enhancing the military status of the armed SS.

Around this time, a number of other small, armed detachments were being created at *SS-Abschnitt* level throughout Germany. Limited to a size of 100 men (the police also raised several such quasi-military units, known as '*Hundertschaften*') and in critical areas, these units were brought together to form the so-called *Politische Bereitschaften*. On 24 September 1934, Hitler decreed that the *Politische Bereitschaften* be brought together to form a new armed SS force to be known as the *SS-Verfügungstruppe*.

In March 1933, Himmler had been appointed Police President of Munich and founded the first concentration camp at Dachau. This was rapidly joined by others at Buchenwald and Sachsenhausen. These, though thoroughly unpleasant places, were worlds apart from the death camps established later during the Holocaust. It was intended that potential enemies of the State who were considered dangerous but who had not been found guilty in court of any specific crime would be detained in these camps for 're-education'. Indeed, though treatment was often brutal, many were subsequently released when no longer considered a threat, a luxury of course not available to later inmates. It was around this time that the first of the *Wachverbände*, or Guard Units, were formed to staff these camps under the command of *SS-Oberführer* Theodor Eicke. By 1935, five full battalions, or *Wachsturmbanne*, of these troops had been formed – *Oberbayern* (at Dachau), *Elbe* (at Lichtenburg), *Sachsen* (at Sachsenburg), *Ostfriesland* (at Esterwegen) and *Brandenburg* (at Oranienburg).

In 1937, further reorganisation saw these battalions formed into three full deathshead regiments: *SS-Totenkopfstandarten Oberbayern* (at Dachau), *Brandenburg* (at Sachsenhausen) and *Thüringen* (at Buchenwald). These units would become officially designated as the *SS-Totenkopfverbände* in 1936. Post-*Anschluss*, a fourth regiment, *SS-Totenkopfstandarte Ostmark*, was established at the concentration camp at Mauthausen in Austria, and in 1939, a fifth, *SS-Totenkopfstandarte Dietrich Eckardt*, was also formed.

From a beginning as little more than brutal thugs guarding hapless concentration camp inmates, the *SS-Totenkopfverbände* (SS-TV) would become a well-trained military force, though no less brutal in its methods, which would in turn provide the *Waffen-SS* with the unit that would become the formidable *3 SS-Panzer Division Totenkopf*.

Meanwhile the SA continued its expansion, and the Army grew ever more concerned at rumours that the brownshirts considered themselves as a revolutionary force which would replace the regular Army. Hitler too was becoming concerned that the SA was slipping beyond his control, seeing its allegiance being owed to its own commander-in-chief, *SA-Stabschef* Ernst Röhm, and Röhm's enemies lost no time in feeding Hitler's mistrust of his once-valued comrade. Eventually, Röhm demanded the formation of a people's army to replace the regular Army, which he would personally command. This was the final straw for both Hitler and the generals of the regular Army. There was now a real danger of civil war, and Hitler was

An *SS-Mann* of the *SS-Totenkopf Standarte Oberbayern*, part of the *SS-Totenkopfverbände*. The *Standarte* '1' is embroidered under the deathshead. He wears the regulation enlisted rank's peaked service cap with leather chinstrap.

determined to eliminate this threat from within his own movement.

To execute his plan, Hitler called up his most trusted men, the SS. He called a meeting of SA leaders for 30 June 1934, at which the unsuspecting SA leaders were quickly arrested by SS troops and those determined as the ringleaders executed. The SS of course also took the opportunity of settling some of its own old scores, and eventually over 300 were executed in what was to become known as the 'Night of the Long Knives'. A new 'puppet' leader,

Viktor Lütze, was appointed to command the SA, with Hitler confident that this weak and colourless individual would prove no threat. He was correct. The SA was reduced to a mere quarter of its former size and at the same time was disarmed. It would no longer pose a threat to Hitler or be a serious obstacle to the development of the SS.

Once again, the SS had proved itself loyal, prepared to act outside the law, and even commit murder when its *Führer* so wished. In reward, Hitler declared the SS to now be a fully independent branch of the Party, no longer subordinate to the disgraced and humiliated SA.

During this period of struggle, the SS had mushroomed to some 200,000 strong. Recruitment criteria had been relaxed due to the need for rapid expansion to allow the SS to better withstand the pressure placed upon it by the resentful brownshirts. With the threat of the SA removed, however, Himmler immediately set about restoring its elite status. Many members were no longer considered appropriate for the new, reborn, elite SS, and over 60,000 men were dropped from its ranks.

In October 1934, an SS officer cadet training school (*SS-Junkerschule*) was opened at Bad Tölz in Bavaria, and was joined in 1935 by a further establishment in Brunswick (*SS-Junkerschule Braunschweig*). Several highly experienced former Army officers were recruited to provide the SS trainees with high-quality military training.

The first full regiment of *SS-Verfügungstruppe* was created around a core of former members of the *Politische Bereitschaften* when three *Sturmbanne* were amalgamated under the title *SS-Standarte I Deutschland* in Munich.

A further regiment, *SS-Standarte 2 Germania*, was formed in Hamburg, and following the 1938 *Anschluss* with Austria, a third regiment was formed in Vienna under the title *SS-Standarte 3 Der Führer*.

With the *Leibstandarte SS Adolf Hitler*, the *SS-Verfügungstruppe* and the *SS-Totenkopfverbände* at his disposal, Himmler now had the requisite raw material to provide the nucleus for the creation of his own SS army.

CHAPTER TWO

RECRUITMENT

Probably the single most important aspect of recruitment into the SS as a whole, and certainly into the *Waffen-SS* and its forerunner, the SS-VT, was that of exclusivity. As the elite branch of the Party, the SS required that all of its recruits be of the highest standards. As it mushroomed in size, these standards did decline quite drastically, and many members of the *Allgemeine-SS* were certainly not of the level of quality the elite nature of the organisation sought to promote.

So far as the armed SS was concerned, however, these recruitment criteria were maintained for as long as possible, until, inevitably, the need for battlefield replacements following the outbreak of war forced a decline in standards.

In considering recruitment into the *Waffen-SS*, three distinctly different areas shall be examined: German SS recruits, foreign volunteers into the 'Germanic' units and finally conscripts into the second-rate units formed during the second half of the war.

GERMAN RECRUITS

From the creation of the SS-VT in 1935, the intent to maintain only the highest standards on selection was clear.

SS volunteers were carefully chosen. There was no requirement for high educational standards; indeed a substantial proportion of recruits came from farming backgrounds with slightly lower than normal educational standards. This, it was reasoned, would provide a force of men accustomed to hard manual work, and therefore with a high level of fitness, and any shortcomings in educational standards would be more than offset by a greater amenability to political indoctrination and willingness to accept strict discipline.

Farming in the 1930s was no easy life, and the SS saw the induction of tough members of rural communities rather than 'soft' city dwellers as a positive advantage. Life in the field, and the ability to 'live off the land' would be a far easier prospect for a countryman than for a 'townie'. This is not to suggest that the SS recruited exclusively from the rural communities, but statistics would seem to bear out that there was a far higher percentage of recruits from the countryside into the SS than was the case with the *Wehrmacht*.

An original SS-VT recruiting leaflet entitled *'Wie komme ich zur SS-Verfügungstruppe?'* (How do I join the SS-VT?) provides the following information for the prospective recruit.

When is the intake for the SS-VT?

On 1 October. Reporting date for the October intake: 1 February.

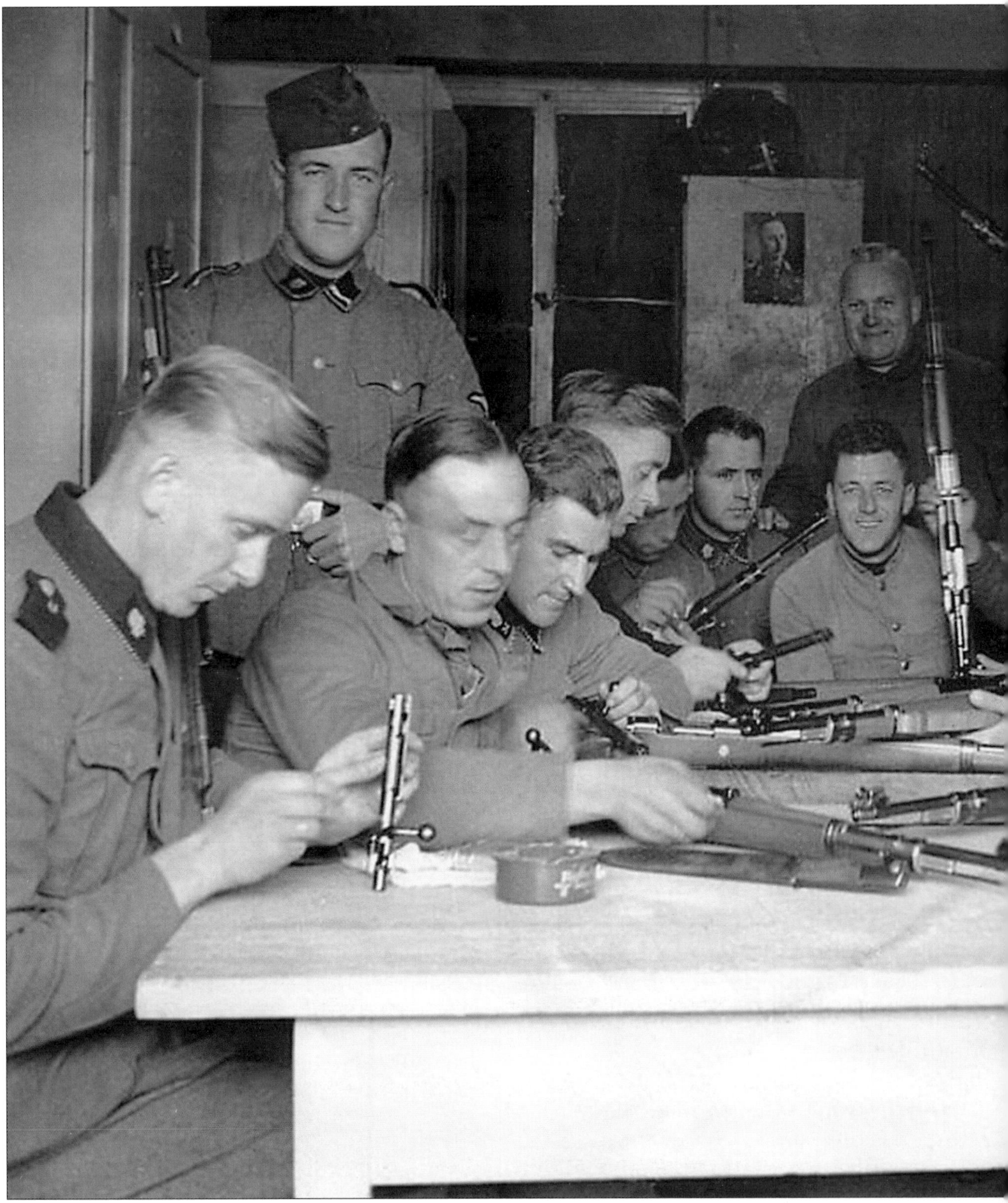

Who can volunteer?

Candidates must be between 17 and 22

Minimum Height for the *Leibstandarte SS Adolf Hitler* 178 cm
Minimum Height for *SS-Standarten Deutschland, Germania* and *Der Führer* 174 cm
Minimum Height for Musicians, Pioneers and Signallers 172 cm

What are the criteria for enlistment?

Each candidate must
  a) be of German nationality
  b) be fit and suitable for the SS (free of any problems of health, and with a National Socialist viewpoint)
  c) be able to establish his antecedents back to at least 1800
  d) be single and not engaged
  e) have completed his obligatory Labour Corps Service
  f) if at the minimum age, have the written permission of his parents or official guardian
  g) if an apprentice, have successfully completed his training, or had the agreement of his journeyman as to the course being cut short
  h) pay for any dental treatment required at the time of acceptance, and have any such work carried out before enlistment
  i) have normal eyesight without glasses
  j) have no criminal record, or criminal proceedings outstanding against him

SS-Totenkopf personnel gather round the table in their barrack room to clean down their weapons after a training session. Like soldiers everywhere, *Waffen-SS* men were taught to treat their personal weapons with care and respect.

Anyone who does not fulfil all these requirements **cannot** be accepted

A career as an officer in the SS is open to all SS members who have completed a minimum of one year's service

How long does the volunteer serve?

Minimum length of service in the SS-VT is 4 years, including 3 months' probationary service. The first two years of service are reckonable towards national military service

Volunteers who wish to follow a career as an NCO must serve for a minimum of 12 years

Where does one apply?

At the recruitment office in the recruiting area appropriate to the applicant's permanent home address, or at the *Allgemeine-SS Standarte* nearest to the applicant's home address

SS-Recruitment Area I
Address *Leibstandarte SS Adolf Hitler*
Berlin-Lichterfelde
Finckensteinallee 63

For applicants whose place of residence lies in the areas of Military Districts I, II, III, IV, VIII

SS-Recruitment Area II
Address *SS-Standarte Germania*
Hamburg
SS-Barracks

For applicants whose place of residence lies in the areas of Military Districts VI, IX, X, XI

SS-Recruitment Area III
Address *SS-Standarte Deutschland*

München 13
SS-Barracks

For applicants whose place of residence lies in the areas of Military Districts V, VII, XII, XIII
SS-Recruitment Area IV
Address *SS-Standarte Der Führer*
Wien XVI
Radetsky Barracks

For applicants whose place of residence lies in the areas of Military Districts XVII, XVIII

Applications, however, may be made from any place within the Reich for the *Leibstandarte*, providing the candidate is 1.78 m or over in height. Applicants are free to elect for service in any particular military trade, but there is no guarantee that a vacancy will available in the chosen field.

How does one make the application?

Along with the completed application, the applicant must provide
   a) the Volunteer Certificate from the Police
   b) two passport-size photos (without headgear)
   c) a CV in the applicant's own handwriting, giving details of: Forename and Surname, Date and Trade, Labour Corps Service, if State Sports Badge is held, Horse Riding Certificate or details of training with a Motor School of the National Socialist Motor Corps, Driving Licence, any knowledge of Morse Code, Signals experience, all in clear handwriting
   d) written agreement of the parent or official guardian where applicable

SS recruits under training. Note that it was common for recruits not to be permitted to wear SS collar patches, or shoulder straps, until their basic training had been completed. The SS arm eagle is the only insignia worn.

Completed applications should be submitted as soon as possible. Those who do not submit these details until just before the date set for reporting run the risk of having their date of entry set off until the following year

What does the volunteer receive?

During the first two years of service, he receives, in addition to free uniforms, accommodation, food and health care, remuneration of RM 0.50 per day

After completion of the first year's service promotion to *SS-Sturmmann*, and after two years' service promotion to *SS-Rottenführer* or *SS-Unterscharführer*, with progress to higher grades possible

In subsequent years, further promotions are possible

After completion of four years' service, the possibility of transfer to a career in the police

Much has been made of the boast that the *Waffen-SS*, at least in its early days, would not accept a candidate even if his only flaw was a single filling to a tooth. In fact, this was likely to be as much for the fairly mundane reason of avoiding the SS becoming

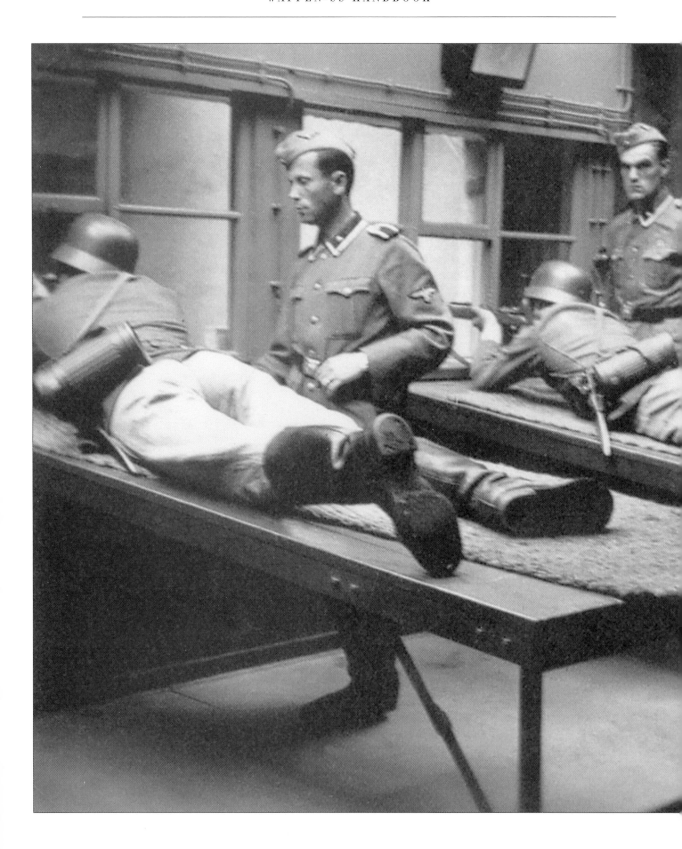

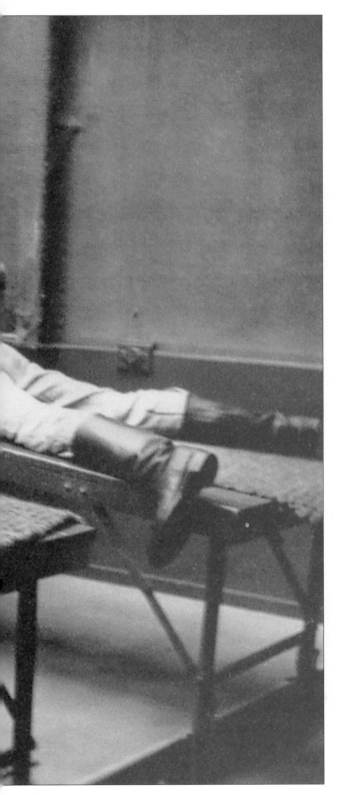

responsible for potential costly and time-consuming dental treatment as for reasons of exclusivity. With the huge number of potential recruits from which to chose, why take on a man with possible dental problems when there were a hundred more without? It is also worth pointing out that even volunteer recruits into the *Wehrmacht* were required to have any dental treatment taken care of before they were accepted.

Initial enlistment into the *Waffen-SS* was for a period of four years for other ranks. For NCOs, the service requirement rose to twelve years and for officers a commitment of twenty-five years was required.

It was not possible to join the *Waffen-SS* as an officer (although those who already held, or had previously held, officer rank in the *Wehrmacht* were often accepted into the SS in an equivalent rank). Generally, potential officers were required to serve for at least a year in the ranks before being permitted to apply for officer training at one of the *SS-Junkerschulen*.

As the war progressed, it is unsurprising that the sheer demand for battlefield replacements, especially after the launching of Operation Barbarossa, the invasion of the Soviet Union, would enforce a slight lowering of standards. Extreme criteria such as the ban on recruits with a tooth filling were dropped, and the age bands expanded, and the pre-war upper age limit of twenty-three was increased eventually to thirty-five.

Ultimately, in the final stages of the war, large numbers of personnel were simply

Two *SS-Unterscharführer* keep a watchful eye on their recruits during training on the rifle range as the soldiers practise firing from the prone position. Both recruits are wearing the light-coloured drill trousers, but with the regulation field-grey service tunic.

Weapons training was of the highest importance. Here, *Waffen-SS* soldiers strip and clean their Mauser Kar 98k rifles. On this occasion, these soldiers, and the others in the background, wear both jacket and trousers in the pale drill material, though the field-grey *Feldmütze* is worn.

transferred en masse from the *Wehrmacht* into the *Waffen-SS*. These tended to be, for instance, *Luftwaffe* ground crews who no longer had aircraft to serve, or *Kriegsmarine* sailors with no ships to man. Many of these inductees were of a standard that would never have allowed them to be accepted into the pre-war SS-VT but they were considered suitable 'cannon-fodder' in the closing days of the war. It must be said, however, that even after it had become clear that Germany could no longer win the war, there were still many keen to volunteer for what they considered the elite branch of the armed forces. A similar situation existed in the Navy, when even long after the Battle of

the Atlantic was lost and few submarines survived beyond their first war cruise, young Germans were still eagerly volunteering to serve in Dönitz's elite U-boat arm.

GERMANIC RECRUITS

Suitable foreign volunteers were seen as a positive advantage for the *Waffen-SS* as early as 1939. Thanks to the Army, severe restrictions were placed on the number of German citizens who could be recruited into the SS, but those ethnic Germans living outside the Reich borders were fair game for SS recruiters. In addition to those who were actually of German ethnic origin, it was decided that those who, though not of German blood, were deemed 'Germanic' would also be accepted.

The SS lost no time in actively recruiting in areas such as the Czech Sudetenland and Austria, which fell under German control. There were also a number of volunteers from countries such as Switzerland, which had a large German-speaking section of the populace.

It was principally after the success of the Campaign in the West, however, that recruitment of the 'Germanics' began in earnest. In particular, Norwegians, Danes, Dutch and Belgian Walloons were actively recruited. The French and Belgian Flemings were initially rejected as not being Germanic peoples, and volunteers were therefore directed towards the German Army rather than the *Waffen-SS*.

In the early years, these recruits signed on for a fixed two-year period of service, after which they were free to return to their native land. In most of these countries there already existed political parties which mirrored the National Socialists (NSDAP) in Germany. In Holland the NSB, in Norway the NS, in Denmark the DNSAP and in Belgium the VNV, all actively encouraged their members to serve with the *Waffen-SS* to some degree. In most cases, however, these men were fervent nationalists and not necessarily pro-German, but saw service in the *Waffen-SS* as a way of fighting in what they saw as the 'Crusade against Bolshevism'. Although they were offered German citizenship as a prize for their service, this was something that was by no means always seen by these volunteers as something to be particularly valued. Technically they were not considered as SS members *per se*, but were merely attached to the SS for their period of service.

Although many professed similar political beliefs to German SS men, and were deemed acceptable for service in the SS by Himmler, their German counterparts did not always accept them. Many of the Germans saw themselves as infinitely superior and resented this dilution of the SS elite. It took intervention by Himmler himself and the sacking of many SS training instructors, and their substitution with those more sympathetic to their Germanic comrades, to avoid a total breakdown in morale among the volunteers. In the event, when they finally reached the front line, these volunteers were to prove themselves steadfast and reliable in battle, and some of the best troops to have fought within the *Waffen-SS*.

OTHER RECRUITS

The nadir of SS recruitment standards came in 1943 when the original desire for quality above quantity was finally laid to rest as Himmler's ambitions for his own personal army resulted in the formation of many low-quality foreign volunteer units, the character of which dismayed many of the old original veterans who were drafted in to form the cadres for these new units. What a veteran from the earliest days of the SS, schooled in the ideology of Nazism, which saw those races from the East as 'inferior' in almost every way, must have thought as he watched his new recruits to the *Handschar* Division, wearing the traditional fez, and kneeling on their prayer mats as they faced towards Mecca and began their prayers to Allah, can only be imagined.

Of course, by this time, many of those original SS men who still survived had lost many of their ill-conceived ideological beliefs, forced into much more pragmatic viewpoints by the realities of war on the Eastern Front. If the troops they observed with considerable scepticism had proved themselves in battle (as indeed a few succeeded in doing), then these battle-hardened veterans may have accorded them a grudging respect. In fact, many of these units were unmitigated disasters, with desertion endemic within them, and were disbanded after being in existence for only a short time.

Probably worst of all those who served in the *Waffen-SS* were those who had not volunteered at all, but were forced into service. The most appalling example of this was the despicable *Dirlewanger* Brigade, manned by those dredged from prisons and concentration camps, or posted to the unit for punishment. This unit was responsible for some of the worst atrocities committed during the war.

CHAPTER THREE

TRAINING

As we have already seen, in general every member of the *Waffen-SS* was obliged to begin his career 'at the bottom' and train initially as a common soldier. The training was extremely tough in physical terms. As a basic minimum each recruit had to prove himself capable of completing a 3-km battle march in full field uniform with weapon and steel helmet and carrying 100 kg of equipment, in just 20 minutes.

Given, however, that Germany expected all members of its male youth to serve first with the *Hitler Jugend*, where military training and field craft was part and parcel of normal training, then undergo a period of service with the RAD (*Reichs Arbeitsdienst,* or State Labour Service), where even more robust physical training and military style exercises were carried out, the extremely hard physical training which was experienced when joining the *Waffen-SS* was possibly not quite so much of a shock to the system as it might have been for recruits to elite units in other countries.*

The *Waffen-SS* was also a great exponent of the use of live fire training, where recruits went about their combat training under live small arms and even artillery fire.

While relatively safe, the fire being aimed above their heads, this was only so if the recruit kept his nerve. Anyone who panicked under fire and ran was in great danger of being mown down, and indeed casualties did occur in such circumstances.

Great emphasis was also placed on close-quarter battle training, with hand-to-hand fighting skills using pistols, machine pistols, fighting knives and even entrenching tools being taught.

There are many wild stories related about some of the methods of training used in the *Waffen-SS* (and indeed the Army also), one of the most often recounted being the practice of ordering a recruit to stand to attention, then balancing a live hand grenade on top of his helmet and expecting him to stand stock-still while it detonated. The theory was that the blast would be deflected safely upwards and the recruit would suffer nothing worse than mild concussion from the explosion. If, however, his nerve faltered and he shook, the grenade would roll off his helmet, fall by his feet and on detonating would at least blow his legs off, if not kill him outright. Thus the value of keeping one's nerve would be effectively proved.

---

* The RAD was a uniformed organisation, arranged along military lines and with a military-style rank structure, but involved in constructional work, working on the land, etc. Photographs, however, often show RAD personnel involved in drill movements where the shovels they carried over their shoulders are clearly obvious substitutes for rifles.

This interesting pre-war photograph shows a very unusual form of insignia being worn. The *SS-Verfügungstruppe* officer is on attachment with the Army, undergoing specialist training, and because of this uniquely wears the Army national emblem over his right breast pocket.

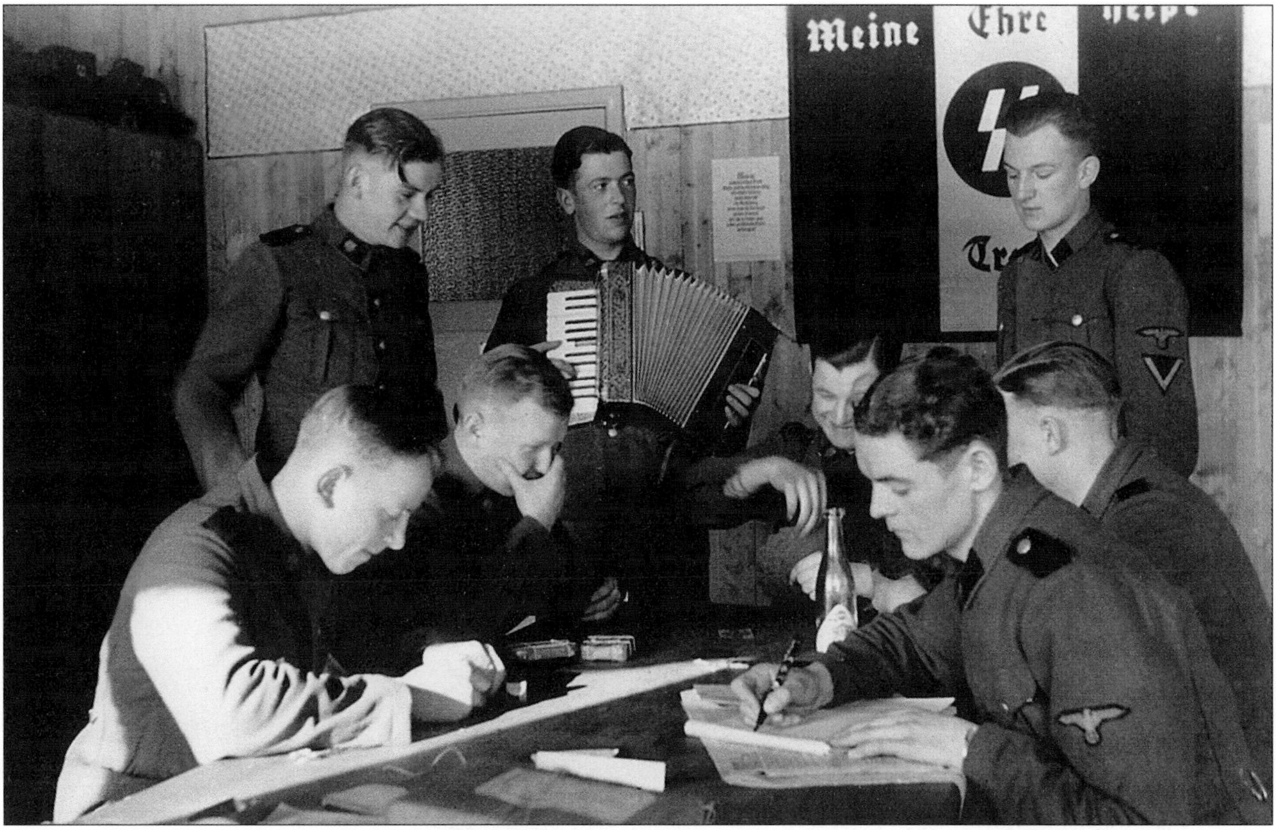
Meine
Ehre

Soldiers from an *SS-Totenkopf* unit relax in their billet while off duty, though, it has to be said, this is clearly a posed propaganda photograph.

Unfortunately, such stories, though they emphasise well the ethos of *Waffen-SS* toughness, are grossly exaggerated. Although every soldier knew of such stories, the author has been unable to find one single veteran who either underwent or witnessed such a training method. The fact is that a powerful hand grenade, going off balanced on a soldier's helmet, would probably kill him either way.

Other equally frightening methods, however, were indeed used. One of the most nerve-wracking of these was the training in digging slit trenches, where a recruit would be told to dig himself in with the news that enemy tanks were approaching. After a few moments, tanks would appear and begin to roll over the trenches that had been hastily dug. Of course if the soldier had dug a reasonably good-sized one-man trench or foxhole, he would be perfectly safe as the tank rolled over his position, its tracks straddling his foxhole. If the trench was not deep enough to allow clearance for him with his backpack, etc. in the ground clearance space between the earth and the underside of the tank's hull, he would be in serious danger. Even worse, if his nerve broke when the tank was just about to roll over him, and he leapt up and tried to make a dash for safety, he stood a good chance of being crushed. Once again, casualties were not unknown in such training. In some cases the realism of such training was

Kit inspection. Here recruits have their weapons and personal kit laid out for inspection by their platoon commander. Two NCOs are in attendance, no doubt ready to note the names of any whose kit is not fully up to expected standards.

Barrack-room accommodation of an *SS-Totenkopf* unit. Note the bunk beds in the background, and the steel helmets and gas mask canisters neatly stacked on top of the lockers.

enhanced by the use of real captured enemy tanks of exactly the type these soldiers would soon face.

In addition to this realistic combat training, physical fitness was a high priority, and *Waffen-SS* training NCOs were every bit as harsh as their counterparts in the *Wehrmacht* when it came to putting their recruits through their paces. A 6 a.m. start each morning was followed by a full hour of strenuous PT before trainees were able to partake of a rather basic and meagre breakfast. Weapons training, hand-to-hand combat and range-firing exercises would follow prior to lunch. The afternoon would typically consist of drill sessions, fatigue duties and a battle march, or at least two hours of sporting activity.

Apart from normal PT exercises, the greatest tool at the disposal of the training NCO was the forced march. Recruits were regularly kitted out in combat gear, wearing steel helmet and carrying weapons plus a full load of kit, and occasionally wearing their gas masks at the same time, and marched until they had reached the limits of their endurance. Wearing their best uniforms, they would be told to 'take cover', usually just as they were passing a suitable pool of muddy water, a patch of thorns or some nice slushy snow, anything in fact that would render their uniforms filthy, thus

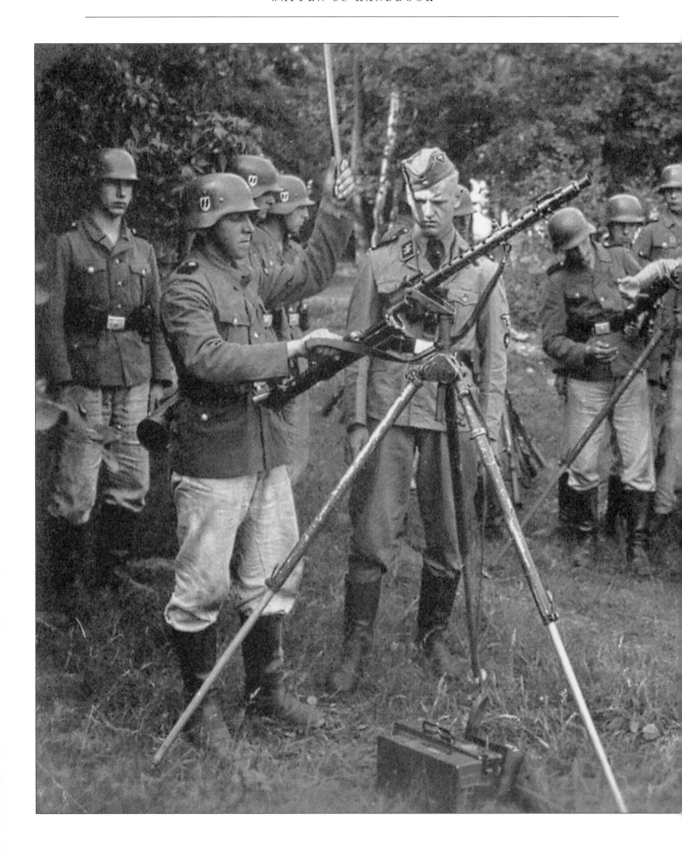

giving the recruits one more onerous task in making their uniforms immaculate again before their next inspection.

Barrack-room inspections, of course, were gone through with ridiculous attention to detail, with the slightest imperfection or imaginary speck of dust being enough to send the inspecting NCO into a paroxysm of rage, throwing the soldier's kit and belongings about the floor or even out of the window. That there was seemingly no end to the inventiveness of the training NCOs in devising new tortures for their recruits was little different from the situation in other armies throughout the world.

These were not, however, simply exercises in sadism, though many of the soldiers undergoing this treatment may have been forgiven for thinking so. These training routines had a definite purpose, helping the recruits to bond together into a unified group, supporting each other against the enemy, in this case the NCO bullying them. It also instilled into them, even if initially only through fear of the NCO, the instinct to instantly obey orders.

One particularly difficult task recruits had to master was the *Parademarsch*, or so-called 'goose-step'. This exhausting step put considerable strain on the leg muscles, and even by trained men could only be kept up for a very short period. As the war progressed, however, there was less emphasis on parade drill and more on combat exercises.

One aspect of *Waffen-SS* training which is often misunderstood was political education,

Recruits undergo training on the MG34 machine-gun, a weapon capable of laying down a devastating rate of fire. The instructors are wearing the SS-VT pattern field cap and lightweight earth-grey uniform.

Off-duty troops relax in their billet with a few bottles of beer.

or as some would have it, indoctrination. This certainly took place, and the SS hierarchy assuredly considered a National Socialist outlook, or 'Weltanschauung', to be essential for all SS men. Whether the trainees took much notice of these lectures is another matter. It must be borne in mind that these were fit, healthy young men anxious to fit in and be part of what was widely considered to be the elite military force of the nation. They had passed through the Hitler Youth and the *Reichs Arbeitsdienst* and had been brought up during a period when the National Socialists had brought Germany from a beaten, virtually bankrupt nation to one of the most powerful countries in the world. In most

cases they either did not see or chose to ignore the darker side of Nazism. Not surprisingly, most were already firm supporters of their country's political leadership and political indoctrination was hardly necessary.

Most *Waffen-SS* veterans will confirm that they did indeed receive political education classes, but that they fail to remember what was discussed, mostly because they were bored witless by being stuck in a stuffy classroom listening to political debate they barely understood and cared even less about. Most would far rather have been out in the fresh air involved in sporting activities.

Waffen-SS soldiers were, however, encouraged to revoke their membership of any organised Church or religion, though not forced to do so, and to declare their religion simply as *'Gottglaubigkeit'*, indicating a vague belief in God but no specific affiliation.

While foreign recruits did initially seem to have problems with bullying from German NCOs while undergoing training, in the case of West European recruits at least these were rapidly resolved, and most were treated no differently from German recruits. One Danish volunteer who had formerly served with the Danish cavalry actually commented that his Danish recruit training was harsher than that he received with the *Waffen-SS*.

As previously mentioned, potential officers and NCOs were selected from the ranks, recruits being monitored for the correct attributes. Every member of the SS from the enlisted *'Schütze'* to the *Reichsführer-SS* himself was designated an *SS-Mann*, and it is this title that was considered the important one. The military rank held was then considered to be simply a reflection of the individual's performance. By declaring every rank to hold the honorary status of *SS-Mann*, all full members of the SS then held equal status as far as their membership of the organisation was concerned.

From April 1934, SS potential officers were trained at the *Führerschulen* (later

A favourite part of the instructor's repertoire was the battle march in full kit with loaded pack. Recruits were expected to be able to cover 3 km in 20 minutes carrying a full load.

Officers, too, were expected to be proficient with a range of weapons. Here an *SS-Totenkopf* officer practises firing from the prone position with the Gewehr 98 rifle. This is distinguishable from the similar Kar 98k by the way in which the bolt projects horizontally rather than being turned down.

renamed *Junkerschulen*) at Bad Tölz in Bavaria and in Braunschweig. A number of senior ranks within the SS-VT/*Waffen-SS* were former Army soldiers who had already done their training through the Army's own officer training system (for example Paul Hausser, Felix Steiner). Some 85 per cent of SS officers had served during the First World War and around 25 per cent in the postwar *Reichswehr/Wehrmacht*. It was therefore, initially at least, the junior officer ranks (from *Untersturmführer* to *Hauptsturmführer*) in which the *Junkerschule* graduates proliferated. As the war dragged on, numbers of these were promoted to field-grade ranks (*SS-Sturmbannführer* to *SS-Standartenführer*), but *Junkerschule* graduates at general rank were few and far between.

The *Waffen-SS* method of recruiting its officers direct from the ranks had pitfalls as well as advantages. On the positive side it encouraged good performance, each soldier knowing that if he proved himself, displayed the desired attributes and showed potential, he had as good a chance of being selected for officer training as any other, regardless of educational or social background. On the other hand, leaving selection up to the individual company commanders inevitably brought the possibility of bias. Indeed the failure rate was often rather high due to candidates being chosen who, though they may have been adequate or even very good enlisted soldiers, were not particularly suitable as officers.

Eventually the training process did become more structured and to some degree, standardised, with the training syllabus centrally decided. After serving from nine months to a year with their units, the selected candidates would undergo squad leader training with their units, lasting up to two months. The candidate, now known as an *SS-Junker*, would then at least join his course of training at the *SS-Junkerschule*, having already gained a minimal degree of leadership skills.

After five months of both practical and theoretical training, tests were taken and the successful candidates promoted to *SS-Standartenjunker*. At the end of ten months' training and a further set of practical and theoretical tests the successful soldier would then be promoted to *SS-Standartenoberjunker*. The final stage of the training would be a large-scale field-training exercise which could last up to two weeks and was generally followed by a platoon commanders' course at the SS training school at Dachau. Assuming all went well here, the candidate would return to his unit, and around six months after completing his training he would become eligible for promotion to the rank of *SS-Untersturmführer*.

Subjects covered in the training syllabus at the *SS-Junkerschulen* included the following.

IDEOLOGICAL TRAINING

This aspect of SS training is a somewhat contentious issue. On the one hand, many point to this political indoctrination as being part of the reason why so many SS officers are claimed to have shown contempt for what were considered 'lesser'

Waffen-SS infantry training with the Kar 98k rifle. The instructors on this occasion are experienced enlisted men, not NCOs.

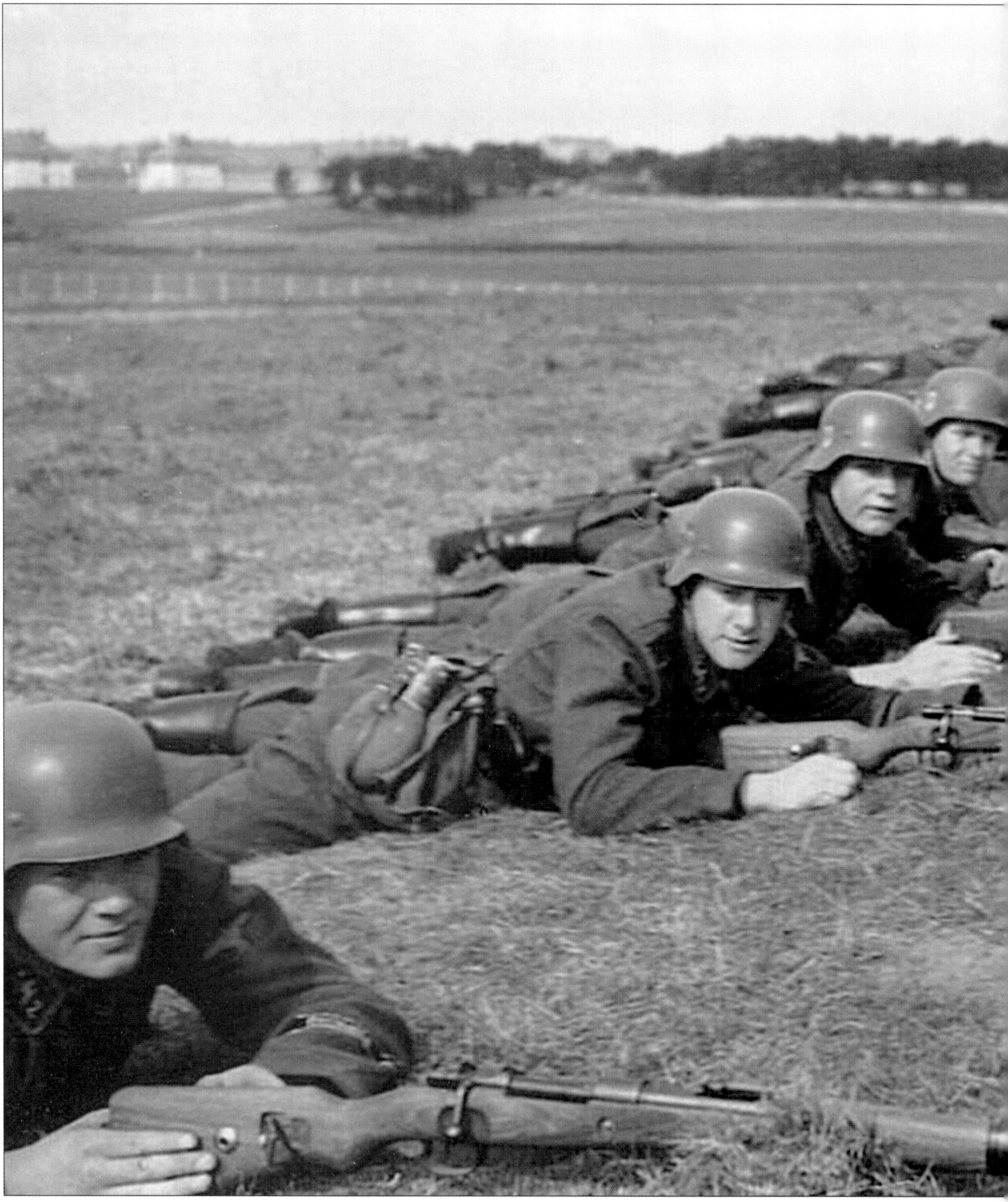

peoples, particularly during the Campaign in the East. On the other hand, many former SS officers claim that this aspect of their training was not taken too seriously and that far more emphasis was placed on their military role. The truth probably lies somewhere in between. Certainly, with SS officers being selected from the ranks, irrespective of their social background, there is no doubt that many would have found this overwhelmingly theoretical instruction dull in the extreme. However, the fact that this training seems to have been aimed at producing in the future *Waffen-SS* officer a sense of identity with National Socialist ideology, so that any attack on Nazi values would be seen as a personal attack on him also, when considered alongside the seemingly fanatical loyalty of many such officers, seems to suggest that some of this training at least was taken on board.

However, one must also consider that towards the latter stages of the war the fact that the loyalty of the average *Waffen-SS* man of whatever rank seemed no longer to be directed towards the regime or its hierarchy, but to his comrades in arms, would seem to call into question whether the ideological training given to *Waffen-SS* officers was any more effective than that given to officers of the Army or *Luftwaffe* through their own political educational officers.

SERVICE REGULATIONS

Waffen-SS officers were taught a wide range of military regulations, including aspects such as the Army Penal Code, the State Criminal Code, the Military Code of

Firing practice, in steel helmet and full kit, on the ranges. The weapon here is the Kar 98k – note the turned-down bolt.

Range training with the MG42. A young *Waffen-SS* soldier is watched by a combat-experienced *SS-Hauptsturmführer* and bearer of the Knight's Cross of the Iron Cross. The photograph was no doubt specially posed for propaganda purposes.

Physical fitness was given a high level of priority in the *Waffen-SS*, and sporting activity was a regular feature of training. Here a group of SS troops are pictured in their sports kit, consisting of black shorts and white vest with a prominent SS runic emblem on the chest.

On Parade! A company of *Waffen-SS* troops are inspected by their company commander. Just visible on the original print is a small lighting bolt in front of the runes on this officer's collar patch, denoting his membership of the *SS-Nachrichtensturmbann*. Note the brocade dress belts and swords worn by officers on ceremonial occasions, and the aiguillette worn by the adjutant on the extreme left.

Honour, Administration of Official Documents, Disciplinary Regulations, Defence against Espionage, Subversion, and Professional Duties of the German Soldier.

SS AND POLICE REGULATIONS

These were added after the abortive July 1944 assassination attempt on Hitler.

PHYSICAL EDUCATION

The SS officer candidate was expected to participate in an almost endless round of physical and sporting activities, route marches and cross-country runs. Possession of the State Sports Badge and the SA Sports Badge was expected of every SS man and was an essential before promotion to officer rank could be considered.

In addition to this classroom-based theoretical training, and the obvious need for any soldier to prove himself physically fit, the future *Waffen-SS* officer was trained to equip himself in his role as a combat leader with training exercises in tactical skills (including map reading, weapons training, troop training and drill), combat engineer skills, signals and communications skills, paramedical training and motor transport training.

Generally speaking, the number of officers of the *Waffen-SS* who went on to show high levels of leadership skills as well as personal gallantry, and inspired considerable loyalty and trust within their men, so much so that their troops would quite literally follow them anywhere, suggests that for many, the training given at the *SS-Junkerschulen* was highly successful.

CHAPTER FOUR

ORGANISATIONAL STRUCTURE

The most senior post within the *Waffen-SS*, and indeed in the entire SS, was that of *Reichsführer-SS*, a post held throughout the brief life of the *Waffen-SS* by one man, Heinrich Himmler, who was answerable only to Hitler.

The SS as an organisation was divided into a number of main offices, or *Hauptämter*. The SS structure changed and evolved over a period of years. Those with which the *Waffen-SS* would have regular direct involvement were as follows:

Hauptamt Persönlicher Stab Reichsführer-SS
This was Himmler's own personal staff element.

SS-Hauptamt
    SS-Gruppenführer Kurt Wittje
    SS-Gruppenführer August Heissmeyer
    SS-Obergruppenführer Gotlob Berger

It was the main SS central office, responsible primarily for recruitment, which was heavily involved in the formation of the numerous foreign volunteer units in the *Waffen-SS*, and also responsible for propaganda (including the publication of numerous papers and periodicals) and education and physical training. It also acted at the personnel and records office for NCOs and enlisted men of the *Waffen-SS*.

SS-Führungshauptamt
    SS-Obergruppenführer Hans Juttner

This was the operational headquarters of the SS. Among its many functions was that of ensuring that SS personnel were regularly paid and trained and adequately supplied. It was also responsible for putting into effect promotions and appointments.

SS Wirtschafts- und Verwaltungshauptamt
    SS-Obergruppenführer Oswald Pohl

This was the main economics and administrative office. Among many other interests, it controlled factories that were involved in making military equipment and uniforms for the *Waffen-SS*, and was responsible for the construction of housing and barracks.

Hauptamt SS-Gericht
    SS-Gruppenführer Paul Scharfe until 1942
    SS-Gruppenführer Franz Breithaupt 1942–45

This was the SS Legal Department; it was involved in punishing offences which broke the SS disciplinary code.

A mixed group of *Polizei* and *Waffen-SS* officers. The former wear normal police service dress, but note that as full members of the SS the two officers in the centre of the group wear a set of silver-wire-embroidered SS runes just below the left breast pocket.

SS Personalhauptamt
    SS-Obergruppenführer Walter Schmitt
    until 1942
    SS-Obergruppenführer Maximilian von
    Herff 1942–45

This was the personnel branch of the SS, which also effectively acted as the 'manning and records office' for officer ranks in the *Waffen-SS*.

There were a large number of smaller offices within the SS, but it is generally only within the above list that branches will be found which had regular and direct involvement with the *SS-Verfügungstruppe* and *Waffen-SS*.

Originally created as branches of the *Allgemeine-SS*, these *Hauptämter* continued to carry out the same functions for personnel of the *SS-Verfügungstruppe* and *Waffen-SS*. On

A group of *SS-Unterscharführer* in cold-weather gear wearing the field-grey wool greatcoat. This was manufactured with dark green or field-grey collar, both styles being widely issued. The field cap is the SS-VT pattern, with metal deathshead button to the front and embroidered eagle and swastika insignia on a black triangular patch on the left-hand side.

the outbreak of war, Himmler's personal staff element sprouted a *Feldkommandostelle*, or field headquarters, organised along military lines, which accompanied Himmler during any trips outside Germany and into the occupied areas. This was no small administration element, but a fully functioning military unit, peaking at around 3,000 men and including combat troops, flak elements, military police and Himmler's personal train, known as *Sonderzug Heinrich*.

So it can be seen that the *Waffen-SS*, as but one part of the SS as a whole, was supported by a massive administrative structure covering almost every possible aspect of the *Waffen-SS* soldier's life. Political considerations, however, principally Hitler's wish to avoid alienating his senior military commanders, resulted in *Waffen-SS* units serving in the field joining those of the *Wehrmacht* under military rather than SS command during wartime. Although SS divisions would serve as part of *SS-Korps* and even SS armies, these would ultimately come under the control of the *Oberkommando der Wehrmacht*.

On 1 October 1936, the first of the organisational structures specifically created for the military elements of the SS was established. This was the *Inspektion der SS-Verfügungstruppe*, or Inspectorate of SS Military Formations. From this point until 1940, the inspectorate functioned as the operational command of the SS-VT. Heading this inspectorate was SS-*Brigadeführer* Paul Hausser, a former Army officer until then commanding the SS-*Junkerschule* at Bad Tölz.

This inspectorate, however, remained firmly under the control of the *SS-Hauptamt* and was subjected to much internal interference. The *Rasse und Siedlungs Hauptamt* had authority over the SS-VT in terms of ideological indoctrination; commanders of the various *SS-Oberabschnitte* were entitled to take command of SS-VT units in emergencies and could even commandeer SS-VT units to assist in the military training of the Hitler Youth and *Allgemeine-SS*. Even within the SS-VT itself, the inspectorate did not exercise full control. The *Leibstandarte SS Adolf Hitler* (LSSAH), the premier armed unit of the SS, was under the direct control of Himmler himself. Hausser was to find himself in conflict with the commander of the LSSAH, *Obergruppenführer* Sepp Dietrich, on several occasions.

Running parallel with the development of the SS-VT was the expansion of the *SS-Totenkopfverbände* (SS-TV). These troops, under the control of Theodor Eicke as *Inspektor des Konzentrationslager und Führer des SS-Wachverbände*, were formed to staff the various concentration camps. Eicke was ambitious and was also a rather accomplished organiser. Within a few months of taking office, he had reformed the concentration camp system, reducing the number of camps and organising the guard units into formal battalion-strength units. Between 1935 and 1938 the SS-TV expanded from a total of just under 2,000 men to around 9,000. These battalions were

subsequently reorganised into three regiments, Oberbayern, Thüringen and Brandenburg, based at the three largest concentration camps – Dachau, Buchenwald and Sachsenhausen. Like Hausser, Eicke's achievements were gained against a backdrop of interference and hostility from the *SS-Hauptamt*.

Unlike the SS-VT, in which service time was counted as being equivalent to that in the *Wehrmacht* as far as completion of the statutory period of conscripted military service was concerned, the *Wehrmacht* considered the SS-TV inferior and thus discounted any time served within its ranks. This was a double-edged sword, however, as it meant that the *Wehrmacht* could not in any way interfere with an organisation which it did not recognise.

By 1938, the armed units of the SS (SS-VT and SS-TV) consisted of the following elements.

Leibstandarte SS Adolf Hitler
SS-Standarte Deutschland
SS-Standarte Germania
SS-Standarte Der Führer
SS-Nachrichtensturmbann
SS-Pioniersturmbann
SS-Sturmbann Nürnberg
SS-Junkerschulen
SS-Inspektion
SS-Sanitätsabteilung
SS-Totenkopfstandarte Oberbayern
SS-Totenkopfstandarte Brandenburg
SS-Totenkopfstandarte Thüringen

In all, this represented over 23,000 men.

These SS units were by this point organised along military lines, the *SS-Standarte* being broadly equivalent to an Army regiment and the *Sturmbann* to an Army battalion. Thanks to far-sighted officers such as Hausser, the training given to SS troops was also along Army lines.

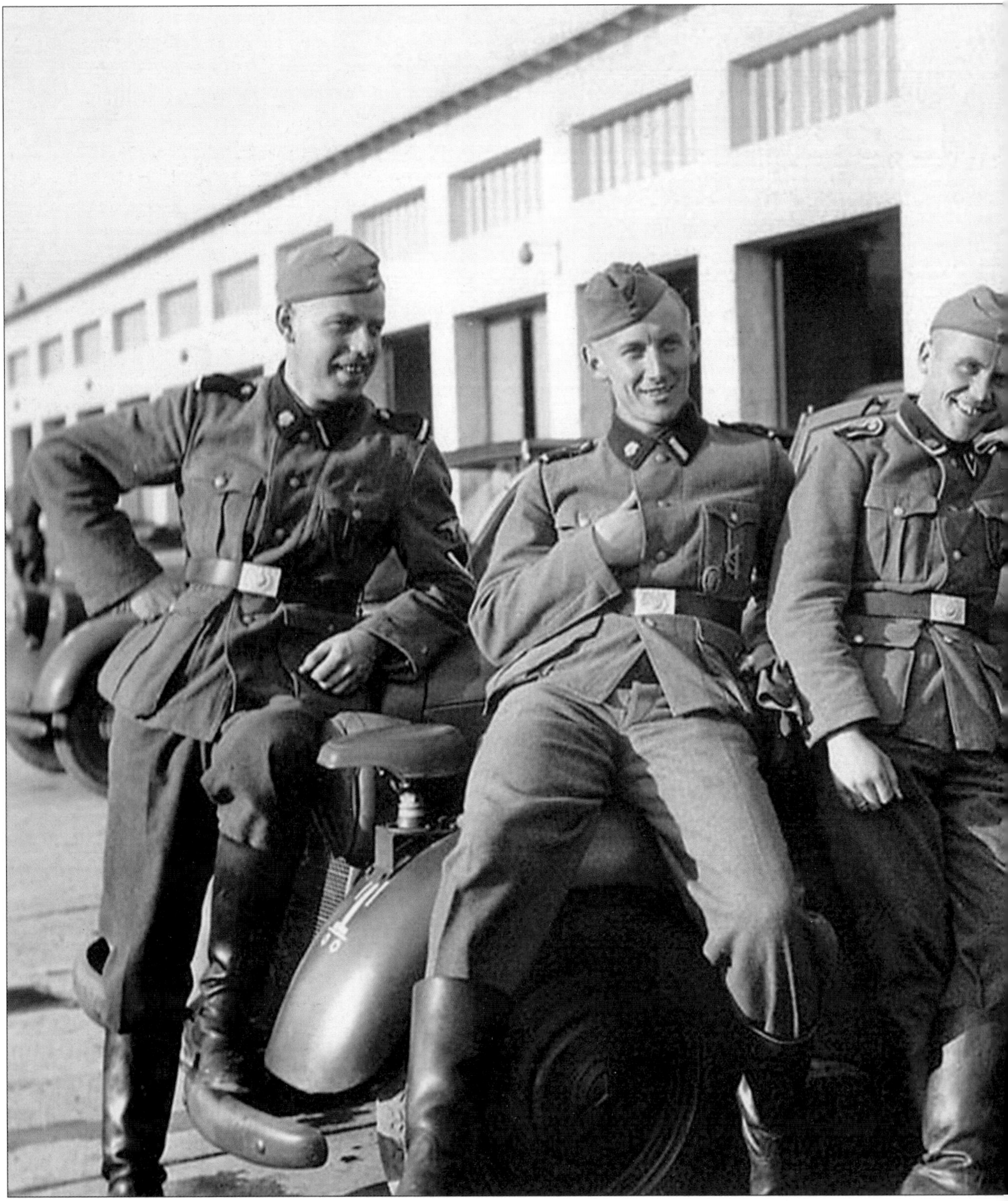

Throughout this period, resentment and open friction between the SS and the ever-suspicious *Wehrmacht* grew apace. The *Wehrmacht* saw no need for the arming and military training of a political organisation and was fiercely proud of its status as the sole *'Waffenträger'*, or bearer of arms, in the defence of the nation. Added to this, it was enraged at the deliberate and often open poaching of good-quality manpower by the SS.

Finally, on 17 August 1938, Hitler issued a proclamation defining the role of the armed units of the SS. In it, it was declared that the SS as a whole (the *Gesamt-SS*) was to be used for political duties and required no military training. However, the armed SS formations, the *SS-Junkerschulen* and the *SS-Totenkopfverbände* were to be excepted from this general rule. These units were declared to be neither part of the *Wehrmacht* nor of the police, but were defined as a 'standing armed formation exclusively at the disposal of the *Führer*'. The armed SS units were now formally permitted to recruit directly from the pool of manpower available for military conscription, and service in the armed SS would count officially as fulfilling the obligation for national service. The SS-TV, however, was restricted to recruiting from those who had already fulfilled their obligation for military service.

As far as their use in war was concerned, Hitler declared that in the case of mobilisation for war, the armed units of the SS would be 'subordinated to the Army in the field, under the orders of the *Oberbefehlshaber des Heeres*'. They would also be subject

SS-Totenkopf troops relax down at the motor pool. It is interesting to note that the enlisted man at right wears the old mirror-image collar tabs, while the others wear the rank patch on the left collar.

An NCO of the
SS-Polizei-Division.
The field blouse
worn is of basic
Army-issue
M1936 pattern
with traditional
collar bars rather
than SS-insignia.
Note, however,
the SS-style
sleeve eagle. An
SS issue belt
buckle is also
being worn, but
the field cap is
Polizei pattern.

exclusively to 'military laws and directives', but would remain a part of the NSDAP. Hitler also retained the right to direct the armed SS to be used 'internally', at which stage they would answer, not to the high command of the Army, but to Himmler as *Reichsführer-SS* and Chief of the German Police.

In the event of war, it was decreed that the SS-VT would in the first instance draw their replacements from the reserves of the SS-TV. First-line SS-TV units in turn would provide reserves for the police, while older *Allgemeine-SS* reservists would undertake the duties of the SS-TV.

One month later, on 17 September 1938, an order promulgated by the *Oberkommando der Wehrmacht* stated that on mobilisation, personnel of the armed SS who found themselves subordinated to Army control were 'to be considered part of the Army for the duration of their incorporation and subordination to the C-in-C Army'. They were to have 'the same rights and duties as soldiers or officials of the *Wehrmacht*' during this period. Army units were also henceforth to take part in joint military manoeuvres with the SS, as well as sporting and other off-duty functions intended to assist in the assimilation of the SS-VT into the military.

A further decree from Hitler on 18 May 1939 provided the final essential step in the full militarisation of the SS-VT when he declared that the armed SS units were to be consolidated into an SS division, complete with its own integral artillery, recon-naissance, anti-tank and anti-aircraft elements. In view of these developments, the three *SS-Totenkopfstandarten* were brought together to form the *SS-Totenkopf Division*, and members of the Orpo (*Ordnungspolizei*), which of course was also under Himmler's direct control as Chief of the German Police, began to be brought

together to form a police division. The *Waffen-SS* had arrived – in all but name.

The term was in fact first used in an internal SS document dated 7 November 1939, in which *Allgemeine-SS* members were instructed to 'apply to become reserve officers in the *Waffen-SS* and Police'. Henceforth, the term *Waffen-SS* was used almost exclusively when referring to what had been the SS-VT.

One month later, a decree issued by Himmler described the *Waffen-SS* as comprising

The *SS-Verfügungs Division*
The *SS-Totenkopf Division*
The *SS-Polizei Division*
The *SS-Junkerschulen*
The *SS-Totenkopfstandarten*.

From these small beginnings, the *Waffen-SS* grew tremendously. Its final Order of Battle saw it fielding a total of thirty-eight divisions, albeit many of these were divisional in name only, often never exceeding regimental strength or even matching it.

The structure of the *Waffen-SS* in the field saw the 'Army' as its largest formal structure. There were two *Waffen-SS* armies, the first being *6 SS-Panzerarmee*, which was formed in autumn 1944 from various armoured units, re-formed after being destroyed during the battles in Normandy. It took part in the Ardennes Offensive, in Hungary and finally in the defence of Vienna in 1945. The other was *11 SS-Armee*, formed in February 1945 on the Eastern Front and filled with stragglers from various battered units. It saw out the war in northern Germany.

Moving further down the organisational ladder, there were several SS corps-level organisations. As with the 'Army', the corps was not a fixed entity, but rather a command-

Waffen-SS soldiers in camouflage gear during field-training exercises. The camouflage smock and camouflage helmet cover are being worn. Note the field cap sitting inside the steel helmet.

level organisation whose constituent divisions could vary from time to time. The following corps were formed around SS divisions.

I SS-Panzerkorps. Formed in 1942, it fought on both the Western and Eastern Fronts, finishing the war in the defence of Vienna.

II SS-Panzerkorps. Formed in 1942, it fought in most major battles on both the Eastern and Western Fronts, and also ended the war in Austria.

III SS-Korps. Formed in 1943, its constituent units were the so-called 'Germanic' volunteer divisions. It fought out the war on the Eastern Front.

IV SS-Panzerkorps. Formed in 1943, it served out the war entirely on the Eastern Front.

V SS-Gebirgskorps. Formed in 1943 in the Balkans, and used primarily in the war against the partisans, it was destroyed during the battle for Berlin.

VI SS-Korps. Formed in late 1943 to control Latvian volunteer SS divisions on the northern sector of the Eastern Front, it remained in the East throughout the war.

IX SS-Gebirgskorps. Formed in early 1944 in Croatia, this Corps fought out the war on the Eastern Front, being wiped out in the battle for Budapest.

XI SS-Panzerkorps. Created in 1944, it fought in Poland before being driven back into Germany and destroyed in the battle for Berlin.

XII SS-Korps. This Corps was created in 1944 and served on the Western Front, being destroyed in the battle for the Ruhr Pocket.

XIII SS-Korps. Formed in late 1944 in eastern Germany, this Corps fought on the Western Front and ended the war in the vicinity of Munich.

XV SS-Korps. Formed in 1943, it fought in Croatia against partisan forces. Ending the war in Austria, it surrendered to the Western Allies but was handed over to the Soviets and nothing is known of its fate.

XVI SS-Korps. Formed in late 1944, it was annihilated on the Eastern Front in 1945.

XVII SS-Korps. Established in 1944, it fought on the Western Front, surrendering to French forces in May 1945.

The extent of the expansion of the *Waffen-SS* can clearly be seen in its ultimate Order of Battle.

DIVISIONS

Many of the *Waffen-SS* divisions changed their designation several times throughout their lives. *Das Reich,* for instance, was variously known as the *SS-Verfügungsdivision, SS-Division Deutschland, SS-Division Reich, SS-Division Das Reich* and *SS-Panzergrenadier Division Das Reich* before the final designation as *2 SS-Panzer Division Das Reich* was reached. For the sake of consistency, the titles listed here are the final designations of each unit. The year quoted, however, is that in which the unit was created at, or expanded to, divisional status.

1   *SS-Panzer Division Leibstandarte SS Adolf Hitler* 1942
2   *SS-Panzer Division Das Reich* 1939
3   *SS-Panzer Division Totenkopf* 1939
4   *SS-Polizei Division* 1939
5   *SS-Panzer Division Wiking* 1940
6   *SS-Gebirgs Division Nord* 1941

A fine study of *SS-Polizei Division* troops during the battle for France. Again, the mixture of *Polizei* and SS insignia is apparent. The officer wears a *Polizei*-pattern peaked service cap, but the belt buckle visible at his waist is the SS officer pattern.

7 *SS-Freiwilligen Gebirgs Division Prinz Eugen* 1942

8 *SS-Kavallerie Division Florian Geyer* 1942

9 *SS-Panzer Division Hohenstaufen* 1943

10 *SS-Panzer Division Frundsberg* 1943

11 *SS-Freiwilligen Panzergrenadier Division Nordland* 1943

12 *SS-Panzer Division Hitlerjugend* 1943

13 *Waffen-Gebirgs Division der SS (kroatische Nr 1) Handschar* 1943

14 *Waffen-Grenadier Division der SS (ukrainische Nr 1)* 1943

15 *Waffen-Grenadier Division der SS (lettische Nr 1)* 1943

16 *SS-Panzergrenadier Division Reichsführer-SS* 1943

17 SS-Panzergrenadier Division Götz von
   Berlichingen 1943

18 SS-Freiwilligen Panzergrenadier Division
   Horst Wessel 1944

19 Waffen-Grenadier Division der SS
   (lettische Nr 2) 1944

20 Waffen-Grenadier Division der SS
   (estnische Nr 1) 1944

21 Waffen-Gebirgs Division der SS
   (albanische Nr 1) Skanderbeg 1944

22 Freiwilligen Kavallerie Division der SS
   Maria Theresia 1944

23 Waffen-Gebirgs Division der SS Kama 1944

23 SS-Freiwilligen Panzergrenadier Division
   Nederland 1945

24 SS-Gebirgs Division Karstjäger 1944

25 Waffen-Grenadier Division der SS
   (ungarische Nr 1) Hunyadi 1944

26 Waffen-Grenadier Division der SS
   (ungarische Nr 2) 1944

27 SS-Freiwilligen Panzergrenadier Division
   Langemarck 1944

28 SS-Freiwilligen Panzergrenadier Division
   Wallonien 1944

29 Waffen-Grenadier Division der SS
   (russische Nr 1) 1944

29 Waffen-Grenadier Division der SS
   (italiensiche Nr 1) 1945

30 Waffen-Grenadier Division der SS
   (weissruthenische Nr 2) 1945

31 SS-Freiwilligen Grenadier Division
   Böhmen Mähren 1945

32 SS-Freiwilligen Grenadier Division 30
   Januar 1945

33 Waffen-Kavallerie Division der SS
   (ungarische Nr 3) 1945

33 Waffen-Grenadier Division der SS
   Charlemagne 1945

34 Freiwilligen Grenadier Division der SS
   Landstorm Nederland 1945

35 SS-Polizei Grenadier Division 1945

36 Waffen-Grenadier Division der SS 1945

37 SS-Freiwilligen Kavallerie Division Lützow
   1945

38 SS-Grenadier Division Nibelungen 1945

It will be noted that on some occasions, where a division was disbanded shortly after its formation, its number in the Order of Battle was subsequently re-allocated to another replacement unit.

In addition to these divisions, a number of volunteer 'Legions' were fielded. These were all relatively short lived, and in many cases their personnel were absorbed into one or other of the divisions. Fuller details are provided in the chapter on Foreign Volunteers.

SS-Freikorps Danmark
Formed 1941, Disbanded 1943
SS-Freiwilligen Legion Norwegen
Formed 1941, Disbanded 1943
SS-Freiwilligen Legion Niederlande
Formed 1941, Disbanded 1943
SS-Freiwilligen Legion Flandern
Formed 1941, Disbanded 1943
*Finnisches-Freiwilligen Bataillon der
   Waffen-SS*
Formed 1941, Disbanded 1943
Osttürkische Waffenverband der SS
Formed 1943
Kaukasischer Waffenverband der SS
Formed 1945
Indische Freiwilligen Legion der Waffen-SS
Formed 1944
Britische Freikorps
Formed 1944

The structure of the basic *Waffen-SS* combat division was in essence identical to that of its Army counterpart. The following illustration is for a *Waffen-SS* panzer division in the summer of 1944.

Divisionsstab	Divisional Staff
Panzer Regiment	Tank Regiment
Stabskompanie	Regimental Staff Company
Fliegerabwehrzug	Anti-Aircraft Platoon
I Abteilung	1st Battalion
Stabskompanie	Battalion Staff Company
1 Kompanie	1 Company
2 Kompanie	2 Company
3 Kompanie	3 Company
4 Kompanie	4 Company
Versorgungskompanie	Supply Company
II Abteilung (as for *I Abteilung*)	2nd Battalion
Panzerwerkstattkompanie	Tank Repair Company

Panzergrenadier Regiment 1	
Stabskompanie	Staff Company
I Bataillon	1 Battalion (each with 4 Companies)
II Bataillon	2 Battalion
III Bataillon	3 Battalion
Flak Kompanie	Anti-Aircraft Company
Panzerjäger Kompanie	Anti-Tank Company
Infanterie-Geschütz-Kompanie	Infantry Gun Company
Aufklärungs-Kompanie	Recce Company
Pionier-Kompanie	Pioneer Company

Panzergrenadier Regiment 2
As for *Panzergrenadier Regiment 1*

Panzer-Aufklärungs-Abteilung	Armoured Recce Battalion (HQ and 6 Companies
Sturmgeschutz Abteilung	Assault Gun Battalion (HQ and 3 Companies)
Panzerjäger Abteilung	Anti-Tank Battalion (HQ and 34 Companies)
Panzer-Artillerie Regiment	Armoured Artillery Regiment (HQ and 4 Battalions)
Flak-Artillerie Abteilung	Anti-Aircraft Battalion (HQ and 6 Companies)
Panzer-Pionier-Bataillon	Armoured Engineer Battalion (HQ and 4 Companies)
Nachrichtenabteilung	Signals Detachment (HQ and 2 Companies)

Ancillary units, such as medical, military police, were attached at divisional level.

Rest period and some rations for an SS-VT motorised unit. Note the goggles worn around the neck of all present. The shoulder-strap cipher just visible on one soldier identifies the unit as *SS-Standarte Deutschland*. A mixture of greatcoats and motorcyclist's rubberised coats is being worn.

CHAPTER FIVE

THE COMBAT BRANCHES

On the outbreak of war in 1939, the *Waffen-SS* (strictly speaking at that time still the *SS-Verfügungstruppe*) was still of very modest size. Only one unit, the *SS-Verfügungsdivision* which was in the process of being formed up, could be considered a significant military unit on a par with those in the German Army. The three SS-VT Regiments *Deutschland*, *Germania* and *Der Führer* were combined to form a division, with the addition of a new artillery regiment. In the event, however, the unit never took to the field in the Polish Campaign as a unified body, but was committed piecemeal, various sub-units being attached to larger Army formations.

The *Totenkopf Division* was still struggling to come up to strength, being studiously ignored by the Army, which took a very dim view of this unit, and indeed all SS units, and did what it could to avoid assisting them with the vehicles, weapons and equipment they needed.

The *Leibstandarte*, though well trained and equipped, was still only at regimental strength. The *Waffen-SS* units at this time fielded the basic components of the typical infantry units, with infantry, pioneers, signals, transport, reconnaissance and medical personnel.

After the SS units had performed relatively well in the Polish Campaign, Hitler ordered their full motorisation, and

thus the Army was finally forced to help provide equipment to the *Totenkopf Division* during the build-up for the Campaign in the West. A large proportion of this unit's equipment, however, was still a mixture of obsolescent and captured stock, plus whatever else its commander, *SS-Obergruppenführer* Theodor Eicke, could beg, steal or borrow. The only other unit of significant size on the strength of the *Waffen-SS* was the *SS-Polizei-Division*. The personnel of this unit, formed from members of the *Ordnungspolizei*, were not considered true members of the SS, though numbers of individual unit personnel did hold SS membership and wore a small set of embroidered SS runes on the left breast pocket to indicate this. The unit, though of division strength, was still horse-drawn and not considered ready for a front-line combat role, being held in reserve.

Around this time, *General* von Weichs paid a visit to the *Totenkopf Division* and was sufficiently impressed for his previous prejudice against these troops to be turned to enthusiastic praise.

Following the end of the Polish Campaign, the various elements of the *SS-Verfügungs division* were finally brought together into one unit, though problems were still being experienced in obtaining sufficient heavy artillery from the Army.

This crewman is serving on a 3.7 cm anti-aircraft gun of the divisional *Flak Abteilung*. The gun is mounted on an 8-ton SdKfz 7 half-track. Note the camouflage smock being worn and the camouflaged cover on the helmets sitting on the vehicle's bonnet.

Hygiene in the field was extremely important. This *SS-Sturmmann* is doing what he can to keep his teeth clean, rubbing them with a piece of rag with the aid of an old broken piece of mirror. He appears to be from the *SS-Polizei-Division*, as the *Polizei*-style collar patches can just be seen under his shirt collar. It is also interesting to note his early helmet cover devoid of the usual added loops for holding camouflage material.

The *Leibstandarte* at this time was strengthened by the addition of a light artillery battalion.

The Western Campaign of 1940 saw the combat units of the SS further improving their standing in the eyes of the Army, though there was still no shortage of strong detractors. In this Campaign the SS encountered first-rate French and British troops and began to show the sort of fanatical and reckless bravery that was to become its trademark.

Hygiene in the field yet again. Soldiers living in the field for extended periods quickly attracted lice and other unwanted pests. Here a trooper is given a close-cropped haircut by one of his comrades.

Naturally, captured vehicles were pressed into service wherever possible. Here a British truck captured in France is used by troops from the *SS-Totenkopf Division*.

There was, of course, a kind of logic in the tactics of the SS combat units. Imbued with fanatical loyalty and belief in their cause, as well as in themselves, their tendency to attack with determination and insist on attacking despite heavy casualties often meant that losses in the initial attack were significant, but it could also be argued that the sort of heavy losses taken by SS troops were only suffered for a brief period and usually secured the objective quickly. Taking a more cautious approach might appear to reduce casualties, but losses suffered in smaller batches would soon add up, and the total number of casualties which might mount up with attrition over a longer period taken to secure the objective might not be much smaller in the long run. Nevertheless, the SS methods drew much criticism from the Army.

Only three SS divisions and one regiment had taken part in the Western Campaign, as opposed to some 140 Army divisions. None of the official *Wehrmacht* communiqués even mentioned the *Waffen-SS* and the part it played in the Campaign. Hitler, however, showered the *Waffen-SS* with praise, and in August 1940 agreed to further expansion of the *Leibstandarte* from Regiment to Brigade status. Nevertheless at this point in time he was reluctant to antagonise his generals by allowing large-scale expansion of the *Waffen-*

The *SS-Sturmbannführer* from a *Totenkopf* unit shows yet another variant of the deathshead collar patches, a mirror image set of 'vertical'-pattern patches, a second deathshead symbol replacing the normal left-hand rank patch. His rank is displayed solely by his shoulder straps.

An example of the 2 cm flak gun mounted on an SdKfz 10 of a *Waffen-SS Flakabteilung*.

SS and set a recruitment level at between 5 and 10 per cent of that of the Army.

In order to circumvent to some degree the limitations on further recruitment, Himmler decided to make use of the large number of personnel in the numerous *SS-Totenkopfstandarten*. Over 40,000 served in these units, enough to create two full divisions. In the event, these units were re-designated as *SS-Totenkopf* infantry regiments, and several of them were subsequently used as the core units around which new SS divisions would be created.

Not until June 1941, shortly before the invasion of the Soviet Union, was another new SS division authorised. This, the *5 SS Division Wiking*, was built around the *Germania* Regiment, transferred from the *SS-Verfügungsdivision* and for which it received one of the aforementioned *SS-Totenkopf* infantry regiments as replacement. This new division, which would incorporate most of the then serving Nordic SS volunteers, would become one of the best in the *Waffen-SS*.

The next major stage in the expansion and development of the *Waffen-SS* came in January 1942 when Hitler approved the addition of an integral tank battalion for each of the *Leibstandarte, Das Reich,* and in May 1942 for the *Totenkopf* and *Wiking Divisions.*

September 1942 also saw the creation of the next *Waffen-SS* division, the *6 SS-Gebirgs Division Nord*, again around a nucleus provided by former *SS-Totenkopfstandarte* troops, followed in October by the creation of *7 SS-Freiwilligen Gebirgs Division Prinz Eugen* from the *Volksdeutsche* community in the Balkans and *8 SS-Kavallerie Division Florian Geyer*, the latter once again including former *Totenkopfstandarte* troops.

From this point, the *Waffen-SS* expanded rapidly, eight new divisions being created in 1943, and a further thirteen in 1944. Eleven new divisions were created in 1945, though in many cases these were simply existing units of smaller size which were expanded to divisional status on paper only. Nevertheless, by 1945, the *Waffen-SS* Order of Battle contained thirty-eight divisions, and within these units almost every branch of the combat services was represented. The *Waffen-SS*, although of much smaller size than the German Army, had gone from being the 'poor relation' of the *Wehrmacht*, deprived of sufficient vehicles, equipment and artillery, to become a force which fielded some of the most powerful military units which Germany possessed, and equipped with the most modern and advanced weaponry.

CHAPTER SIX

THE SUPPORT ARMS

SS-FELDGENDARMERIE

Like the various branches of the *Wehrmacht*, the *Waffen-SS* fielded its own military police. These were in the main former members of the *Schutzpolizei*, the civil police. As Himmler also held the post of *Chef der deutschen Polizei*, or Chief of the German Police, this was one area in which the *Waffen-SS* could not be hindered by *Wehrmacht* intransigence. The purposes of the military police were many and varied. Apart from the obvious tasks such as maintaining order and military discipline, the *SS-Feldgendarmerie* were tasked with traffic control and the maintenance and security of lines of communication, combating partisan activity, controlling prisoners of war, duties which in fact mirrored those of the *Feldgendarmerie* of the *Wehrmacht*.

The major difference between Army and *Waffen-SS* military police lay principally in the overall size of the organisation. In the main, *SS-Feldgendarmerie* were organised at *Trupp* or *Kompanie* level, attached to a parent *Division*, and bore the number of that *Division*. As an example, the *Feldgendarmerie* unit within *17 SS-Panzergrenadier Division Götz von Berlichingen* was *SS-Feldgendarmerietrupp 17*. There were also *Feldgendarmerie* units at *Korps* level, and at the *Feldkommandostelle* of the *Reichsführer-SS*. The *SS-Feldgendarmerie*, therefore, was truly a 'field' police force.

Their duties lay predominantly within the sphere of operations of their parent unit. Small in numbers, they would not necessarily be particularly well known, even to soldiers of the *Waffen-SS*. The *Feldgendarmerie* of the Army, however, were far more widespread, and as well as the units operating in the field with their parent divisions, included many units allocated to headquarters and garrison areas within Germany and the occupied countries. Many *Waffen-SS* soldiers would have encountered Army *Feldgendarmerie* when home on leave or in transit, but depending on their own particular duties may never have seen one of their own *Waffen-SS Feldgendarmerie*. This has indeed been confirmed by former veterans.

SS-Feldgendarmerie units were usually commanded by officers with the rank of *SS-Obersturmführer* or *SS-Hauptsturmführer*, high ranks being rare at divisional level. The typical *Feldgendarmerietrupp* would comprise some officers and NCOs with junior ranks. The unit would be equipped with light trucks, field cars and motorcycles. Typically, such units would not be armed with any weapons heavier than rifles, machine-pistols and a few machine-guns.

Like their Army counterparts, *SS-Feldgendarmerie* were identified by orange-red *Waffenfarbe* colouring where appropriate as piping on shoulder boards and headgear. Initially the Army cuffband bearing the title

Members of the military police detachment of the *Totenkopf Division* are presented with awards by their company commander.

Waffen-SS military police from the *Totenkopf Division* questioning a suspect. Military police, or *'Feldgendarmerie'*, are immediately identifiable by the metal gorget plate worn around the neck on a chain.

Feldgendarmerie in grey Gothic script on brown was worn, but this was later replaced by an SS pattern in grey Latin script on black, with the title *SS-Feldgendarmerie*. The standard Army military police gorget plate, worn on a chain around the neck, was also used by *Waffen-SS Feldgendarmerie*.

Though small in numbers, the *SS-Feldgendarmerie* played an important role. In many cases at the end of hostilities the *Feldgendarmerie* elements of captured *Waffen-SS* units were temporarily kept in place to help maintain order and discipline among the surrendered troops.

SS-KRIEGSBERICHTER

Himmler was well aware of the value of propaganda in maintaining a high profile for his SS troops and ensuring that their achievements were publicised. To that end, the *Waffen-SS* featured its own propaganda

troops (effectively, war correspondents, the term 'propaganda' having slightly different connotations in German as compared to English).

Initially, these were gathered in the *SS-Kriegsberichter-Kompanie* and were placed on temporary attachments to *Waffen-SS* units in the field. It is primarily thanks to these troops, many of whom lost their lives by insisting on operating at the front of the combat zones, that so much excellent photographic material on the *Waffen-SS* has been preserved for posterity.

The SS war correspondent company was ultimately expanded to regimental size and was commanded by *SS-Standartenführer* Günther D'Alquen, the editor of the 'in-house' newspaper of the SS, *Das Schwarze Korps*.

War correspondents were identified by the wearing of a cuffband, initially bearing the inscription SS-KB-Abt, later altered to

SS-Kriegsberichter. On being expanded to regimental status, the unit was given the honour title Kurt Eggers and bore this name on its cuffbands.

SS-UNTERFÜHRERSCHULEN

The *Waffen-SS* had access to its own NCO training facilities, specifically the NCO schools or *SS-Unterführerschulen* at Lauenberg and at Radolfzell. Staff at this school were identified by a cuffband bearing the inscription *SS-Unterführerschule* and the letters USL or USR on their shoulder straps as appropriate. During wartime, further training schools were established at Laibach, Lublinitz and Posen-Treskau.

SS-JUNKERSCHULEN

The SS officer training schools provided training for the whole of the SS, not just the *Waffen-SS*. The two main establishments were at Bad Tölz in Bavaria (*SS-Schule-Tölz*) and at Brunswick (*SS-Schule-Braunschweig*). Experienced decorated combat veterans were regularly rotated back from the front line to provide expert training based on first-hand combat experience. Staff and students at both establishments were identified by a cuffband bearing the title of their school, and the staff also by the letters JST or JSB on their shoulder straps. Pre-war, staff at these schools also wore collar patches with a small T or B alongside the regulation SS runes.

In addition to the schools at Bad Tölz and Brunswick opened prior to the war, training courses for officer cadets were also run at Klagenfurt and in Prague. It has been estimated that at least 15,000 officers were trained at *SS-Junkerschulen* during the period 1939–45. Although some *Waffen-SS* officers were transferees from other branches of the military and had already been trained, the vast majority, certainly at the ranks of *SS-Untersturmführer* to *SS-Hauptsturmführer*, were graduates of the *Waffen-SS* officer training system, some indication of the huge contribution made to the military success of the *Waffen-SS* and the aggressive manner in which SS troops were led in combat.

SS-HELFERINNEN

As with the *Wehrmacht*, so the *Waffen-SS* had its own corps of female auxiliaries, the *SS-Helferinnen*. These women fulfilled clerical and administrative tasks, and also served as auxiliaries in the signals branch, staffing telephone exchanges, and operating telex machines.

Female auxiliaries wore a plain grey suit comprising a skirt and jacket, over a white blouse. On the breast pocket was a large oval black patch with silver-grey SS runes, and on the left sleeve the standard SS version of the national emblem. On the lower left sleeve, those who had attended the training school at Oberrhein in Alsace wore a cuffband with the inscription *Reichsschule-SS*. Those employed in the signals branch wore the standard black diamond-shaped patch with lightning flash as worn by their male colleagues, on the lower left sleeve. A black side-cap with the SS version of the national emblem completed the outfit.

It was decreed that only those who had formally trained at Oberrhein were to be considered as *SS-Helferinnen*. Other women drafted in for wartime service, such as those who served as auxiliaries in concentration camps, were designated *Kriegshelferinnen*. These latter female auxiliaries were the responsibility of the *SS-Wirtschafts und Verwaltungs Hauptamt*. Fully trained *SS-Helferinnen* were controlled by the Telecommunications Service (*Chef der Fernmelderwesens*).

CHAPTER SEVEN

FOREIGN VOLUNTEERS

Although Himmler had originally seen the SS as a racially pure, Germanic organisation, the *Wehrmacht*'s opposition to the expansion of the SS had obliged the *Reichsführer-SS* to consider recruitment from outside the borders of the Reich, where the Army's authority over such matters was less robust.

Initially, Himmler, or more specifically, *SS-Obergruppenführer* Gotlob Berger on Himmler's behalf, restricted his recruitment to areas where the indigenous population was considered Germanic. Thus populations such as the Dutch, Danes, Norwegians were seen as suitable recruits to the SS. After the invasion of the Soviet Union in 1941, combat losses on the Eastern Front led to much greater demand for replacements, and so those nations not considered Germanic, but who were nevertheless considered racially acceptable, were permitted to serve with the SS. This brought in countries such as France and Belgium. Interestingly, in Belgium, the two main peoples who made up this nation were divided into Germanic and non-Germanic. The Belgian Flemings were not considered Germanic owing to their links with France, but the northern Walloons, closer to the Dutch, were acceptable as Germanic volunteers.

Towards the latter part of the war, the sheer need for replacements to fill combat losses, coupled with Himmler's still rampant desire for the expansion of the *Waffen-SS*, led to almost anyone willing to serve being recruited or even press-ganged into joining the *Waffen-SS*. Quite what the original members of the black-uniformed elite must have though of the concept of a Muslim SS man complete with fez can only be guessed at.

Fortunately *Waffen-SS* commanders in the field were inclined to be more pragmatic and were usually happy to accept good soldiers, whatever their origin, religion or, with some obvious exceptions, race.*

It may be useful to consider the foreign volunteers within the *Waffen-SS* in three categories, something the *Waffen-SS* itself did, applying three totally separate oaths of allegiance to these three groups.

THE FOREIGN LEGIONS

The concept of raising 'Legions' of foreign volunteers to serve with the *Waffen-SS* was

---

* There have been numerous claims of Jews entering SS service under false identities as a method of escaping detection and persecution, considering the SS as being the last place the SS would think to find a Jew. The author is unaware of any authenticated examples of what must have been an extremely dangerous and risky gamble.

This posed propaganda shot shows Flemish volunteers undergoing training with the Kar 98k rifle. European volunteers, initially at least, were not always well treated by their German instructors.

approved by Hitler on 29 June 1941. These units were raised to take part in Hitler's much-vaunted 'Crusade against Bolshevism'. By selling the concept of service with the *Waffen-SS* as an act contributing not specifically to the support of Germany and the Nazis, but to the defence of Europe against the perils of Bolshevism, the SS was able to gain many recruits who were, as often as not, fiercely nationalistic but not necessarily pro-Nazi.

The oath which was sworn by those who served in the foreign legions reflected the *raison d'être* of these units:

I swear by God, this sacred oath, that in the struggle against Bolshevism, I will unconditionally obey the Commander-in-Chief of the Armed Forces, Adolf Hitler, and as a faithful soldier am ready, at any time he may desire, to lay down my life for this oath.*

* *Ich schwöre bei Gott diesen heiligen Eid, dass ich im Kampf gegen den Bolschewismus dem Obersten Befehlshaber der deutschen Werhmacht, Adolf Hitler,* *unbedingten Gehorsam leisten und als tapferer Soldat bereit sein will, jederzeit für diesen Eid mein leben eizusetzen.*

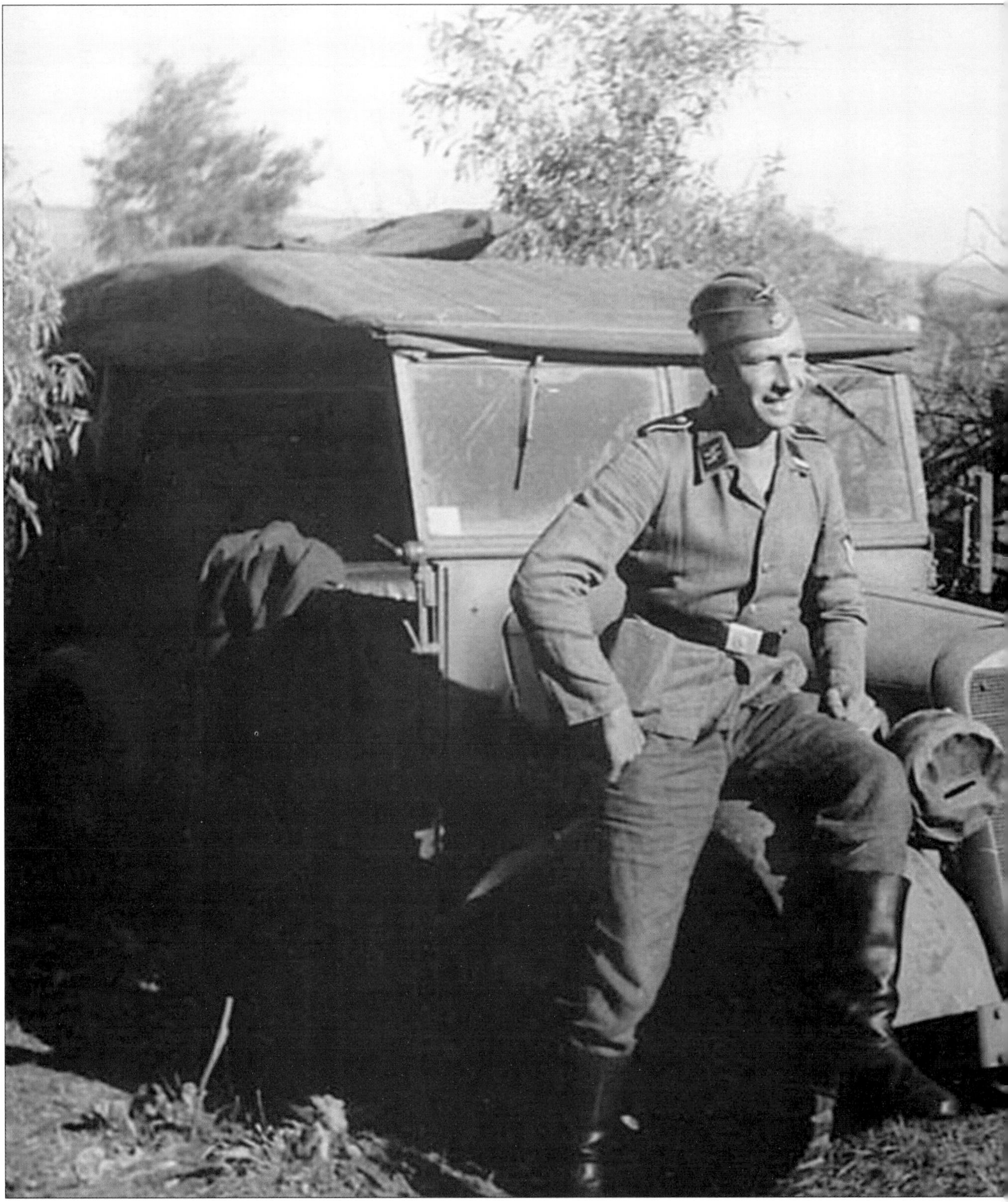

The wording of the oath is particularly interesting. There is no swearing of loyalty to Hitler in person or to Germany, only to obey orders emanating from Hitler in his capacity of C-in-C of the Armed Forces during the struggle against Bolshevism. Recruits signed up for an initial period of service of two years.

The first foreign legion to be raised, the *Freiwilligen Legion Niederlande*, was formed in the Netherlands just after the invasion of the Soviet Union in the summer of 1941. The SS had been recruiting small numbers of Dutch volunteers ever since the conclusion of the Campaign in the West in 1940, and had in fact set up a recruiting office in The Hague.

The German plenipotentiary for the Netherlands, *SS-Obergruppenführer* Artur Seyss-Inquart, appealed for further volunteers to serve on the Eastern Front against the Soviets. In this he was eagerly supported by the Dutch Nazi Party, the NSB. A boost to the nascent legion's morale was received when the highly respected General Seyffardt, former Chief of the Dutch General Staff, offered to lead the new formation.

What initially looked like a very promising level of recruitment was hampered by organisational problems. The Germans, feeling that the levels of training and experience among Dutch officers was inadequate, posted a number of German officers to the legion, and this caused much resentment among the Dutch volunteers, many of whom immediately resigned. In the event, the maximum size reached by the legion was around 2,600 men.

A Mercedes field car, one of a large range of military vehicles built by this prestigious company. The driver appears to be wearing a lightweight pocketless drill jacket but with full insignia added.

Waffen-SS troops examine a knocked-out Soviet light tank on the Eastern Front during the summer of 1941. Though these light tanks posed no threat to the Germans, the excellent T-34 medium tank came as a very nasty surprise.

On completing their training, the Dutch volunteers were committed to the northern sector of the Eastern Front in January 1942, in the area around Lake Ilmen, where they took part in a counter-attack against Red Army forces after several weeks of very heavy fighting. By the end of March, however, the legion had suffered horrendous casualties, losing some 80 per cent of its strength.

Withdrawn from the front line, the legion was brought up to strength once again, but this time the reinforcements included numbers of ethnic Germans as well as Dutch volunteers. Committed to the Leningrad Front once again, the Dutch SS troops fought well and captured the commander of the Soviet 11th Army and several thousand of his troops.

The year 1943 saw the legion still involved in heavy fighting on the Eastern Front, and it was here that on 9 March a young Dutch volunteer, Gerardus Mooyman, received the Knight's Cross of the Iron Cross for knocking out a total of thirteen Soviet tanks with his anti-tank gun during fierce combat. At the end of the following month, the legion was withdrawn from the front and sent back to Holland for a spell of well-earned leave.

It was at around this time that Himmler was pressing ahead with his decision to created a *Panzerkorps* around Germanic volunteer units. This would be part of the *Waffen-SS* proper, and not, as was the case of the legion, a unit simply serving *with* the *Waffen-SS*. This would require the volunteers to swear a personal oath of allegiance to

An *SS-Sturmmann* from the *Freiwilligen Legion Flandern*. Note the unit cuffband and the black rampant lion of Flanders on a yellow shield just above.

Hitler, something that many of the Dutch troops refused to countenance. Accordingly, on 20 May 1943, the legion was disbanded.

In September 1941, Flemish volunteers then serving with the Volunteer Regiment *Nordwest* were merged with a fresh intake of recruits to form the *Freiwilligen Legion Flandern*. After brief training, this new unit was despatched to the northern sector of the Eastern Front, where it took part in fierce defensive fighting before going over on to the counter-attack, proving itself both steadfast in defence and aggressive in the attack. Smaller than the Dutch volunteer legion, the Flemish troops were also to suffer heavy casualties during this period, and by April 1942 it is said that fewer than a hundred remained alive.

A Danish *SS-Untersturmführer* wears the rarely seen collar patch with a red and white Danish flag on the right-hand side.

Re-formed and reinforced, the legion went on to the offensive again against Soviet troops in the Volkhov pocket before being moved to the Leningrad Front, where it took part in fierce defensive actions both here and along the River Neva. By March 1943 it had once again been reduced in strength from just over 1,100 men to somewhere around sixty survivors. These few lucky survivors were withdrawn to their allocated depot in Breslau, where, like their Dutch compatriots, most refused to take the new oath of allegiance to Hitler, and the legion was disbanded.

Within a few weeks of the German invasion of Denmark in 1940, the first Danish volunteers were already coming forward for service in the *Waffen-SS*, though numbers were admittedly rather modest. Most of these found their way to the *Wiking Division*. At the end of June 1941, however, the existence of a new Danish volunteer corps was announced and a Campaign of recruitment of Danes with previous military experience began in earnest. Despite some initial confusion over their status it was ultimately agreed that such volunteers would retain previous Danish Army seniority and pension rights.

On 15 July 1941 the first batch of recruits reached Hamburg for training, and were designated as the *Freiwilligenverband Dänemark*, later to be renamed *Freikorps Danmark*. Within six months the unit had reached a strength of just under 1,200 men. The original commander, *Legions-Obersturm-bannführer* Kryssing, was a fervent Danish anti-Communist who owed no particular allegiance to the Germans, but rather upset them by declaring that as far as he was concerned the only purpose of the legion was to combat Bolshevism. Kryssing was moved sideways into an administrative position and replaced by a more politically acceptable candidate,

On the left is Christian von Schalburg, commander of the *Freikorps Danmark*. He is shaking hands with *SS-Unterscharführer* Soren Kam, a future Knight's Cross winner.

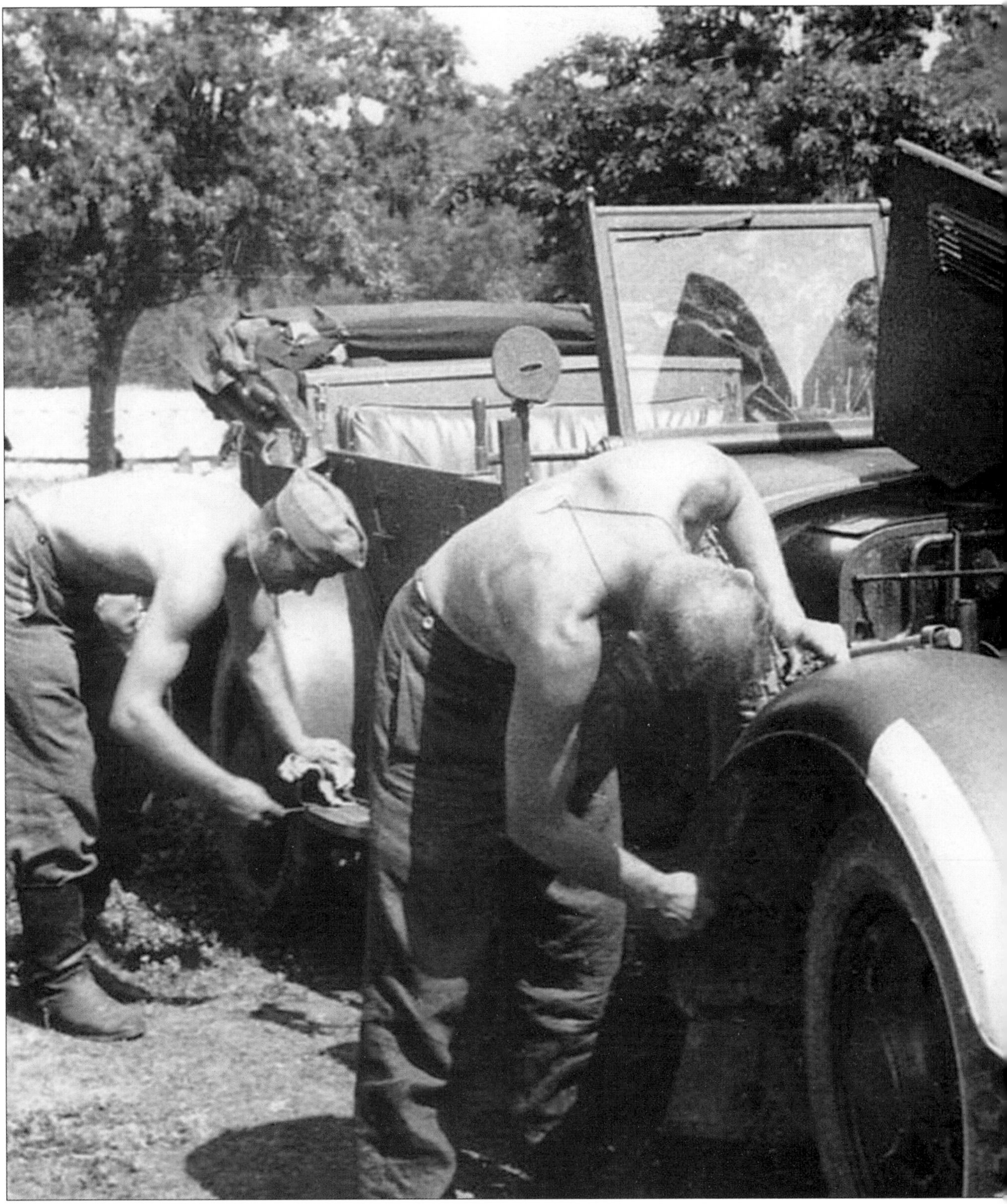

Legions-Sturmbannführer Christian von Schalburg, but this man was killed in action during the unit's first actions. The *Freikorps* was first committed to action in supporting the defence of the Demjansk pocket in May 1942, where it was subordinated to the *SS-Totenkopf Division*. Over the next few weeks *Freikorps Danmark* acquitted itself well, both during an attempt to destroy a Soviet bridgehead and then in the many desperate defensive battles as the Germans fought to prevent the elimination of the pocket by vastly superior Soviet forces.

The Danish volunteers were also instrumental in the recapture of Vassilievshtsina after it had been seized by Soviet troops, earning themselves grateful recognition by their German comrades. Heavy casualties had been sustained during this fighting, and unit strength was reduced to only around 22 per cent of original numbers. The *Freikorps* was relieved in August and given a spell of much needed leave in Denmark. By October, however, it was back on the Eastern Front, where it went into action in the area around Velikije Luki. In late December, after a quiet period in reserve, it saw fierce action around Kondratovo, whence it was ejected by Soviet troops, then it recaptured the village in a determined counter-attack. In late February it was involved in the attack and seizure of a Soviet stronghold at Taidy, after which, reduced once again to around 50 per cent

An Audi staff car is given a good clean and some maintenance work by two *Waffen-SS* soldiers. Many of these vehicles were simply civilian-specification automobiles pressed into military service. This one has lost its sleek glossy black finish. It has been replaced by a dull grey and blackout hoods have been fitted over its headlights.

of strength, it was withdrawn to Germany. Here, in line with the intention to incorporate the volunteer legions into mainstream *Waffen-SS* units, on 6 May 1943 the *Freikorps* was disbanded.

Norway, despite having its own home-grown National Socialist movement, the NS, or *Nasjonal Samling*, proved a less than fertile recruiting ground for the *Waffen-SS*.

Once again, however, despite the lack of enthusiasm for seeming to support Germany *per se*, the invasion of the Soviet Union saw an increase in willingness to serve alongside the Germans in the war against Communism. On 29 June 1941, a Norwegian volunteer legion was announced and recruitment commenced. Shortly afterwards, in August 1941, as the first few hundred recruits were shipped to Germany for training, the new unit was formally established as the *Freiwilligen Legion Norwegen*. It was sent into action on the Eastern Front around Leningrad on 16 March 1942 with a strength of some 1,150 men, under the command of *Legions-Sturmbannführer* Arthur Quist.

The legion suffered badly, taking heavy casualties almost immediately. This particular sector of the front was covered in swamps, marshland and thick forests. Mosquitoes were a particular menace and malaria was rife. Reinforcements were slow in coming, and attrition gradually whittled down the legion's numbers. It was released from the Leningrad Front briefly in late 1942 to serve alongside its Danish equivalent in Byelorussia, but by the end of the year had been returned to the northern sector of the front, where it once again took heavy losses in defensive battles around Uretsk and Krasny Bor. The legion was withdrawn from the front in February 1943 and its men were asked to join a new regular *Waffen-SS* unit being formed. Some agreed and took the new oath of allegiance, but many had had enough and under the terms of their original agreement were permitted to return home to Norway.

GERMANIC *WAFFEN-SS* VOLUNTEERS

Volunteers from the Germanic peoples, and those from the former foreign legions who had agreed to serve in the regular *Waffen-SS*, were required to swear an oath of allegiance to Adolf Hitler in person.

I swear to you, Adolf Hitler, as Germanic Leader, loyalty and gallantry. I vow to you and all those you place over me, obedience until death, so help me God.*

Immediately following the successful Campaign in the West in 1940, Gotlob Berger's recruiting personnel set about acquiring suitable racial stock from these conquered countries to serve in the SS. As most of these lands had, pre-war, their own home-grown equivalents to the Nazi Party in Germany, there was, initially at least, a degree of success for this recruitment programme.

The terms of service were to be similar to those for native German members of the *Waffen-SS*, former ranks and seniority held while serving in the volunteers' own national armed forces were transferable to the *Waffen-SS* and pay and other remunerations were the same as given to German troops. To clarify their legal status,

---

* *Ich schwöre Dir, Adolf Hitler, als germanischen Führer, Treue und Tapferkeit. Ich gelobe Dir und den von Dir bestimmten Vorgesetzten Gehorsam bis in den Tod, so wahr mir Gott helfe.*

As well as being used extensively as officers' staff cars in front-line areas, light field cars such as this Mercedes were fast and agile enough to be used by reconnaissance troops, as is the case here. This example has been camouflaged with a combination of netting and foliage.

they were to wear German uniform, but would wear national insignia (generally a shield in national colours) on their sleeve. As these troops were considered to be serving with the SS but were not actually members of the SS *per se*, they were generally provided with a special collar patch displaying a unique unit emblem, rather than the regulation SS runes, though this practice was often ignored due to availability or otherwise of insignia, and many foreign volunteers may be found in wartime photographs wearing the SS runic collar patch.

These recruits were to be gathered into two *Waffen-SS* regiments, named *Nordland* and *Westland*. To these volunteer regiments was added a German regiment, *Germania*, thus creating the nucleus for a new *Waffen-SS* combat division, which rather confusingly was also at first entitled *Germania*, but shortly thereafter altered to *Wiking*.

A third regiment, entitled *Nordwest*, was formed in April 1941, with the slight difference that recruits were to be considered as serving with the SS but were not to be considered as part of the *Waffen-SS*. By August over two thousand soldiers, a mix of Danes, Dutch and Flemings, were under training. The creating of the various foreign legions, however, meant that there was an insufficient level of volunteer manpower to fill both the legions and this regiment, and it was accordingly disbanded in September in favour of the new volunteer legions.

To the right can be seen the highly effective quadruple 2 cm gun, the *'Flakvierling'*, mounted on the SdKfz 7 half-track.

Meanwhile, the Germanic volunteers serving with the newly created *Wiking-Division* went on to distinguish themselves in action on many sectors of the Eastern Front, earning the respect of their Soviet adversaries, several of whom adjudged the *'Wikinger'* as among the best enemy troops they had encountered. The division quickly earned itself the status of an 'elite' unit, something that by no means all of the foreign volunteer units serving with the *Waffen-SS* achieved. By early 1943, however, it had suffered the inevitable consequences of eighteen months of vicious fighting on the Eastern Front and desperately needed returning to full strength. Himmler decided to take this opportunity to reorganise his Germanic volunteers into a new corps comprising two Germanic volunteer divisions and to be entitled *III (germanisches) Panzerkorps*. To this end a new division was created.

The original *Wiking-Division* would retain the *Germania* Regiment with its good mix of Danes, Dutch and Flemings as well as smaller numbers of Swedes, Finns, Estonians and even Swiss volunteers, plus the existing *Westland* Regiment. In addition, drafts from *Volksdeutsche* communities in the Balkans as well as German-born volunteers gave the *Wiking-Division* a truly 'international' mix.

The new division, entitled *Nordland*, would receive Danes, in the new *Danmark* Regiment, and Norwegians in the *Norge* Regiment. Like *Wiking*, it also received a number of *Volksdeutsche* volunteers and some experienced cadre personnel from *Wiking*. In addition the new corps would receive a brigade of Dutch armoured infantry known as *Nederland*.

Wiking took part in the battles around Kursk in the summer of 1943, suffering heavy losses but gaining an excellent combat reputation. It was converted to a panzer division in October of that year before becoming involved in the encirclement at Cherkassy, from which it broke out only with further heavy losses. Thereafter sent to Poland, it took part in the battles around Warsaw before moving south in late 1944 to participate in the relief of Budapest. It saw its final battles in the defence of Vienna in 1945, where it was virtually wiped out.

Nordland spent the first few months after its creation undergoing intensive training in Croatia before being transferred to the northern sector of the Eastern Front in January 1944. Allocated to *Heeresgruppe Nord*, it took part in the defensive withdrawals through the Baltic states and saw particularly fierce action at Narva. In the second half of September 1944, *Nordland* completed a 250-mile forced march from its positions near Narva to the Latvian capital, Riga, arriving in time to help prevent a major Soviet breakthrough. From here it took part in the fighting withdrawal into the Courland pocket, whence it was evacuated by sea. It saw its final actions as part of the force defending Berlin as the Third Reich collapsed.

The Netherlands also provided two further *Waffen-SS* divisions (though they were divisional in name only, never reaching full strength) when the *Nederland* and *Landstorm Nederland* Divisions were formed in late 1943. *Nederland* was formed around the nucleus of the independent Grenadier Brigade from *III (germanisches) Panzerkorps*. This unit was subsequently numbered as *23 SS-Frewilligen-Grenadier*

An example of the half-track-mounted flak gun being used against ground targets. These light flak guns could provide highly effective suppressing fire in support of infantry operations.

Walloon volunteers from *28 SS-Freiwilligen Grenadier Division Wallonien*, or more likely its predecessor *Sturmbrigade Wallonie*. These troops first served with the German Army before transferring to the *Waffen-SS*, hence the Army rather than SS-pattern Mountain Troop insignia worn on the right sleeve.

Division, with principal units being the Grenadier Regiments *General Seyffardt* and *De Ruiter*. It fought on the Eastern Front and was destroyed in the battle for Berlin.

Flanders also provided the *Waffen-SS* with a combat division. From the remnants of the *Freiwilligen Legion Flandern*, a new assault brigade, *SS-Sturmbrigade Langemarck*, was formed in May 1943. This was expanded to divisional status in October 1944 and numbered as *27 SS-Freiwilligen-Grenadier Division Langemarck*. Although nominally a division, it never exceeded the strength of a reinforced regiment. It distinguished itself

on several occasions on the Eastern Front, taking part in the fighting retreat through Poland, Pomerania and into Germany, where it fought in the defence of the approaches to Berlin.

NON-GERMANIC *WAFFEN-SS* VOLUNTEERS

Volunteers from the non-Germanic peoples who had agreed to serve in the regular *Waffen-SS* were also required to swear an oath of allegiance to Adolf Hitler in person:

I swear to you, Adolf Hitler, as Leader, loyalty and gallantry. I vow to you and all those you place over me, obedience until death, so help me God.*

It is with the non-Germanic units that the greatest variations of quality are to be found. Some of these units were utterly appalling, and of virtually no military value whatsoever, while others were every bit as good as some of the home-grown German *Waffen-SS* units.

Many of the early non-Germanic units (such as the French and Walloons) were initially taken into the German Army, at that point the *Waffen-SS* only being interested in accepting volunteers from nations considered racially Germanic. Eventually, however, pragmatism, to say nothing of Himmler's continued empire-building, saw firstly conscription into the *Waffen-SS* of *Volksdeutsche* in Eastern Europe (for example Romania, Hungary, Slovakia) in mid-1940, then the establishment of SS units from volunteers from the Baltic states in late 1942, and finally in early 1943, the acceptance of Bosnian Muslims saw the end of any pretence of accepting only racially 'pure' Germanic manpower.

A brief summary of the non-Germanic volunteer units (and the term 'volunteer' is used only loosely, as many of the so-called volunteers were conscripted) may give some idea of the great range in quality and effectiveness of these formations.

WEST EUROPEAN UNITS

28 SS-Freiwilligen-Panzergrenadier Division Wallonien
This unit had its origins in *373 Infanterie Bataillon* of the German Army, a volunteer unit composed of Belgian Walloons, who were predominantly members of the right-wing nationalist 'Rexist' movement led by Leon Degrelle. Despite being offered leadership of the military formation, Degrelle had refused, insisting on gaining combat experience in the ranks, and had won both Second and First Class Iron Crosses and earned his commission through skill and determination on the battlefield. His unit had earned the respect of the Germans, but their battlefield successes were only won at the cost of heavy casualties. In June 1943, the unit was absorbed into the *Waffen-SS* as *SS-Sturmbrigade Wallonien*. Attached to the elite *Wiking* Division, it saw heavy fighting in the Cherkassy pocket, from which it eventually broke out – with its reputation enhanced even further, but reduced in strength through battlefield casualties to just over 600 men. Degrelle was decorated with the Knight's Cross for his leadership of the *Sturmbrigade* during this fighting. After regrouping and receiving reinforcements the brigade was once again committed to action on the Eastern Front, fighting in the Battle of Narva and once again suffering heavy casualties. Degrelle became a firm favourite with Hitler, and in the autumn of 1944 added the Oakleaves to the Knight's Cross and the rare Close Combat Clasp in Gold to his decorations. Around this time the brigade was upgraded to divisional status, though this was only ever a paper exercise, the unit never reaching anything like full divisional strength. By 1945 the division was fighting around Stettin, being pushed ever further westwards by the relentless advance of the Red Army. Eventually, down to a handful of troops, it

---

* *Ich schwöre Dir, Adolf Hitler, als Führer, Treue und Tapferkeit. Ich gelobe Dir und den von Dir bestimmten Vorgesetzen Gehorsam bis in den Tod, so wahr mir Gott helfe.*

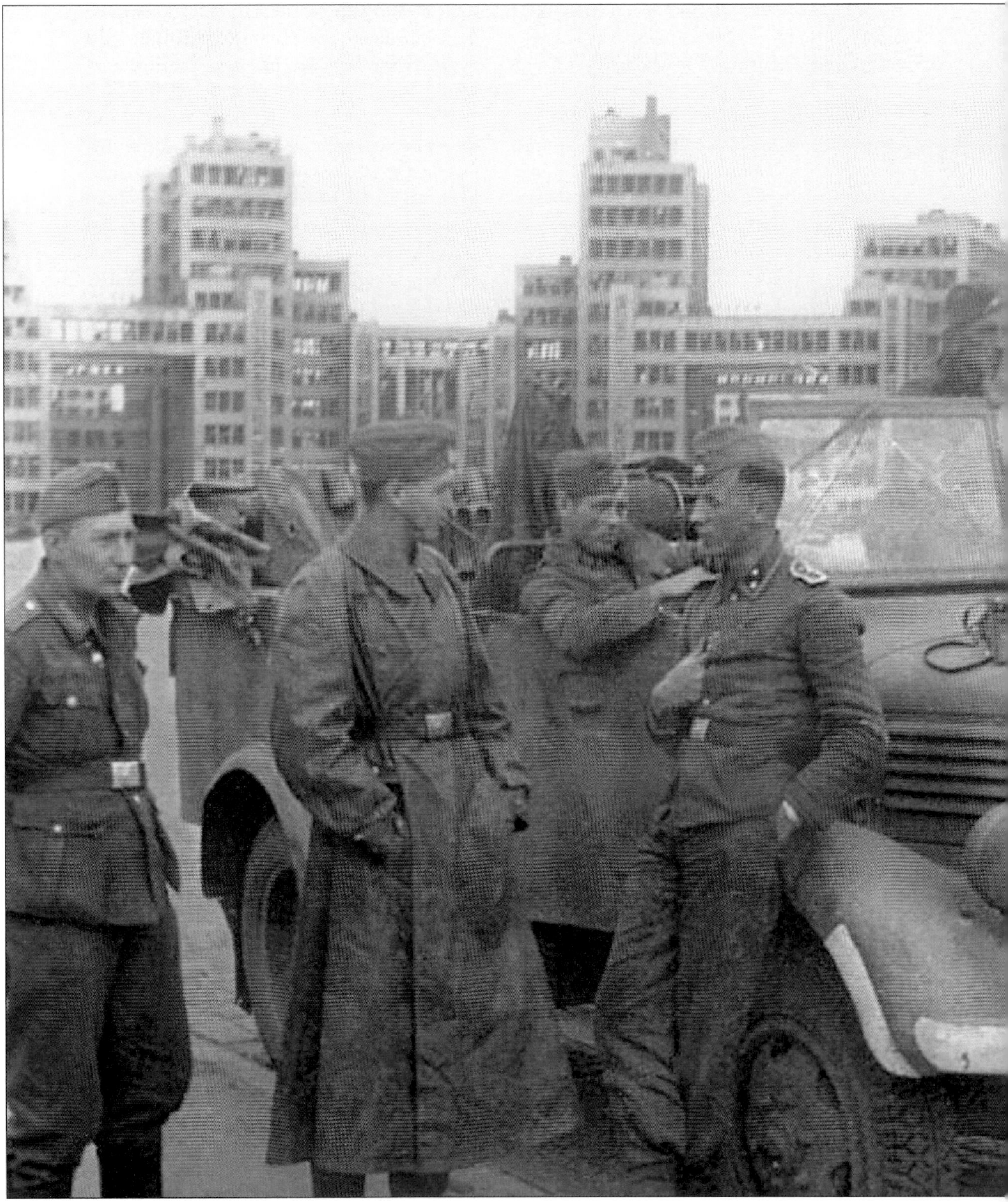

was withdrawn into Denmark, whence Degrelle made his escape by aircraft into Spain. Here he lived out the remainder of his life, totally unrepentant and surrounded by mementoes of his military career, and even occasionally appearing in uniform with full decorations.

29 Waffen-Grenadier Division der SS (italienische Nr 1)

On the surrender of the Italian government in 1943, there remained sizeable numbers of pro-Fascist soldiers in the Italian military who were perfectly prepared to continue fighting. The Germans lost no time in making use of this resource, and within months had formed a volunteer legion of several thousand Italian troops, though these were led in the main by seasoned German officers and NCOs. By the end of 1943, well over 15,000 troops had flocked to this new unit.

This newly created 'Sturmbrigade' was initially used in internal security operations against Italian partisans, but in early 1944 it was reorganised and sent to Germany for training in preparation for its use as a front-line combat unit. Despite the fact that these troops were loyal Fascists, prepared to fight on even after their country's government had surrendered, Himmler refused to consider them as 'true' Waffen-SS soldiers. The unit carried the typical 'Waffen-Grenadier' prefix used by non-Germanic volunteers, and the soldiers were not permitted to wear full SS insignia. Instead their badges were worked on a red rather

This Mercedes heavy field car is a direct equivalent of the Horch shown later. Many such vehicles were produced by different manufacturers but with broadly similar utilitarian bodies. They could also be used to tow light artillery pieces.

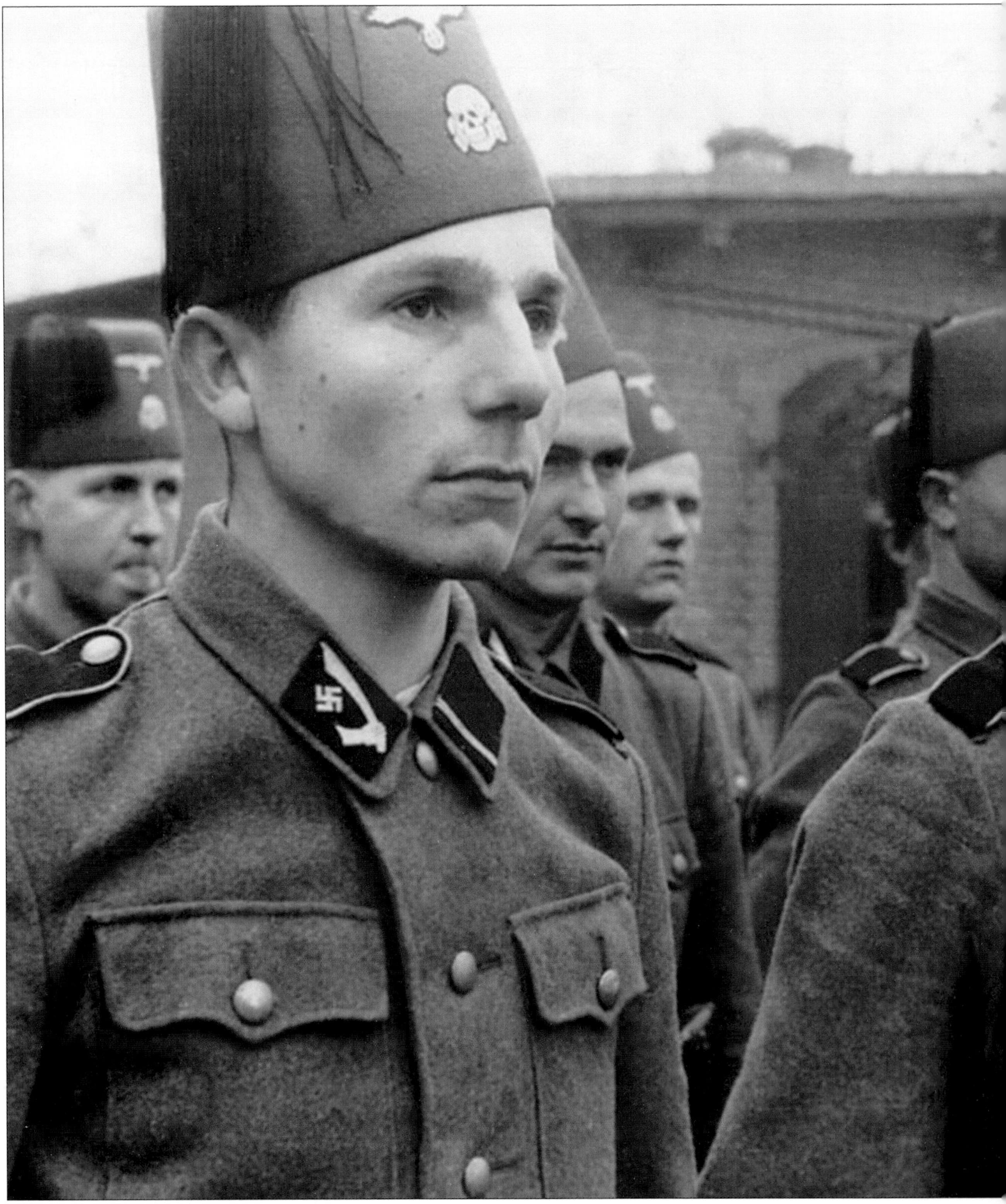

than black background and the eagle insignia they wore carried a fasces rather than a swastika in its talons.

In April 1944, these Italian SS troops were committed to the battle for Anzio and performed very well, so much so that Himmler ordered that the sub-units involved could thereafter wear regulation SS insignia.

These Italian SS troops fought consistently well both against partisans and front-line Allied combat units. In the closing stages of the war, they were upgraded to divisional status, though this was a simple paper exercise. In the final days of the war part of the division was fortunate enough to surrender to US forces. The remainder were still in action against partisan forces around Lake Como. Knowing the likely fate that would await them if captured, they fought to the very last bullet. When their ammunition ran out, they were captured by the partisans and massacred.

33 Waffen-Grenadier Division der SS Charlemagne

The first French combat soldiers to fight with the Germans were the *Légions Volontaires Français*, or LVF, a formation raised in 1941 and controlled by the German Army. It saw action in the central sector of the Russian Front in 1941–2, but suffered so heavily that it was withdrawn from the front and from 1942 to 1943 was used in rear-area security and anti-partisan duties.

Re-formed and reinforced, but still not up to full strength, it was committed to front-line action again in the summer of

This interesting shot shows Bosnian Muslim volunteers from the *Handschar Division*. Of particular interest is the traditional fez worn as headdress but with SS insignia, and the special collar patch of this unit.

1944, acquitting itself so well that in its area of operations the Red Army thought it was facing not one under-strength unit, but two full divisions of French volunteers.

In September 1944, the French volunteers were taken over by the *Waffen-SS* and redesignated as an *SS-Freiwilligen-Sturmbrigade*. Before this unit could see any major action, it was decided to pull together all French volunteers serving in other units (a number were attached to *18 SS-Freiwilligen-Panzergrenadier Division Horst Wessel*) and add these to the *Sturmbrigade* to create a new division.

This new unit was committed to the fighting on the Eastern Front in Pomerania in early 1945, where the sheer weight of Soviet forces facing it saw the unit smashed into three separate fragments, two of which were totally annihilated by the Soviets. The third managed to retreat to the Baltic coast, whence it was evacuated by sea to Denmark. From there it made its way to the area around Neustrelitz in the closing days of the war. Here the divisional commander, *SS-Brigadeführer* Krukenberg, released the survivors from their oath of allegiance. Around 500 or so, however, expressed willingness to fight on and were sent into the battle for the defence of Berlin. These few remaining troops fought with great courage, three of their number winning Knight's Crosses.

Those who had not wished to continue the fight could hardly have expected a hero's welcome on their return to France, but few would have guessed the fate that awaited them. While making their way westward into captivity they were intercepted by a column of Free French soldiers who unleashed a torrent of abuse at these 'renegades' for fighting in German uniform. When one of them was fool enough to make a scathing response about the Free French fighting in American uniforms, the enraged commander had the *Charlemagne* survivors executed on the spot.

This French volunteer unit was one of the best foreign volunteer units to serve in the *Waffen-SS*.

EAST EUROPEAN UNITS

7 SS-Freiwilligen Gebirgs Division Prinz Eugen

Formed on 1 March 1942 from a core of *Volksdeutsche* from Serbia and Croatia, with a number of Hungarians and Romanians, this was partly a volunteer force but with a sizeable proportion of conscripts. The principal function of this division was to combat Tito's Communist partisans in Yugoslavia, and as a unit intended for what were considered 'internal security' duties it was denied the latest high-quality weapons and equipment and was primarily issued with captured French, Yugoslav, Czech and Italian material. The unit was in almost constant bitter combat with Tito's partisan units from the day it took to the field until October 1944, when it was tasked with covering the withdrawal of German forces through Yugoslavia and came into contact with regular Red Army units. Here it suffered badly with severe losses, including its commander *SS-Obergruppenführer* Artur Phleps, who was captured and executed by Soviet troops. Although not one of the best *Waffen-SS* divisions in terms of its combat achievements, it was far from being the worst, and six soldiers from the division earned the Knight's Cross of the Iron Cross.

13 Waffen-Gebirgs-Division der SS Handschar

This quite appalling unit was formed in February 1943, being raised from Croatian Muslims in a blatant attempt to utilise the traditional Muslim enmity against the Christian Serbs who provided the bulk of

Tito's partisan forces. The unit again was composed of a mixture of volunteers and conscripts, some of very poor quality. During its training period in France in the second part of 1943, the division mutinied and murdered a number of its German officer cadre. Amazingly, in a *Waffen-SS* where membership of any organised religion was superseded by the *'Gottglaubig'* concept, this unit was allowed to have its own Imams and Mullahs and its personnel were permitted to make their religious devotions every day. Once committed to combat actions against Tito's partisans, its performance was mediocre to say the least, and its appearance was usually followed by reports of atrocities against the local populace. Himmler eventually tired of the unreliability of this unit and disbanded the Muslim element, retaining only the trusted German and *Volksdeutsche* cadre personnel to form a regimental *Kampfgruppe*. In this form, the remnants of *Handschar* saw combat against units of the Red Army and acquitted itself well.

It must also be mentioned that the *16 SS-Panzergrenadier Division Reichsführer-SS* was on a number of occasions referred to in movement orders as the *Handschar Division*, in a ruse intended to confuse the enemy over its true identity, and some reports of the latter fighting well may in fact relate to the former. The sad truth is that the amount of time and resources lavished on recruitment and training of this unit could have been much better spent, resulting as it did in a formation which for a good part of its existence was little more than a mutinous rabble of dubious military value. Five of the division's soldiers were decorated with the Knight's Cross, but it should be pointed out that these were all members of the German cadre, and the awards were all made after the discharge of the Muslim personnel.

14 Waffen-Grenadier Division der SS (galizien Nr 1)

Attempts to recruit anti-Communist Ukrainians into the *Waffen-SS* were encouraged by the military commander of the region, *SS-Brigadeführer* Wächter, and in March 1943 permission for the raising of a volunteer division was given. The issue met with overwhelming success in its early stages, with over 100,000 volunteers coming forward. Unfortunately many, though enthusiastic, were of poor quality, but over 30,000 were accepted – enough to form a full division. The spurious 'Galician' tag was because recruitment was supposed to have been restricted to that part of Poland that had been part of the former Austro-Hungarian empire and thus fitted with the racial stereotype of the ideal SS man. It also aided Himmler in avoiding the issue that he was in fact recruiting Slavs, whom he had previously declared racially inferior. Himmler even gave permission for this unit, composed mostly of Catholics, to maintain its own divisional clergy, something unheard of in German SS units.

The division, once trained, was committed to the central sector of the Eastern Front, and sent into action around the Tarnow-Brody pocket, where it was all but annihilated, losing around 80 per cent of its strength in bitter fighting. Its remnants were withdrawn from the front for refitting and never saw serious action again. It is reported, however, that survivors of this fighting roamed the area for several years after the end of the war, engaging in guerrilla actions against the Soviets.

Despite its mauling, the division was gradually rebuilt, and by 1945 had reached a strength of some 13,000 men. It was sent into Czechoslovakia to help put down the Slovak uprising, and from there it moved into Yugoslavia for action against the partisans, but in the event saw little action in the closing stages of the war. It gradually moved westwards and surrendered to the Western Allies, the bulk of its manpower avoiding capture by the Soviets and the almost certain death that such capture would bring. Only one member of the division, its commander, *SS-Brigadeführer* Fritz Freitag, was decorated with the Knight's Cross.

15 Waffen-Grenadier Division der SS (lettisches Nr 1)

Latvian volunteer units had been formed as early as 1941, when police and security units were raised to help keep rear areas free from Soviet partisan activity. In 1943 some of these units were attached to *Heeresgruppe Nord*, gaining front-line combat experience.

Subsequently, permission was given for the raising of a Latvian legion, and substantial numbers of volunteers, in excess of 30,000, came forward. Command of the new unit was given to the former Latvian Minister of War, Rudolf Bangerskis, who was given the rank of *SS-Gruppenführer*.

The new unit first went into action in November 1943, facing a new Soviet Winter Offensive, and suffered heavy losses. The Latvian troops fought with great determination as the Red Army approached their homeland, earning considerable respect from their German comrades. Although the unit was pulled out in time to escape encirclement when Latvia fell in October 1944, the volunteers lost much of their heart once their homeland had fallen. The division was gradually pushed westwards and was fortunate enough to surrender to the British in April 1945. Five soldiers from the division were decorated with the Knight's Cross.

19 Waffen-Grenadier Division der SS (lettisches Nr 2)

Formed in March 1944 following the favourable response to the recruiting

Campaign which resulted in the formation of *15 Waffen-Grenadier Division*, this new division reached a strength of just over 10,000 men and, like its companion Latvian unit, fought with great courage to defend its homeland from the approaching Red Army. The division was pushed into the Courland pocket, whence some of its personnel were evacuated by sea to Germany, the remainder being captured by the Soviets when the pocket finally surrendered at the end of the war.

This division was one of the best of the foreign volunteer units, with eleven of its soldiers being awarded the Knight's Cross.

The Soviet Union had annexed Latvia prior to the outbreak of the Second World War, and so considered Latvians as Soviet citizens. Most captured Latvian volunteers were therefore deemed to be traitors and executed.

20 Waffen-Grenadier Division der SS (estnisches Nr 1)

Estonia had suffered the same fate as Latvia prior to the Second World War, having been forcibly annexed by the Soviet Union. Many Estonians were already fighting guerrilla actions against the Soviets when the Germans attacked Russia in 1941. Not surprisingly the Germans were seen as liberators, and when the Germans, astutely, asked for volunteers to serve against the Red Army on the anniversary of the liberation of the Estonian capital Tallinn from the Soviets, the response was extremely favourable. Like their Latvian counterparts, Estonian volunteers were already serving with the German Army, but on the decision to form a new Estonian division for the *Waffen-SS* in 1944, most of these troops joined the newer recruits into the SS to create the new division. Committed to the front in mid-1944, they too fought well, particularly distinguishing themselves at the Battle of

Narva. It was eventually pushed back into the Courland pocket, whence it was evacuated by sea to Germany. Returned to the Eastern Front once again, it was pushed back into Poland, being badly mauled in the fighting in Silesia and retreating into Czechoslovakia, where the bulk of the division ended the war surrendering to the Red Army. Most of them were executed. A fortunate few made their way west and surrendered to the Anglo-American forces.

21 Waffen-Gebirgs Division der SS (albanisches Nr 1) Skanderbeg

Albania had been under Italian control until the Italian surrender in 1943, at which point the Germans took over. Himmler lost no time in attempting to recruit Albanian Muslims for the war against the Communist partisans. This new Albanian Division was formed in April 1944 but recruitment was slow, quality poor and the numbers disappointing. Only 6,000 or so Albanians were adjudged suitable for service in the *Waffen-SS*, and this number was padded out with drafts of *Volksdeutsche* and German cadre personnel.

It was finally sent into action in August 1944 and its performance proved abysmal. In just two months well over 3,000 of its troops deserted. Those who did remain seemed more intent on settling scores with their personal enemies, resulting in a number of atrocities being committed. Himmler even resorted to drafting in thousands of German sailors in an attempt to make up numbers, but little could be done to turn this unit into a worthwhile fighting force and it was disbanded in early 1945.

23 Waffen-Gebirgs Division der SS (kroatisches Nr 2) Kama

Another failed attempt, this unit was created from Bosnian Muslims with a cadre of *Volksdeutsche* and German personnel. A

number of trained Muslim NCOs and officers were also drafted in from the *Handschar Division*. Ten months after its formation, the division was still in training. Discipline problems were rife, and mindful of the mutinous conduct of the *Handschar* troops during their training in France, Himmler ordered its immediate disbandment.

25 Waffen-Grenadier Division der SS (ungarisches Nr 1) Hunyadi

This unit, formed in mid-1944, was composed of Hungarian ethnic volunteers. It was still under training and working up to combat readiness when Hungary was overrun by the Red Army. It was nowhere near ready for use and was swiftly annihilated.

26 Waffen-Grenadier Division der SS (ungarisches Nr 2)

Formed in the autumn of 1944, this Hungarian unit was bolstered by the addition of *49 SS-Panzerbrigade Gross* as well as drafts of Hungarian and Romanian Army troops retreating westwards. Despite this, like *25 Waffen-Grenadier Division* it was nowhere near ready for use when it was overrun by the Red Army.

29 Waffen-Grenadier Division der SS (russisches Nr 1)

One of the worst military units ever to have been created, the origins of this formation lay in early 1942 when the mayor of the town of Lokat in central Russia sought permission from the Germans to raise a 'self-defence' force to protect the inhabitants from partisan attacks. The original 500-man force was extremely successful. Unfortunately, however, the mayor, who personally led the force, was killed in action, and his replacement, though an educated and intelligent man, was one of the cruellest despots in modern history.

Bronislav Kaminski had a fanatical hatred of Communists, and having been a prisoner of the Soviet system himself, lost no opportunity to extract revenge on his former tormentors. He pursued the Communist partisans with determination and total lack of mercy. Atrocities were common, and as the Kaminski unit grew in size it began to resemble some medieval private army, the arrogant and corrupt Kaminski answering to no one and on occasion treating his own men almost as brutally as he treated the partisans.

To the Germans, however, Kaminski was a valued resource, as partisan activities in the areas in which he operated almost invariably ceased. By late 1943, over 10,000 men were serving with Kaminski and he had been decorated with the Iron Cross.

In 1944, the unit adopted the grandiose title of the Russian People's Liberation Army, or RONA. Himmler adopted the Kaminski unit as *SS-Sturmbrigade* RONA. Ultimately raised to divisional status, though it never in reality grew to more than regimental size, it was undergoing training when the Warsaw Uprising began. Kaminski's troops were committed to the battle for Warsaw, and began a brief but horrific reign of terror the like of which had not been seen since medieval times. Men, women, children, sick and wounded were butchered with equal enthusiasm. As well as their enthusiasm for killing, Kaminski's troops were dedicated to filling their pockets with loot stolen from their victims. Their behaviour shocked even some of the hardened SS anti-partisan units. Kaminski's rabble even threatened to shoot German troops who tried to interfere with their savage rampage. The senior commander in charge of operations, *SS-Obergruppenführer* Erich von dem Bach-Zelewski, was finally persuaded by the sheer volume of complaints flooding in from German units

about Kaminski's behaviour that action was essential. Kaminski was arrested and charged with looting, conveniently ignoring the countless murders committed by his men. After a brief field court martial he was found guilty and swiftly executed, his death being covered up by means of a fake partisan ambush, the remnants of his unit being transferred to former Red Army General Andrei Vlassov's Russian Army of Liberation.

30 Waffen-Grenadier Division der SS (russisches Nr 2)

Volunteers from the largely anti-Communist population in Byelorussia had been serving with the Germans since the autumn of 1941, generally in police and anti-partisan units, and although the generally pro-German attitude waned somewhat as the war drew on, when the decision to form a further *Waffen-SS* division was taken in the summer of 1944, there were still many willing volunteers. The unit, after training, was sent into action in France, to combat the resistance fighters of the Maquis. The unit's performance was entirely sub-standard and many of its members deserted. This resulted in the 'division' being downgraded to brigade status. It was easily swept back by the advancing Allies, and in early 1945 its personnel were turned over to Vlassov for incorporation into his Russian Army of Liberation. Captured by the Red Army in May 1945, most were executed out of hand.

Mention should also be made of the large number of Cossacks who served with the German forces. These men were originally under the control of the German Army and remained so until 1944, when they were absorbed into the SS. This, however, appears to have been an entirely administrative move, and the Cossacks retained their original uniforms and the various German cadre and liaison staff serving in these units remained Army rather than *Waffen-SS* personnel.

In addition to the units considered above there were a number of smaller units, mostly of little or no military significance, but nevertheless of some historical interest and in some cases of great propaganda value to the Germans.

SPAIN

A considerable number of Spanish volunteers had seen service with the German Army on the Eastern Front with the famous 'Blue Division'. When Generalissimo Franco, under pressure from the Western Allies, withdrew his troops in 1943, a small number elected to remain and continue the fight against the Soviets. These men were formed into two companies, *SS-Freiwilligen Kompanie (span.) 101* and *102*, which were committed to battle around Krasny Bor. Given the small number, it did not take long for these units to be whittled down by battlefield casualties. The survivors went into action in the battle for Berlin, and the handful remaining alive at the end of hostilities were taken prisoner by the Red Army.

SWEDEN

Probably no more than 130 Swedish volunteers served in the *Waffen-SS*. Most of these were gathered in *SS-Aufklärungs Abteilung 11*, part of the elite *Nordland* Division which contained so many other Nordic volunteers.

FINLAND

Finland contributed a battalion of volunteers to the *Waffen-SS*. Formed in June 1941, this small contingent was to become the *Finnisches-Freiwilligen-Bataillon der Waffen-SS*. It served briefly with the *Wiking-Division*, but in 1943 it was disbanded and its personnel returned to serve with the Finnish Army.

INDIA

In April 1943 a number of Indian troops who had served with the British Army were persuaded to join forces with the Germans. Sufficient numbers of supporters of the nationalist leader Chandra Bose came forward to justify the creation of a full regiment, *Indisches Infanterie Regiment 950*. It seems unlikely that the German Army ever seriously considered committing this force to front-line combat, and most probably considered its worth more in terms of propaganda than military value. The unit was absorbed into the *Waffen-SS* in November 1944, and although a special SS-style collar patch bearing a tiger's head was manufactured it is considered doubtful if these troops ever wore anything other than the standard lightweight German Army tropical issue uniforms they were originally issued with.

GREAT BRITAIN

A small number (sources vary, but the total number was probably between fifty and sixty) of British POWs in German hands were persuaded to agree to serve with this so-called 'Corps' in early 1944. They were a rather motley crowd, prone to serious indiscipline problems, and were probably more of a liability than an asset to the Germans. A mere handful may have seen some action with the *Nordland-Division*, and it is believed that a few may have been killed during the battle for Berlin, but in reality their military worth was virtually nil, although the Germans no doubt derived some satisfaction from being able to claim that British troops were serving with the SS in its 'Crusade against Bolshevism'.

CHAPTER EIGHT

UNIFORMS AND INSIGNIA

The number of different uniform types worn by the *Waffen-SS* in the period from its earliest days through to the final days of the war in May 1945 was quite astonishing. To cover each and every variant would take far more space than can be devoted to this complex subject here. Accordingly, only a brief overview of the subject, covering those uniform types the reader is most likely to encounter in typical wartime photographs, is provided here. For those who wish to study the subject in greater depth, a number of books are recommended in the Bibliography.

THE BLACK SERVICE UNIFORM

During its earliest days, the SS-VT used the same black service uniform as the *Allgemeine-SS*. This comprised either black shoes with trousers or black jackboots with breeches, worn together with a four-pocket, open-collar tunic and a black visor cap, steel helmet or field cap. A black greatcoat could also be worn. The long trousers featured white piping to the outer seam of the leg.

The tunic, first introduced in 1932, was a smartly cut garment, fastened by four aluminium pebbled-finish buttons. It featured two pleated patch-type breast pockets with button-down flaps, and two unpleated skirt patch-pockets with an external button-down slanted flap. At each side seam at waist level were alloy belt-support hooks, and at the top of the single skirt vent on the jacket rear were two further pebbled-aluminium buttons, which also served to support the belt.

The open collar was piped in twisted black/white cord for lower ranks, twisted black/silver cord for NCOs and in silver twist cord for officers. From October 1934 the black/white twisted cord was deleted and black/silver twist-cord was worn by all non-officer ranks.

From May 1933, a single shoulder strap was worn on the right shoulder, the design of which reflected the wearer's rank grouping as follows:

SS-Mann–SS-Hauptscharführer
Straight twisted black/silver cord braids
SS-Untersturmführer–SS-Hauptsturmführer
Straight twisted silver cord braids
SS-Sturmbannführer–SS-Standartenführer
Plaited silver cord braids – 4 loops
SS-Oberführer–SS-Oberstgruppenführer
Plaited silver cord braids – 8 loops

Collar patches were worn, piped in a similar manner to the collar itself, showing the rank insignia on the left collar and the unit insignia on the right. Generally speaking, enlisted-rank collar insignia are most often encountered in machine-embroidered silver-grey thread, and officers in hand-embroidered aluminium wire, though some NCO ranks wore officer-quality patches, but with their own black/silver twist piping rather than the distinctive silver officer piping.

On the upper left arm was worn the regulation armband, in red wool with a circular white disc in the centre, bearing a black swastika, but bearing the addition of a stripe of black tape material just inside the upper and lower edges of the band.

Where appropriate, the unit cuffband was worn on the lower left sleeve along the upper edge of the turn-back cuff. The bands were woven in 3 cm wide black rayon with interwoven aluminium thread edging some 3 mm wide. Once again, the most likely form to be encountered would be with the lettering machine-embroidered in silver-grey thread for enlisted ranks and hand-embroidered, or machine-woven aluminium thread for officers. Again, however, lower ranks were known to wear officer-quality bands.

The black service tunic was worn with a brown shirt and black tie by lower ranks and with a white shirt and black tie by officers.

In cold weather, a black wool greatcoat was used. This full-length double-breasted coat was worn with full insignia on shoulder strap, armband, collar patches and cuffband, the collar being trimmed in the same style of piping as the jacket.

Officers wore a black leather belt with a circular, silvered-metal buckle showing an eagle and swastika surrounded by the SS motto 'Mein Ehre Heisst Treue', which was adopted in 1931. Enlisted ranks also wore a black leather belt, but in this case the buckle was rectangular, with a circular central motif showing a design similar to that on the officer buckle, but for the eagle having a larger wingspan. A leather cross-belt was also worn by both officers and enlisted men. This was passed under the shoulder strap on the right shoulder and attached to the belt to the left of the waist-

This *SS-Sturmmann* from the *SS-Totenkopfverbände* wears a later version of the black service dress. Note that no numeral is worn on the collar patch and the steel helmet is of the modern, smaller, M35 pattern with the standard decal of black runes on a silver shield, and with a white rather than brown shirt.

belt at front and back. By the outbreak of war use of the cross-belt had all but ceased and formal orders ending its use were issued in May 1940.

Enlisted ranks wore standard black leather cartridge pouches for the Gew 98 rifle or Kar 98 carbine. For parade duties, the *Leibstandarte* had the distinction of wearing white leather accoutrements rather than black.

HEADGEAR

The visor cap worn with this uniform had a shiny black lacquered *vulkanfiber* peak, a black wool or tricot top and a black band in either wool/tricot for lower ranks or velvet for officers. Piping to the crown and upper and lower edges of the band was in white for all ranks, with the exception of *SS-Oberführer* and above, who wore woven aluminium braid piping.

The lower ranks' cap was worn with a leather chinstrap retained by black buttons, and the officers' cap with aluminium braided chin cords, retained by aluminium buttons.

Insignia consisted of a deathshead emblem on the front of the band, and an eagle and swastika emblem on the front of the crown. Prior to 1935, the deathshead pattern used was of the old hussar style, without lower jaw. From 1935 onwards a distinct SS pattern with full lower jaw was used.

In 1936, the eagle and swastika national emblem also changed, from a small type as used on other party headgear to a larger, distinct SS style.

The field cap (*Feldmütze*) worn with the black service dress by lower ranks was cut from black wool and featured a scalloped front portion to its flap. A small silvered-metal button embossed with a deathshead was worn on the front of the flap, and a small national eagle and swastika emblem, embroidered in silver-grey thread on a triangular piece of black wool, was stitched to the left-hand side of the crown.

The steel helmet worn with the black uniform was of the First World War style (M16 or M18) with the large rim and projecting vent lugs, replaced in 1935 with the new, smaller and neater M35 pattern with rolled rim and non-projecting vent bushes. The helmets were finished in semi-gloss black paint. On both sides just below the vent were decals as follows:

Early 1934–autumn 1934
Right side, white runes on black shield.

Left, national colours tricolour.
Leibstandarte only

Autumn 1934–autumn 1935
Right side, black runes on silver shield.
Left, national colours tricolour.
Leibstandarte only

Autumn 1934–autumn 1935
Right side, black runes with white border within black circle with white border.
Left, white bordered black 'mobile' swastika. SS-VT

Autumn 1935–May 1945
Right side, black runes on silver shield.
Left, red shield with white disc and black swastika. All SS units

Although not commonly seen on photographs of *Waffen-SS* personnel, the standard edged weapons (daggers and swords) as introduced for wear with the black service dress were worn with all forms of dress by SS-VT and *Waffen-SS* troops on appropriate occasions. These are described in Chapter Ten.

EARTH-GREY UNIFORMS

At the same time as the introduction of the four-pocket tunic to replace the older, traditional brown shirt, a version of the new-style tunic in a colour designated 'earth-grey' was produced. Although worn initially, the swastika armband was soon deleted from the earth-grey tunic as being far too conspicuous for use in the field. At first the single shoulder strap on the right shoulder as worn on the black service dress was featured, but this later changed to the military style of wearing shoulder straps on both shoulders.

As well as breeches, long trousers and 'boot-trousers' (for wear with jackboots

The circular alloy buckle worn by SS officers in the field. Its clasp, however, was prone to opening unexpectedly in combat, and so many officers opted to wear the plain Army officer's belt with double claw buckle.

rather than shoes) were also manufactured in earth-grey. Unlike the black trousers, the earth-grey versions did not feature white piping to the outer seam.

An earth-grey field blouse was also introduced in 1935. This was similar to the earth-grey service tunic, but with split cuffs and with Army-style belt-hook supports on the front and rear on each side, rather than the side hooks and rear button support arrangement on the tunic.

Around this time, the M16 and M18 steel helmet began to be painted in a brownish-grey shade, and around the end of 1935 a grey version of the visor cap was introduced for officer ranks. Again this retained the same form as the previous version used with the black service dress, but had the crown

manufactured from so called 'earth-grey'-coloured wool. The band remained black.

In 1936, a grey version of the *Feldmütze* was introduced. This was identical in cut to the earlier black version and used the same insignia, though the metal deathshead button was usually painted in a grey-green colour. Around this time, stocks of the new M35-style steel helmet began to see issue to SS troops.

It should be noted that a mix of both black and earth-grey uniform parts being worn at the same time was far from uncommon, due to the staggered introduction times of each part. Photographic evidence suggests that some elements of the old pre-war earth-grey service dress were still being used during the early part of the Second World War.

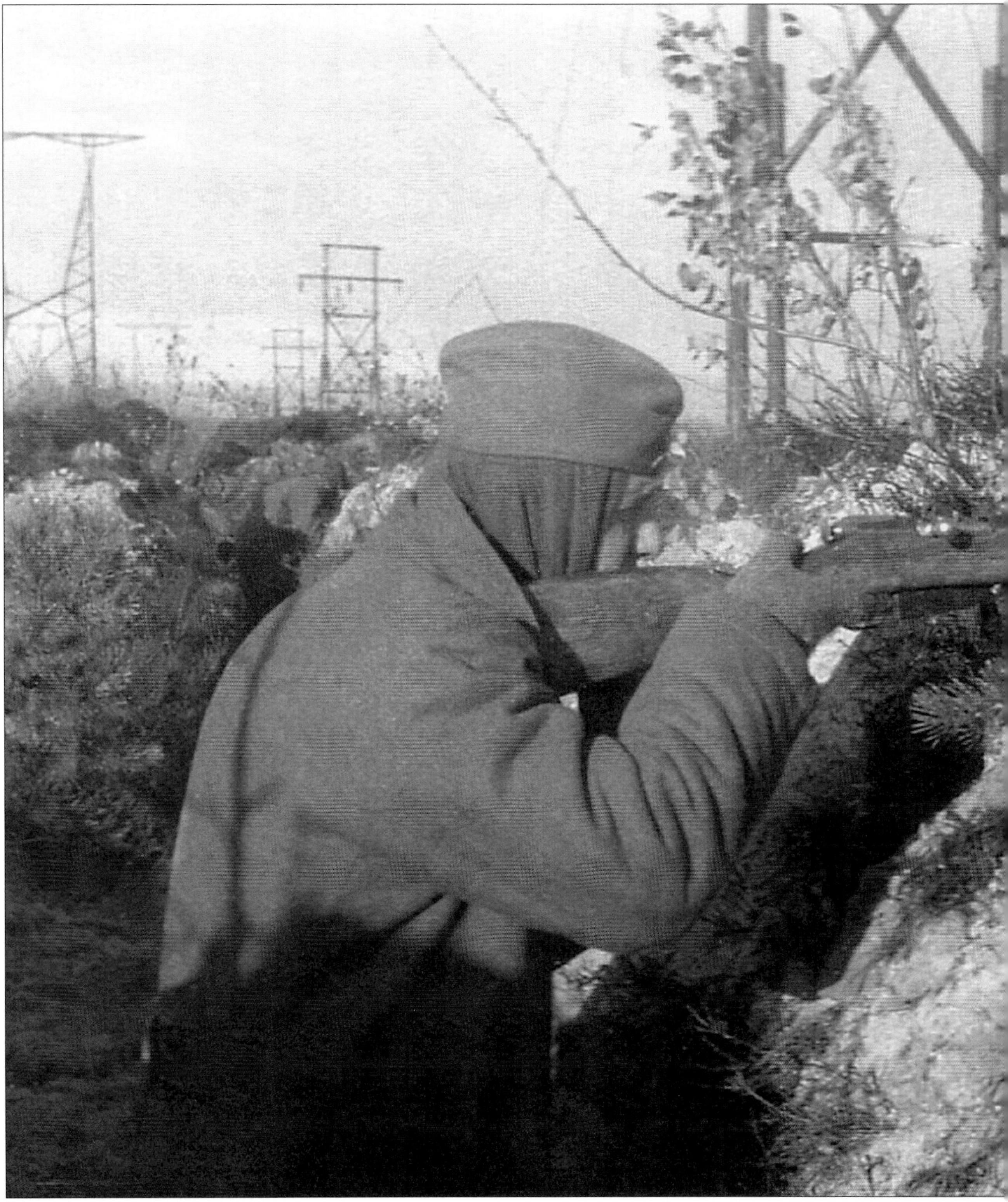

FIELD-GREY AND WARTIME UNIFORMS

In 1935, the *Leibstandarte* began to receive a version of the four-pocket tunic cut from the same field-grey woollen cloth as were the uniforms of the Army. This was part of the continuing efforts to 'militarise' the *Leibstandarte* and emphasise its elite status. It was with the field-grey version of this tunic that the distinctive SS arm eagle made its first appearance, though its initial form was somewhat different from that finally established.

The new tunic was of the same basic design as the black service dress, but was cut from field-grey wool. It retained the open-collar style and four-button fastening but also had the facility to be fastened at the neck. It also retained the two pleated breast patch-pockets, turn-back cuffs and slanted pocket flaps on the skirt.

A newer field-grey blouse was introduced in 1936 and was authorised for wear by all SS-VT personnel. In this new tunic, the cuffs were split, with button-down adjustment, and two sets of holes for the metal belt-support hooks were provided at front and rear of the tunic. The skirt pockets remained the slanted- flap type. Initially at least, the collar of the SS-pattern tunic was provided with aluminium/black twist piping (silver for officers), though this was later deleted. In 1939, the SS-pattern tunic was ordered to be fitted with a dark green contrasting collar, as with the Army versions. Such tunics are still easily identified on old photographs through the slanted lower

A soldier on watch during the winter months. He wears the regulation field-grey wool greatcoat and has added a woollen 'toque', a simple knitted tube which is pulled on in balaclava style, to protect the side and rear of his head. The basic field cap offered little protection.

An *SS-Unterscharführer* from the *SS-Totenkopf Division* shows one of the many variants of collar patch worn by these troops. This is the so-called 'horizontal' type, more often seen than the rarer 'vertical' pattern. This soldier has seen some combat service, as evidenced by the Iron Cross ribbon in his buttonhole.

pocket flaps as opposed to the external pleated patch-pockets on the skirt of Army tunics.

Because of the inability of the SS to meet demand for tunics for its own armed units, actual Army uniforms of the M36 pattern were issued to SS troops in considerable numbers. These Army field blouses had four pleated patch-pockets, with scalloped button-down flaps, and a five-button front, the tunic buttoning right up to the neck and being provided with a hook-and-eye fitting to hold the collar closed. The cuffs were also split, with button fastening to allow for adjustment. These tunics were worn with field-grey wool trousers and jackboots.

As the war dragged on, many minor detail changes were made to the basic M36 field blouse, and in 1940 the dark green collar ceased being fitted at the manufacturing stage, though many blouses after this point still had it retrofitted.

From 1941 onwards, although many Army-issue field blouses continued to be worn in the *Waffen-SS*, the organisation produced its own specific SS-pattern field blouse. While the Army moved to a six-button front fastening, the SS retained the original five-button style, though earlier-style pleated patch-pockets with scalloped flaps were retained. The SS 1941-pattern blouse featured a plain field-grey collar.

Officers were required to provide their own uniforms from the officer's clothing allowance, and generally purchased the same-style tunics as their Army counterparts. These were closely modelled on the M36-style blouse, with dark green collar, but made from finer-quality materials, and usually with the turn-back cuffs widely sported by officer tunics. Some officers had tunics made for them from coarser, harder-wearing wool, and with similar features to enlisted men's tunics, such as adjustable cuffs and provision for belt-support hooks. Others actually wore enlisted men's issue tunics, and simply badged them up for officer rank. This practice was eminently sensible as well as economical, making them harder to tell apart from their men by enemy sharpshooters.

NCOs wore flat aluminium braid, some millimetres wide around the edge of the collar, exactly as their Army counterparts, and those with the rank of Company First Sergeant (*'Der Spiess'*) wore two rings of the same braid around each lower sleeve. This aluminium braid was later replaced by matt grey artificial silk braid on later wartime blouses.

The next major change came in 1942, when the field-blouse pockets lost their central pleat and the number of belt-support hook holes at each position was reduced from three to two. In 1943, the scalloped edges to the pocket flaps were replaced by a straight edge, a further simplification in the manufacturing process.

Finally, in 1944, a short waist-length jacket, modelled closely on the British battledress blouse, was introduced. By this point, the quality of material had degraded even further, and many examples had a drab brownish-grey colour distinctly different from the smart field-grey tunic of 1936. This tunic had but two patch breast pockets, and featured a wide integral waistband. This late war garment never came near to replacing the earlier styles, and indeed photographs of it in wear are rather uncommon.

In parallel with the field blouse, a field-grey greatcoat was developed. The regulation SS versions of this calf-length double-breasted coat had plain field-grey collars, while the Army version, also used by the SS, had a contrasting dark green collar. SS greatcoats normally featured full insignia, including collar patches, sleeve

An *SS-Oberscharführer* from the *Leibstandarte* wearing the regulation NCO service cap. Note the central metal loop on the chinstrap. The extremely small-size LAH metal monograms on his shoulder straps are a rare pattern intended for the rank of *SS-Stabsscharführer*, where the three metal pips of this rank would leave insufficient space for the normal larger-sized monogram.

These *Waffen-SS* grenadiers from the *Leibstandarte* are wearing the padded reversible camouflage winter parka with attached hood and matching overtrousers.

eagles and cuffbands where appropriate. Greatcoats worn by SS officers of general rank had pale grey facings to the lapels. There was also a slight difference in the rear half-belts provided on SS and Army-pattern greatcoats. The dark green collar was subsequently dropped from the Army greatcoat, and by 1944 manufacture of the SS pattern greatcoat itself ceased. Thereafter, the standard Army pattern was used.

A large loose-fitting surcoat in field-grey material was also produced, which was designed to be worn over the standard greatcoat.

CAMOUFLAGE SMOCKS

The most innovative aspect of SS uniform production was certainly their pioneering of the use of camouflage materials. As early as 1938, SS-VT units had begun using smocks cut from cotton duck material printed in camouflage colours. These were pullover smocks with elasticated waist and cuffs, with a lace-up neck fastening. Slash openings on the front panel allowed access to the field blouse worn below. Later examples of the smock featured various loops sewn to the shoulders and upper

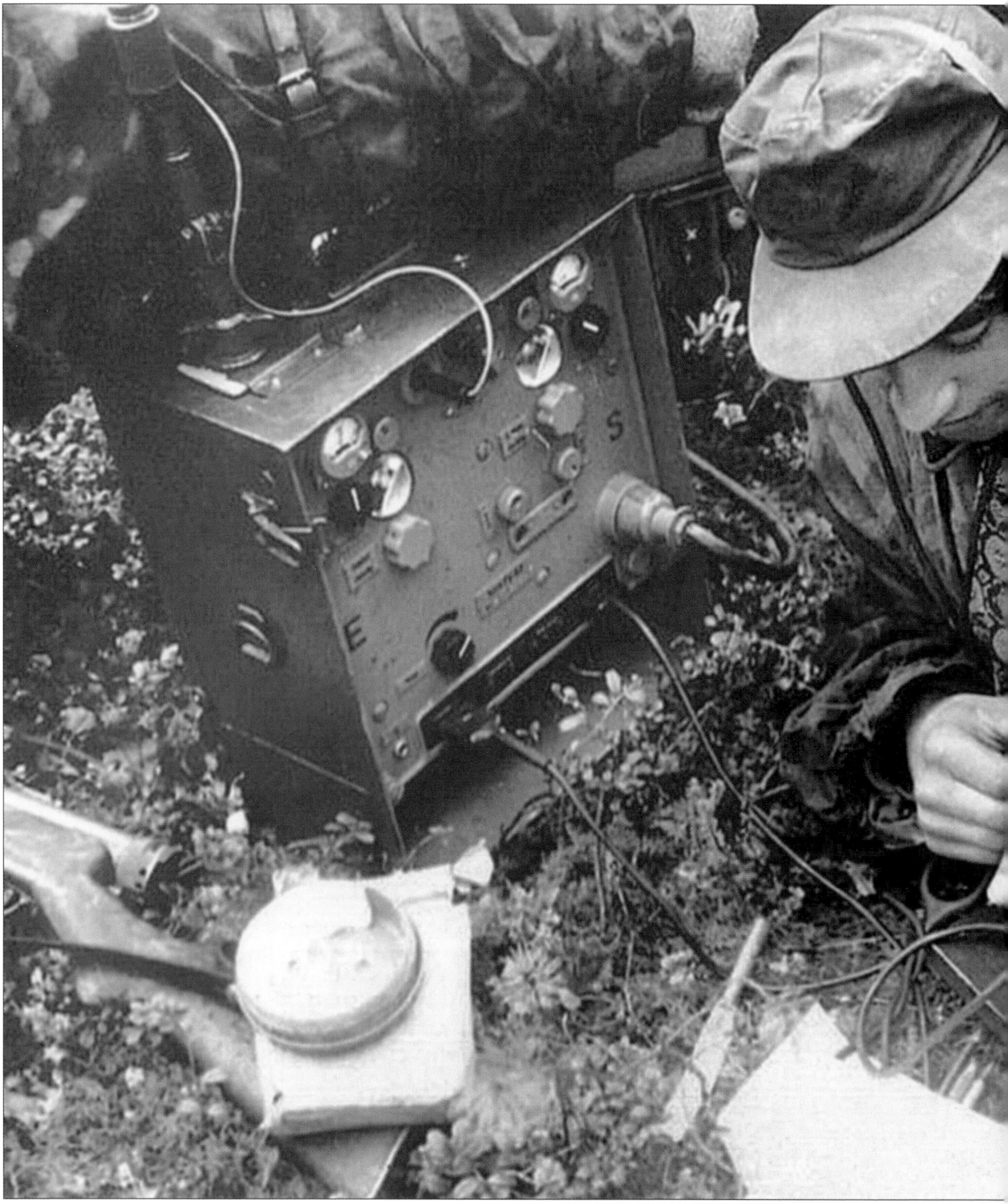

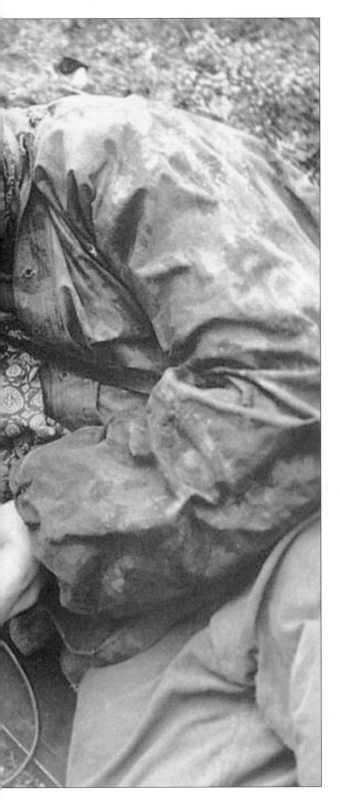

sleeves to allow further camouflage materials, such as foliage, to be attached, and also featured pockets to the lower front. The smock was double sided, one side being in predominantly green shades for summer use and the other in browns for autumn use. The smock was originally intended to be worn over the belt, ammunition pouches and equipment, being fairly loose fitting around the skirt to allow access. It was common, however, for equipment to be worn over the smock and for the skirt to be rolled up to allow easy access to the skirt pockets of the field blouse. Various camouflage patterns were used, some of which, being made in smaller numbers, are now exceedingly rare.

Along with the smock, a camouflage cover in the same patterns was produced for the steel helmet. A strip of material at the 'peak' of the cover allowed it to be looped over the helmet peak, and the sides and rear were then held in place by spring-loaded alloy clips. It too was reversible. Initially it was made without additional cloth loops for the attachment of foliage, but these were soon added.

Completing the issue of camouflage material in the early part of the war was the camouflage shelter quarter, poncho, or 'Zeltbahn'. This was a triangular sheet of camouflaged material, equipped for button fastening around its sides to allow several to be joined to form a tent, and with a slit in the centre for the wearer's head, allowing it to be worn as a waterproof poncho.

A *Waffen-SS* radio operator in the field. Note the visored field cap made from camouflage material matching that of his smock, and that his ensemble is completed by a civilian silk scarf!

Although the *Waffen-SS* had numerous special camouflage garments, recourse was often made, as here, to local materials such as reeds to aid concealment.

Poland, September 1939, and a group of armoured personnel from the *Leibstandarte* inspect a captured enemy artillery piece. They wear the early black wool-beret-covered crash helmet. Note also that for security purposes they wear cloth patches stitched over their collar insignia.

SPECIAL UNIFORMS

Although beginning their lives as basic motorised infantry units, the *SS-Verfügungstruppe* were soon provided with armoured vehicles such as armoured cars, and in 1937 adopted similar special black panzer clothing to that used by the Army since 1934.

The panzer uniform consisted of loose-fitting black wool trousers worn bloused at the ankle into short-shaft jackboots or lace-up boots. With these was worn the *Panzerjacke*, or armoured jacket. This was an extremely stylish waist-length double-breasted jacket cut from black wool. Its

buttons were concealed behind a fly-front and large lapels and collars were fitted. Initially, Army-pattern jackets were worn, but sometime around 1940–1 a specific SS version was produced which was slightly different from that used by the Army. Army jackets had angled fronts, whereas the front on the SS jacket was straight. Army lapels tended also to be slightly larger than those on SS jackets, and the Army jacket had a seam down the centre of the rear panel, whereas SS jackets had the rear panel cut from a single piece of material. As with the field-grey blouse, however, substantial numbers of Army-issue jackets were also

A *Waffen-SS* panzer officer in the turret of his tank. Note the officer's silver piping to the collar of the jacket and the flap of his (Army-pattern) field cap. He wears the Panzer Assault Badge and on his right sleeve the badge for single-handed destruction of an enemy tank.

issued to, and worn by, SS armoured-vehicle crews because of shortages of their own distinct version.

Whereas Army jackets, at least in the early models, had collars piped in the rose-pink branch of service colour of the armoured troops, SS jackets only carried piping to the collar for officers, this being in twisted silver cord. Enlisted ranks' jackets had no collar piping, except in the few cases where this was added unofficially, or where an Army-pattern jacket was worn which still retained its pink collar piping.

In 1941, a further armoured vehicle crew uniform was introduced, identical in cut to the black uniform, but cut from field-grey wool. This was worn by the crews of certain other armoured vehicles, such as self-propelled guns, and eventually by some *Panzergrenadier* units. Uniquely, NCOs in the *Leibstandarte* wore NCO aluminium braid edging to the collar of this jacket. This was the only unit recorded as having done so.

The armoured vehicle uniforms, though smart and highly popular, were not particularly suitable for wear in the extremely hot interior of a tank during combat in summer months. To improve the comfort of crews, a lightweight version, introduced in the autumn of 1941, was also produced in

SS panzer crewmen pose near a *Panzer III*. Note that none actually wears the special black uniform for tank crews, but rather more comfortable and practical lightweight drill clothing for temperate climates.

cotton, in a field-grey colour for both tank crews and the crews of other armoured vehicles. It was almost identical in cut to the wool uniform, but had the additional of a large and extremely useful patch-pocket on the left breast. In general, only shoulder straps were worn with this lightweight ensemble, though some did have sleeve insignia also added. This loose-fitting jacket could also be worn over the black *Panzerjacke*.

It is worth noting that special leather versions of the black panzer clothing were also produced. These should not be confused with the single-breasted collarless jackets of the type worn by engine-room crews in the German Navy, which were also used to a considerable degree by SS tank crews. As well as these well-documented leather jackets, leather versions of the black panzer jacket itself were manufactured. Identical in cut to the black wool jacket, these were cut from supple black leather. Tank troops of the Army and *Luftwaffe* are also known to have used this style of leather *Panzerjacke*. The shiny finish to these leather jackets would soon dull with use, and in black and white wartime photographs it can be difficult to tell at first glance that such leather jackets are being worn. Clearly identified examples of both Army tank crews and *Luftwaffe* tank crews from the Hermann Göring Division wearing such leather jackets have been found, and the survival of original examples in this cut suggests almost beyond doubt that such garments saw issue to *Waffen-SS* tank troops as well.

A heavy, lined, one-piece overall was also provided to tanks crews for wear during winter months. This was field-grey on one side, reversible to white.

TROPICAL UNIFORMS

SS troops operating in warm climates (for example Italy and the Crimea) during the summer months were issued with SS-pattern lightweight tropical clothing from 1943. This was manufactured from tan-coloured cotton and consisted of either shorts or long baggy trousers, and a four-pocket open-neck field blouse. Either jackboots or short ankle-boots could be worn with this dress.

The first-pattern SS tropical tunic was very similar to that worn by the *Luftwaffe* in tropical climes, and was provided with four patch-pockets with button-down flaps. All buttons were held in place by metal split rings to allow easy removal for cleaning. Collar patches, though occasionally worn, were often omitted from this blouse, which generally featured only shoulder straps and sleeve insignia.

As well as the regulation tropical jacket, SS troops also made widespread use of a second pattern garment similar to the Italian style Sahariana jacket. This had the distinctive feature of a yoked shoulder, the forward part of the yoke on each side forming the flap for the breast pocket.

CAMOUFLAGE UNIFORMS

These are being treated separately from the camouflage smocks mentioned earlier simply because the former were single garments, whereas those that follow were complete outfits in their own right.

A special one-piece 'boiler-suit'-type overall was produced in camouflage-print lightweight material for wear by tank crews from January 1943. This was generally worn with the special insignia for camouflage clothing, but frequently had shoulder straps added for personal preference. It too was reversible. Originals of this garment are now of the greatest rarity.

In January 1944, a special version of the panzer uniform began to be issued in camouflage colours. These jackets appear to have been made both in double-sided

A group of *Waffen-SS* soldiers in tropical service kit. The jacket is the Italian 'Sahariana' style, with the edges of the yoke forming the flap for the breast pockets. The tan tropical field cap was similar in style to that worn by the *Afrikakorps* but lacked the false edge flap of the former.

cotton duck material and also printed on single-sided lightweight cotton, the jacket being similar in cut to the standard black and field-grey armoured-vehicle uniforms, and generally being worn in the summer, though it could be worn over the black jacket in colder weather if necessary. It was issued with matching lightweight trousers, also in the special cut for panzer crews. Although originally intended for wear only with the special insignia for camouflage uniforms, many, if not most, seem to have been fitted with shoulder straps and in some cases also arm eagles.

In March 1944, a special two-piece camouflage suit consisting of trousers and field blouse was introduced. This was cut from lightweight herringbone-twill material and could be worn over the standard field-grey clothing if appropriate. It was made in the so-called 'pea-pattern' camouflage print, and was cut in a similar style to the basic M43 field uniform. Most commonly, this blouse seems to have been worn with shoulder straps and usually also with the sleeve insignia, but not with collar patches.

For wear during winter months in particularly cold climates, a special heavy

An SS rifleman on the Eastern Front wears the padded reversible winter suit. He has also pulled the side-flaps of his field cap down to protect the tops of his ears.

padded winter suit was also introduced in 1943. This consisted of padded over-trousers worn over the standard wool trousers, with drawstring fastening to the ankles, cloth braces, and with a large flap-type fly front. These were worn together with a heavy padded parka-type jacket with two skirt pockets and with flaps allowing access to the tunic worn beneath. This had drawstring fastening to the waist and skirt, and adjustable cuffs. It also featured an integral hood. This suit was reversible, with white 'snow' camouflage on one side, and predominantly brown SS-pattern 'autumn' camouflage colours on the other. It was issued along with padded winter mittens in the same materials, and could also be used with a separate hood. A padded face mask in identical materials was also produced.

HEADGEAR

By 1937, the SS-pattern *Feldmütze* was also being manufactured in field-grey as well as black and earth-grey wool.

Steel helmets of the M16, M18 and M35 pattern were produced with a light grey-green paint finish, relatively smooth, giving it a semi-gloss sheen, though this would later change to a rough paint finish to avoid reflection and increase camouflage prop-erties. In 1940, the national colours shield began to be omitted from new helmets, its red/white/black colours being rather too conspicuous for combat use. In 1942 a new form of helmet was introduced, the manufacturing methodology being changed for reasons of economy, giving the rim of the helmet a wider and more flared look due to the edge being unrolled, and having integrally embossed rather than separately bushed vents. From 1943, decals were omitted completely from SS helmets.

In 1938, the SS visor cap began to appear with a field-grey rather than earth-grey

This excellent shot of an *SS-Mann* shows the steel helmet decal to good advantage. The shape of the runes on the collar patch are also slight variants on the normal design in their width and angle.

crown, both officer and enlisted ranks caps being manufactured in this manner. In 1940, permission was given for caps to be piped in the branch of service colour as worn on the shoulder straps, instead of the basic white hitherto used. Although this permission was rescinded shortly thereafter, a number of caps with colour piping were manufactured and worn.

A special version of the field cap, more akin, visually at least, to the visor cap, began

An SS machine-gunner with the
Czech MG26(t). This is clearly a
training exercise, as the magazine
has not been fitted to the weapon.
The swastika banner decal is clearly
shown on the left-hand side of the SS
steel helmet.

Portrait study of an *SS-
Hauptscharführer* wearing an officer-
quality tunic. The leather chinstrap
to the cap is Army pattern, lacking
the central metal loop on the
normal SS strap.

to appear in 1938. This cap had no chinstrap, and had a peak made from field-grey cloth rather than black *vulkanfiber*. It was worn with the standard metal insignia. This cap was exceptionally popular with enlisted ranks and even some officers. Authorisation for its wear was rescinded in 1939, though examples remained in use long after this date due to authorisation for existing examples to be 'worn out'.

Many officers had field caps made to the Army 'Old-Style Field Cap' pattern. Once again, these closely resembled the standard visor cap, but were much lighter in weight and lacked much of the padding and stiffening found in regular visor caps. They also had a soft black leather peak. This allowed them to be rolled up and stuffed into the pocket if the need arose to change this soft cap for a steel helmet. These caps generally had woven insignia, metal clearly being inappropriate for such a cap, though some do seem to have been worn with the standard metal insignia.

In December 1939 a new-style field cap was introduced for officer ranks. It was modelled on the *Luftwaffe* style, and was known as the *'Schiffchen'*, or 'Little boat' due to its resemblance to an upturned boat. This style lacked the scalloped portion to the front of the flap as found on the older-style cap. Cut from field-grey coloured wool, it carried an SS-pattern woven deathshead insignia on the front of the flap, and a woven SS-pattern national emblem on the front of the crown. Normally cut from finer material, it featured silver braid piping around the flap. This was later altered to white piping for officers and silver braid piping for generals, in line with that used on the visor cap. It seems, however, that this was generally ignored, and silver piping continued to be worn by all officer ranks.

Before the introduction of the officer model of the *Feldmütze*, most SS officers

An *SS-Unterscharführer* of the *Leibstandarte* wearing the awards of a combat veteran. As well as the ribbons of the Iron Cross and Eastern Front Campaign Medal, he wears the General Assault Badge and Wounded Badge in silver. His cap is not the peaked service cap, but the old-style field cap, without chinstrap and with soft leather peak.

acquired Army officer M38-pattern field caps and rebadged these with SS insignia. In some cases full SS insignia were used, while in others the Army national emblem was retained and a metal SS deathshead simply pinned over the Army national-colours cockade.

An enlisted-ranks version of this cap, generally in a coarser-grade material, and

A garment not often seen is the lightweight officers' raincoat worn here by this *SS-Standartenoberjunker*. This coat was modelled on the regulation greatcoat but in lightweight waterproof cotton.

without the piping to the flap, was introduced in 1940. Until 1942, these caps were produced with an inverted chevron of braid in the wearer's branch of service colour over the deathshead on the front of the flap.

This cap was also produced in black wool for wear with the special black panzer clothing. Once again, because of supply shortages, a mixture of the correct SS

An *SS-Untersturmführer* wearing an enlisted-grade tunic but with officer insignia, a common fashion for officers in the field. Note the aluminium braid officer piping to the flap of his field cap. On his pocket are the Iron Cross First Class and General Assault Badge.

The *Waffen-SS*-pattern black panzer 'wrapover' jacket is worn by this *SS-Unterscharführer*. Almost certainly an armoured car crewman, he wears the Infantry rather than Panzer Assault Badge and the cuffband of the *Deutschland Regiment*, an armoured infantry, not a tank, unit. He also has the embroidered one-piece form of insignia for the M43 cap, this being rarely seen in wartime photographs due to the late date of its introduction.

panzer pattern, Army panzer patterns and even the old black *Allgemeine*-pattern *Feldmützen* are known to have been worn by SS panzer troops.

Personnel serving with SS mountain troop units wore a special cap known as the *Bergmütze*, or mountain cap. Closely modelled on the cap worn by mountain infantry during the First World War, this cap featured a short stubby peak, and sides which could fold down to cover the rear and sides of the head in cold weather, with a short strap which could be buttoned under the chin. When not unfolded, this fastening sat at the front of the cap just above the peak. As well as the standard deathshead and national emblem worn on the front of the cap, just above the buttoned flap, a machine-embroidered edelweiss flower, the

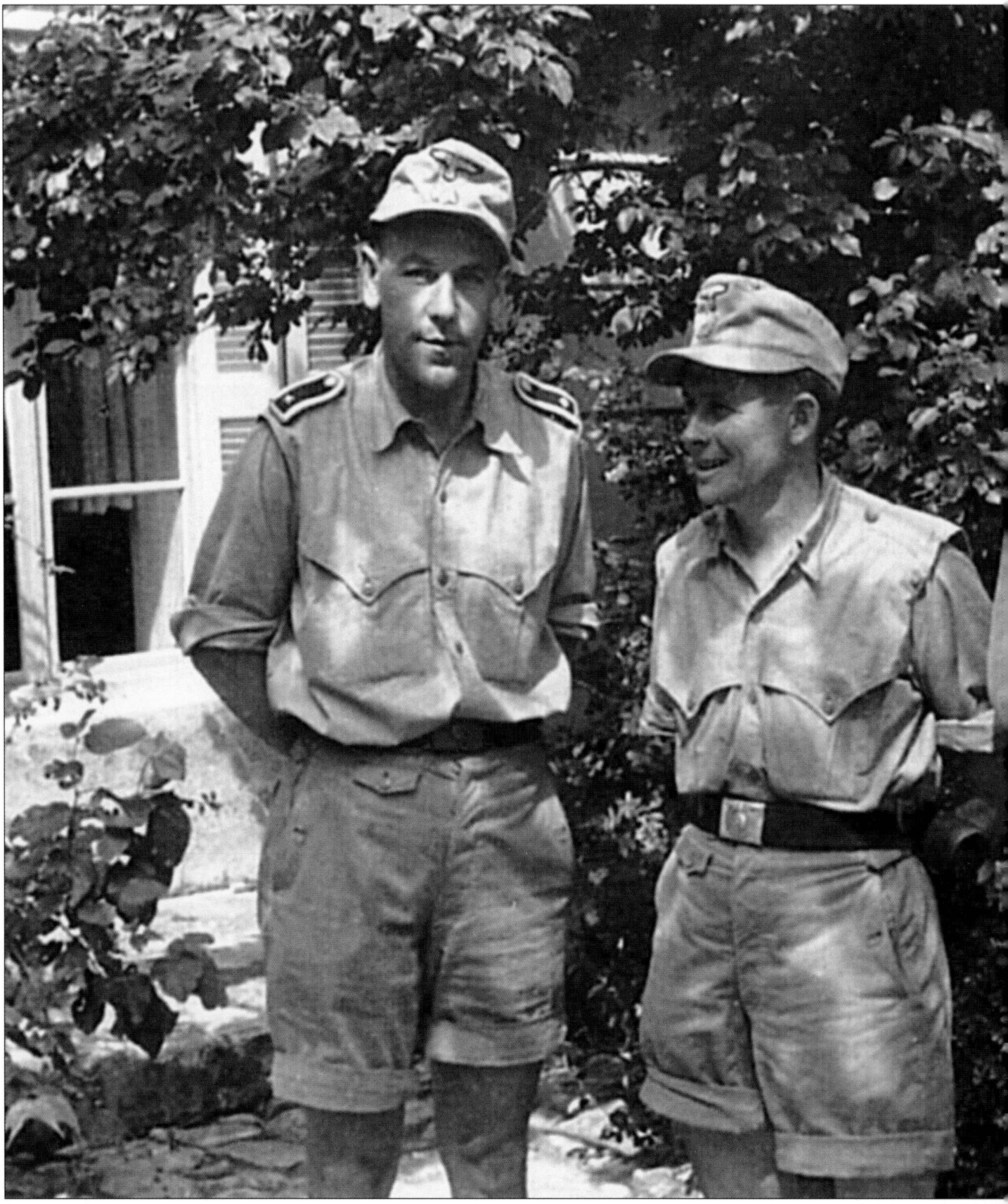

symbol of the mountain troops, was worn on the left side, on the flap, at an angle of some 30 degrees.

In 1943, a new field cap was introduced with a view to replacing the numerous existing types with a single standard piece of headgear. This cap, known as the *Einheitsfeldmütze*, is generally referred as the M43 field cap. It was based on the *Bergmütze* previously described but had a longer peak and generally a lower crown. Even within the parameters of this design, there are variations, with both single-button and double-button fastening of the flap.

Officer versions are usually found with aluminium braid piping to the crown, and with a partial leather sweatband on the forward part of the cap. Some original examples of these caps also feature either single or double metal-grommet-type air vents to the side of the crown.

On the version with a single button fastening to a relatively narrow chin-flap, both the SS-pattern woven deathshead and SS-pattern national emblem, as two separate insignia, were worn on the front of the cap. On types with the wide two-button fastening flap, the deathshead was worn to the front of the cap and the national emblem on the left side flap. Special one-piece insignia with both the deathshead and national emblem woven or machine-embroidered on to a single trapezoid-shaped backing were also used on some caps, the smaller size of the insignia in this case allowing them to fit comfortably into the space above the double-buttoned flap.

The M43-style cap was also manufactured in black wool for use by panzer troops.

This group of soldiers in tropical kit shows the matching shirt, also of Sahariana style, with the yoke forming the pocket flap.

TROPICAL HEADGEAR

For use with the tropical-pattern uniform previously described, a special variant of the *Feldmütze* was produced. Two versions were made, both cut from golden-tan-coloured lightweight cotton material. One was modelled closely on the *'Schiffchen'*-style cap, the other was based on the peaked tropical cap favoured by *Wehrmacht* personnel. The SS version, however, lacked the false side-flaps featured on the Army-pattern tropical peaked field cap.

In both cases the standard two-piece insignia were worn, but woven in tan on black. Officer versions of the cap would normally feature woven aluminium braid piping.

Less commonly worn, but still seen from time to time in wartime photographs, was the tropical sun helmet. This traditionally styled sun helmet was made from cork, and covered with panels of tan-coloured canvas, the edge to the brim being bound in tan-coloured leather.

On the left side of the crown a small metal shield in silver with embossed black runes was worn. On the right was a similar metal shield, but with the red field with white disc and black swastika. Given the scarcity of original wartime photographs of this form of headgear being worn, it can be assumed that it was less than universally popular.

SPECIAL HEADGEAR

Prior to the outbreak of war, a special beret was issued to SS panzer troops. This was based on a similar item worn by Army panzer soldiers and consisted on a large floppy beret that was pulled over a padded crash helmet. The standard SS insignia of an eagle with swastika over a deathshead were worn, but of a distinct pattern, the eagle having a much larger wingspan than normal, and the deathshead being of the older, 'chinless' style. Surviving examples of this piece of headgear are of the greatest rarity.

A similar 'beret' made from field-grey wool was worn in very small numbers by crew-members of SS assault guns and self-propelled artillery. These are even rarer than the black version and very seldom encountered.

One of the most bizarre pieces of headgear worn by SS units was the traditional Muslim fez used by *13 SS-Division Handschar*. This very simple piece of headgear comprised a compressed woollen felt fez made in both maroon (for dress use) and field-grey (for field use) colours, and with a long black tassel. It had no lining, but a small artificial leather sweatband was provided. Insignia were the basic two-piece machine-woven emblem of eagle and swastika over a deathshead. Although the steel helmet was worn under combat conditions, this is one unusual piece of headgear that did see widespread use, as evidenced by original photographs. Even some of the German cadre officers, who would have been entitled to wear the normal field cap or visor cap, are known to have sported the fez, perhaps in an effort to show solidarity with their Muslim charges.

A similar form of headdress was worn by some members of the Albanian SS Mountain Division *'Kama'*. The *Handschar* fez was of the traditional truncated cone shape, whereas the version worn by the Albanian Muslims was more akin to a conical skullcap.

One of the most popular forms of SS headdress was the camouflage field cap introduced in June 1942. This was cut from cotton duck material printed on both sides with the same patterns as used on the camouflage smock. The unlined cap was fitted with a sweatband on the interior. This sweatband was simply a fold in the basic material of the cap. The normal exterior side was in the predominantly green spring patterns, and the interior side, with the sweatband, in the autumn brown shades. Various types exist. Some have no vent holes. Others have vent holes with embroidered reinforcing, while still others have metal grommets for ventilation. Examples of this cap are known from wartime photographs to have been locally manufactured, perhaps by unit tailors, as they may rarely be seen with button-fastened drop-down side-flaps similar to those found on the *Bergmütze*, or M43 cap.

Most commonly, this cap was worn without insignia, and indeed initial regulations stated it was to be worn in this way. From December 1942, however, specials versions of the SS cap eagle and deathshead were produced in a rust brown or dark green on black weave for wear on the autumn or spring sides of the cap respectively. Original examples of this cap with factory-fitted insignia are extremely rare.

Despite the oft-claimed German tendency towards regulation and order, even once the M43 standard field cap was introduced a wide range of differing 'regulation' caps continued to be worn, to say nothing of locally manufactured non-regulation items. The items mentioned here, however, should allow the reader to identify most uniform and headgear items that will be encountered.

INSIGNIA

THE NATIONAL EMBLEM

The national emblem, or *Hoheitszeichen*, worn by SS units consisted of an eagle clutching a wreathed swastika in its talons. On the early black service uniform this emblem was worn only on the cap, and in its

An SS officer candidate. Such ranks were permitted to wear officers' aluminium chin cords on the peaked service cap and officers' twist-cord piping to the NCO collar patches. The sleeve eagle worn is also of the hand-embroidered officer-quality type.

initial form was of the same style as worn by the SA Stormtroopers. In 1936, however, a new pattern was introduced specifically for the SS. This style had a greater wingspan than the early type and was unique in that the central feather of the wing was longer than the others, giving the profile of the wing a 'pointed' effect. This eagle was worn in metal on the crown of the visor cap, and in cloth on the field cap and on the sleeve of the tunic. The exception to this was the special pattern worn by the Italian SS units in which the eagle clasped fasces rather than a wreathed swastika in its talons. This latter type was embroidered on both red

The senior sergeant in each company was designed as *'Der Spiess'*, the nearest equivalent to the British CSM or RSM. This was an appointment rather than a rank, however, and was designated by two rings of aluminium braid on each sleeve. The cuffband being worn is for *SS-Standarte Deutschland.*

and black backing cloth. Apart from the earliest form of SS sleeve eagle, which was also embroidered on field-grey backing, all SS pattern sleeve eagles were worked on black.

The SS sleeve eagle was manufactured in hand-embroidered bullion wire, in machine-embroidered silver-grey yarn, and in machine-woven form. In this last form it was woven in grey or white on black for enlisted men, in aluminium thread on black for officers (also worn by some NCOs and enlisted ranks), in tan on black for tropical tunics, and very rare variants were made in green on black and brown on black for wear on camouflaged clothing, though these were not often used.

The version of the SS national emblem worn on the cap was most commonly the machine-woven version, in the same colours as for the sleeve eagle.

THE DEATHSHEAD

Like the national emblem, the SS deathshead emblem was manufactured in two patterns. The earliest was based on the traditional hussar skull, devoid of a chin, and of almost identical design to the deathshead worn on the collar patches of Army panzer uniforms, but larger.

In 1935, a new version was introduced, more anatomically accurate and with a full chin. This was worn in silvered metal on the band of the visor cap.

A woven cloth version, in the same colours as for the machine-woven sleeve and cap eagles, was worn on the field cap. Original embroidered versions exist but are rare, the machine-woven pattern being by far the most common form.

SHOULDER STRAPS AND COLLAR PATCHES

Shoulder straps worn by early SS-VT units were of the *Allgemeine-SS* pattern, worn only on the right shoulder, but in 1935 Army-style straps began to be worn on both shoulders. The typical *Waffen-SS* shoulder strap was cut from black wool (with either field-grey or black wool undersurface) and was piped in the appropriate colour of *Waffenfarbe*, or Branch of Service colour, for the wearer's unit. Enlisted ranks wore a plain strap, while those for NCOs were trimmed in woven aluminium or artificial silk braid and with metal rank pips as appropriate.

Junior officers wore straps made from rows of straight matt silver-grey braid on a black wool, base, with *Waffenfarbe* intermediate underlay between the braid and black base. Field-grade officers' straps were made from similar materials, but had the braid in an interwoven pattern, and finally ranks equivalent to Army generals wore interwoven silver/gold braid on a pale grey base. The full range of rank attributes was as follows.

Collar patches worn by SS units were dual purpose. That worn on the right displayed the SS runes or other special identifying insignia, while that on the left indicated the wearer's rank. As a general rule, enlisted and NCO patches were worked in silver-grey thread and officer patches in aluminium thread, though in some cases officers wore enlisted-grade patches and enlisted men officer-grade patches. More often the real indicator of the wearer's status, certainly as far as the right-hand patch was concerned, was the presence of twisted silver braid cord edging on officer patches.

Junior NCOs also had the wearer's rank indicated by a series of sleeve patches/ chevrons on the left sleeve just below the national emblem. The full range of standard rank insignia worn by *Waffen-SS* units may be summarised as follows:

Rank	Shoulder Strap	Collar Patch
SS-Schutze	Plain	Blank
SS-Oberschutze	Plain	Blank
SS-Sturmmann	Plain	Single braid strip
SS-Rottenführer	Plain	Two braid strips
SS-Unterscharführer	Braid edging around sides and end, but not base	One pip
SS-Scharführer	Braid edging all round	One pip, one braid strip
SS-Oberscharführer	Braid edging all round, one pip	Two pips
SS-Hauptscharführer	Braid edging all round, two pips	Two pips, one braid strip
SS-Sturmscharführer	Braid edging all round, three pips	Two pips, two braid strips
SS-Untersturmführer	Straight matt silver braid	Three pips
SS-Obersturmführer	As above but with one metal pip	Three pips, one braid strip
SS-Hauptsturmführer	As above but with two metal pips	Three pips, two braid strips
SS-Sturmbannführer	Interwoven matt silver braid	Four pips
SS-Obersturmbannführer	As above but with one metal pip	Four pips, one braid strip
SS-Standartenführer	As above but with two metal pips	One oakleaf
SS-Oberführer	As above	Two oakleaves
SS-Brigadeführer	Interwoven silver-gilt braid	Three oakleaves
SS-Gruppenführer	As above, with one metal pip	Three oakleaves, one pip
SS-Obergruppenführer	As above, with two metal pips	Three oakleaves, two pips
SS-Oberstgruppenführer	As above, with two metal pips	Three oakleaves, three pips
Reichsführer-SS	Interwoven braid of unique pattern	Three oakleaves within oakleaf wreath

The full range of collar insignia authorised for wear by *Waffen-SS* troops (not all were actually issued) in wartime service, and many of which may be seen in this handbook, were as follows:

SS	All units not authorised a specific collar patch
SS T	*SS-Schule Tölz*
SS B	*SS-Schule Braunschweig*
Deathshead	*SS-Totenkopfverbände/ Totenkopf Division*
Rampant Lion with Axe	Norwegian Volunteer Legion
Horizontal 'Wolfsangel' Rune	Dutch Volunteers
Trifos (three-legged swastika)	Flemish Volunteers
Sonnenrad (sun-wheel swastika)	*Nordland Division*
Odal Rune	*Prinz Eugen Division*
Scimitar with Swastika	*Handschar Division*
Rampant Lion	*14 SS-Division*
Swastika	*15 SS-Division*
Sun/Stars Patch	*15 SS-Division*
E with arm holding sword	*20 SS-Division*
SA *Kampfrune*	*Horst Wessel Division*
Cornflower	*Maria Theresia*
Danish Flag	*Freikorps Danmark*
H	*Hunyadi Division*
Fasces	*29 Waffen-Grenadier Division der SS (ital. Nr 1)*
Crossed Rifles over Grenade	*Dirlewanger Brigade/ Kampfverband Dora*
Flaming Grenade	*Landstorm Nederland*
Three Lions Passant	*Britisches Freikorps*

An *SS-Scharführer* from *SS-Standarte Deutschland*. His early-pattern shoulder straps bear a large Gothic letter 'D' and his collar patch the original *Standarte* number '1'.

An *SS-Unterscharführer* serving as an instructor on the staff of the SS NCO training school (*Unterführerschule*) at Lauenberg, a position indicated by the embroidered initials USL on his shoulder straps.

A variety of collar patches as worn by volunteers in the *Waffen-SS*. Top left to bottom right: 7th (*Prinz Eugen*) Division, 11th (*Nordland*) Division, *Freikorps Danmark*, 13th (*Handschar*) Division, 14th (Galician) Division, 15th (Latvian) Division, 18th (*Horst Wessel*) Division, 19th (Latvian) Division, 20th (Estonian) Division, 22th (*Maria Theresia*) Division, 23th (*Nederland*) Division, 25th (*Hunyadi*) Division, 27th (*Langemarck*) Division, 29th (Italian) Division, 34th (*Landstorm Nederland*) Division, Dirlewanger Brigade, *Britische Freikorps* (the last being a postwar replica).

In addition, the blank right collar patch also associated with SD personnel was often worn by units which had not yet received any special insignia but were not deemed eligible for wearing the SS runes.

The following patches were designed and manufactured, but as yet no evidence has emerged to suggest they were ever issued and worn.

Viking Ship Prow	*5 SS-Panzer Division Wiking*
Helmet with Goat-Head Crest	*21 Waffen-Gebirgs Division Skanderbeg*
Sunburst	*23 Waffen-Grenadier Division der SS Kama*
Cross of Burgundy	*28 SS-Freiwilligen-Grenadier Division Wallonien*
Maltese Cross with Crossed Swords	*29 Waffen-Grenadier Division der SS*
Wolf's Head	*30 Waffen-Grenadier Division der SS*
Tiger's Head	*Indische Freiwilligen Legion der SS*

The most distinctive piece of insignia worn by *Waffen-SS* troops was, without doubt, the unit cuffband. These were worn with enormous pride, as a further indication of the soldier's elite status. In the closing stages of the war, when Hitler felt that his *Waffen-SS* soldiers had not fought with sufficient determination in the offensive around Lake Balaton, he ordered that they be stripped of their cuffbands as a punishment. In fact most had already removed their cuffbands in order to conform with orders to avoid the true identities of the units involved being detected by the enemy. It was, nevertheless, an indication of the high regard in which this particular form of insignia was held.

The following insignia were actually manufactured and worn by *Waffen-SS* troops.

Battalion

SS-VT Signals Battalion	*SS-Nachrichtensturmbann*
SS-VT Pioneer Battalion	*SS-Pioniersturmbann*
SS-VT Medical Battalion	*Sanitätsabteilung*
SS-Inspectorate	*SS-Inspektion*

	Division	**Regiments**
1 SS-Panzer Division	*Adolf Hitler*	*Adolf Hitler*
2 SS-Panzer Division	*Das Reich*	*Deutschland*
		Der Führer
		Germania
		Langemarck
		(1942–43)
3 SS-Panzer Division	*Totenkopf* Theodor Eicke*	*Thule*
		SS-Heimwehr Danzig
4 SS-Polizei-Panzer-grenadier Division	*SS-Polizei Division*	
5 SS-Panzer Division	*Wiking*	*Nordland*
		Germania
		Westland
6 SS-Gebirgs Division		*Reinhard Heydrich*
		Michael Gaissmair
7 SS-Frw. Gebirgs Division	*Prinz Eugen*	
8 SS-Kavallerie Division	*Florian Geyer*	
9 SS-Panzer Division	*Hohenstaufen*	
10 SS-Panzer Division	*Frundsberg*	
11 SS-Panzer-grenadier Division	*Nordland*	*Norge*
		Danmark
		Hermann von Salza
12 SS-Panzer Division	*Hitlerjugend*	
16 SS-Panzer-grenadier Division	*Reichsführer-SS*	
17 SS-Panzer-grenadier Division	*Götz von Berlichingen*	
18 SS-Frw.-Panzer-grenadier Division	*Horst Wessel*	
21 Waffen-Gebirgs Division der SS	*Skanderbeg*	
23 SS-Frw.-Panzer-grenadier Division	*Nederland*	
27 SS-Frw.-Grenadier Division	*Langemarck*	
28 SS-Frw.-Grenadier Division	*Wallonien*	
33 SS-Waffen-Grenadier Division	*Charlemagne*	
34 SS-Frw.-Grenadier Division	*Landstorm Nederland*	
Frw. Standarte Nordwest	*Nordwest*	

Here we see the *Trifos*, or three-legged swastika, worn by Flemish volunteers from the *Langemarck Division*.

Britisches Freikorps	*Britisches Freikorps*
SS-Freikorps Danmark	*Freikorps Danmark*
Frw. Legion Flandern	*Frw. Legion Flandern*
Frw. Legion Norwegen	*Frw. Legion Norwegen*
Frew. Legion Nederland	*Frw. Legion Niederlande*
	Frw. Legion Nederland

BRANCH CUFFBANDS

Military Police	*SS-Feldgendarmerie*	Officer School Brunswick	*SS-Schule-Braunschweig*
War Correspondents	*SS-Kriegsberichter* *SS-KB-Abt Kurt Eggers*	Medical Academy	*SS-Ärztliche Akademie*
NCO School	*SS-Unterführerschule*	Brunswick Music School	*Musikschule Braunschweig*
Officer School Bad Tölz	*SS-Schule-Tölz*		

* Former members of the *SS-Totenkopfverbände* often wore the cuffband of their former units, the band showing the SS deathshead being popular, as were *Thüringen*, *Obergayern* and *Brandenburg*.

117

A range of original *Waffen-SS* cuffbands illustrating several different manufacturing types. Top to bottom:
1 SS-Panzer Division,
2 SS-Panzer Division,
3 SS-Panzer Division,
5 SS-Panzer Division,
9 SS-Panzer Division,
10 SS-Panzer Division,
12 SS-Panzer Division.

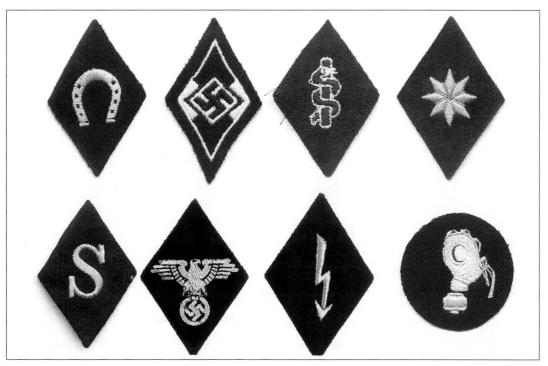

Specialist badges worn on the lower left cuff. Top left to bottom right: Farrier, former member of the *Hitler Jugend*, Medical Orderly, Administration Officer, Technical Sergeant, Press and War Economy Department, Signaller, Gas Defence Specialist.

It should be noted that as far as the *Horst Wessel* and *Charlemagne* bands are concerned, only anecdotal evidence from former unit members exists that the bands were issued on a very limited scale.

In addition, the following cuffbands were certainly manufactured, but no evidence for their actual wear is known.

7 SS-Frw.-Gebirgs Division	Artur Phleps
23 SS-Frw.-Panzer-grenadier Division	General Seyffardt De Ruiter
1 Ostmussel-manisches SS-Regt	Osttürkischer Waffenverband der SS

SPECIALIST INSIGNIA

In similar form to the Army, certain specialist personnel within the *Waffen-SS* wore identifying insignia on the lower left cuff. These were embroidered on a diamond-shaped black wool patch.

Technical Sergeant	Letter 'S'
Technical Officer	Cogwheel
Armourer NCO	Crossed Rifle/Machine-Gun
Legal Officer	Five-petal Flowerhead
Administration Officer	Eight-Pointed Star
Musical Director	Lyre
Farrier	Upturned Horseshoe
Signaller	Lightning Flash
Medical Officer	Aesculapius Rod/Snake
Medical Orderly	As above but outline shape only
Veterinary Officer	Snake
Former HJ Members	HJ Diamond Insignia
Former Police Member	Police Eagle within wreath
Former Member of the SA	SA *Kampfrune*
Mountain Troops	Edelweiss patch on right sleeve Edelweiss on left side of field cap

CHAPTER NINE

AWARDS AND DECORATIONS

There were very few awards and decorations introduced during the period of the Third Reich which were awarded solely to one single branch of the armed forces. Generally speaking, if a member of one branch could show that he had completed the requisite criteria, even for an award intended for a totally different branch, then that award could be bestowed. This is why, for example, sailors may be seen wearing an infantry combat badge, an SS soldier wearing a *Luftwaffe* paratrooper badge. There were some awards, however, which were predominantly bestowed upon particular branches, SS included.

To cover all of the military awards of the Third Reich which could be won by members of the SS would take far more space than is available here. Once again the reader is directed to the Bibliography, where a range of detailed works on this subject may be found, for those who wish to study this aspect in greater depth. For the purposes of this handbook, a general overview of most of the significant awards that will actually be seen worn by SS troops, as opposed to those which could theoretically be earned, is provided. These are considered in three basic categories: gallantry awards, general service and Campaign awards, and those with a particular connection with the SS.

All awards were issued with a certificate of possession (*Besitzzeugnis*) confirming the wearer's entitlement to the award, and an appropriate entry would be made in the soldier's military records, including his personal ID book (*Soldbuch*).

GALLANTRY AWARDS

The premier German gallantry award during the Second World War was the Iron Cross. Re-instituted on 1 September 1939, after various amendments to its statutes, its final range of classes stood as follows:

> Iron Cross Second Class
> 1939 Clasp to 1914 Iron Cross Second Class
> Iron Cross First Class
> 1939 Clasp to 1914 Iron Cross First Class
> Knight's Cross of the Iron Cross
> Oakleaves to the Knight's Cross
> Oakleaves with Swords to the Knight's Cross
> Oakleaves with Swords and Diamonds to the Knight's Cross
> Golden Oakleaves with Swords and Diamonds to the Knight's Cross
> Grand Cross of the Iron Cross

The last two mentioned above can be discounted for the purposes of this work, as both were only awarded once, and in each case, to a member of the *Luftwaffe*. All other

A regimental commander, accompanied by his adjutant, bestows military decorations on his men, all of whom, from the awards already worn, are combat veterans.

grades, however, were awarded to members of the *Waffen-SS*.

It was necessary for a prospective recipient to have earned the previous class before being eligible for the next. On the rare occasions where a soldier's achievements were such that the Knight's Cross was warranted immediately, the simple expedient of awarding the Second and First Classes at the same time as the Knight's Cross ensured that the 'rules' were adhered to.

SECOND CLASS AND CLASP

The Iron Cross Second Class consisted of a blackened iron core within a silvered frame,

the obverse centre bearing a swastika in high relief and the year of re-institution, 1939, in the lower arm. The reverse was plain but for the original year of institution, 1813, in the lower arm. A suspension ring was attached to the edge of the upper arm and the award suspended from a black/white/red/white/black ribbon. Generally, the award was worn only on the day of its bestowal. Thereafter its ribbon alone was worn from the tunic buttonhole or on a ribbon bar above the left breast pocket.

For those who had been decorated with the Iron Cross Second Class in the First World War, a special clasp was introduced, which was to be worn on the ribbon of the

A young *SS-Sturmmann* from the *Leibstandarte SS Adolf Hitler* proudly sports his newly awarded Iron Cross Second Class. The award itself was worn in this fashion solely on the day of the award, and thereafter only the ribbon was worn. The shoulder straps bear the LAH monogram of the *Leibstandarte*.

1914 Iron Cross. This consisted of an eagle clasping a wreathed swastika, all on a trapezoid-shaped bar with the year 1939. This was attached to the ribbon by means of prongs on its reverse.

The Iron Cross Second Cross and its clasp could be awarded for minor acts of distinction in leadership or gallantry (such as, for example, leading a particularly successful patrol behind enemy lines).

FIRST CLASS AND CLASP

This next class was a pin-back award. Its obverse design was identical to that for the Second Class, but its reverse had a plain flat silvered face to which was attached a hinged pin fitting, or in the case of some privately purchased awards, a screw-back fitting. It was worn on the left breast pocket, above the level of lesser awards, such as the infantry combat badge. Unlike the Second Class, the award was worn at all times.

As with the Second Class, a Clasp was introduced to reward those who had already won the Iron Cross First Class of 1914 and went on to further distinguish themselves in the Second World War. It was of similar design to the Second Class Clasp, but with a wider wingspan, and like the Iron Cross First Class itself, featured a pin-back fitting. The Clasp was to be worn on the left breast pocket just above the Iron Cross First Class of 1914. Again, privately purchased pieces could have a screw fitting instead of a pin. Some examples were also made with the Clasp directly attached to the upper arm of a replacement 1914 Iron Cross First Class.

As with the Second Class, the First Class would be awarded for minor acts of leadership and gallantry, such as, for example, successfully capturing an enemy bunker against determined opposition.

THE KNIGHT'S CROSS

This was a new award, intended to bridge the gap between the First Class and the Grand Cross, and at the same time replace Imperial awards such as the famed *'Pour le Mérite'* or 'Blue Max' which had neatly filled this gap. The award was basically identical to the Second Class in its physical appearance, but was slightly larger and had a frame made from silver. The suspension consisted of a loop shaped rather like a paper clip, passing through a small 'eye' on the edge of the frame, allowing the Cross to be suspended from a ribbon around the neck. This highly regarded award was bestowed in recognition

The Iron Cross, Germany's premier gallantry award. On the left the Second Class, on the right the pin-back First Class, and in the centre, the Knight's Cross, worn at the neck.

of particularly distinguished acts of military leadership or personal gallantry. A total of 638 Knight's Crosses were awarded to members of the *Waffen-SS*.

THE OAKLEAVES

Introduced in 1940, the Oakleaves were a traditional German device to recognise those who had won a gallantry award and had then gone on to carry out further acts of distinguished leadership or gallantry. In the case of the Knight's Cross, the attendant Oakleaves clasp consisted of a spray of three leaves with the centre leaf overlaid on the lower two, all die-struck from real silver. On the reverse face of the Oakleaves was affixed a replacement ribbon suspension loop, allowing the Oakleaves to be neatly clipped to the existing eye on the Knight's Cross frame once the original suspension loop had been removed.

A total of seventy-six Oakleaves clasps were awarded to members of the *Waffen-SS*.

THE OAKLEAVES WITH SWORDS

Introduced in 1941 for those Oakleaves winners who had continued to distinguish themselves in combat, this award consisted of the standard Oakleaves clasp, to the base of which were soldered two tiny crossed swords. This rare award was bestowed only twenty-four times on soldiers of the *Waffen-SS*.

THE OAKLEAVES WITH SWORDS AND DIAMONDS

This stunning decoration was also introduced in 1941 for award to those rare few for whom even the Oakleaves with Swords was insufficient recognition of their achievements. Two examples of the clasp were given to the recipient, one in platinum and set with diamonds on both the Oakleaves and the Sword hilts, and another, for everyday wear, in silver with imitation stones. Each was individually hand-assembled from several parts, had the stones set and was hand-finished by skilled jewellers. Only two were awarded to members of the *Waffen-SS*.

THE GERMAN CROSS

Introduced in September 1941, this award was another 'gap-filler' intended to reward deeds greater than those that could be recognised by the award of the Iron Cross First Class, but which would not be sufficient to earn the Knight's Cross.

It was a large, multi-piece award, consisting of a large radiant sunburst silver star on top

of which was a slightly smaller black star. In the centre was a silvered disc with a black enamelled swastika, and a circular ring of red enamel. On to this ring of red enamel was set a wreath of laurel leaves with the year of introduction, '1941', at its base.

The award was in two classes, Silver and Gold, the colour being that of the laurel wreath. The silver award was bestowed for acts of military merit which contributed to the war effort, but did not involve combat. The gold award was given to those who had carried out repeated acts of distinguished conduct, leadership or gallantry in direct combat with the enemy.

The award was worn on the right breast pocket and was also produced in an embroidered form. A total of 894 were awarded to members of the *Waffen-SS*.

THE HONOUR ROLL CLASP

This award, introduced in January 1944, was to recognise those whose deeds had led to their names being listed on the Roll of Honour of the German Army (*Waffen-SS* troops also being eligible). It consisted of a small gilded wreath of laurel leaves, in the centre of which was a large swastika. It had four prongs on the reverse, by which it was pinned to the ribbon of the Iron Cross Second Class in the wearer's tunic buttonhole. Recipients of this award had to have already been decorated with the Iron Cross First Class.

THE WAR MERIT CROSS

This was a new decoration, created in October 1939, which was intended to recognise the recipient's contribution to the war effort by his meritorious conduct. It was created in three Classes: War Merit Cross Second Class, War Merit Cross First Class and Knight's Cross of the War Merit Cross.

It was necessary to possess the Second Class before being eligible for the First, and the First before being eligible for the Knight's Cross. The award was in two grades, with and without Swords. Those without Swords were generally issued to those, for example, in industries contributing to the war effort, and were predominantly civil awards, whereas those with Swords were awarded to military contributions to the war effort. The War Merit Cross was awarded to many troops, such as transport drivers, vehicle recovery mechanics and military policemen whose efforts may not have involved combat but whose contribution to the war effort was nevertheless immense.

The award consisted of an eight-pointed, so-called 'Maltese' cross, with a circular wreath of oakleaves in its centre. In the obverse central field was a swastika and on the reverse the year of introduction, 1939. The swords were crossed through the centre of the award, emerging from the wreath of oakleaves. The sword hilts were at the base of the award.

The Second Class was in a bronze colour and had a suspension loop set into the notch of the upper arm. It was suspended from a black/white/red/white/black ribbon. As with the Iron Cross Second Class, the award was normally only worn on the day of its bestowal, thereafter only the ribbon being worn.

The First Class was a pin-back award with a silvered finish and was worn on the left breast pocket. Like the First Class Iron Cross, it could also be procured with a screw fitting rather than a pin.

The Knight's Cross was slightly larger than the Second Class, and was struck in solid silver, a ribbon suspension loop being passed through a small eye attached to the cross by two small arms emerging from the notch in the top arm. It was worn around the neck. The Knight's Cross of the War Merit Cross was a rare award, being bestowed only seventeen times to members of the SS.

THE WOUND BADGE

This award had originally been created for the Kaiser's Army in Imperial times, and was re-instituted in modified form in September 1939. The award consisted of a vertical oval wreath of laurel leaves with a pebbled central field. Two crossed swords lay over this field, and superimposed upon them was an M35-pattern steel helmet emblazoned with a large swastika.

The badge was awarded in three grades: Black – for one or two wounds, Silver – for three or four wounds, Gold – for five or more wounds. The number of wounds could be overlooked and a higher-grade badge awarded in the case of a single serious wound such as the loss of a limb.

Given the high casualty rates suffered by the *Waffen-SS*, the issue of Wound Badges to its troops was of a high order.

GENERAL SERVICE AND CAMPAIGN AWARDS

A number of award badges, or battle badges (*Kampfabzeichen*), were created for the German Army to recognise the participation of the wearer in a laid-down number of combat actions. Troops of the *Waffen-SS* were eligible for all such Army awards. The most important of these were as follows.

THE INFANTRY ASSAULT BADGE (*INFANTERIE STURMABZEICHEN*)

Introduced in December 1939, this badge consisted of a vertical oval wreath of oakleaves topped by a *Wehrmacht*-pattern eagle with swastika. Across the centre of the wreath from bottom right to top left was laid a representation of the Kar 98k, the basic weapon of the German infantryman, with bayonet affixed.

The badge, silver in colour, was worn on the left breast pocket, and was issued after the recipient had participated in at least three individual combat actions with the enemy. In 1940, a second version was introduced in a bronze colour, specifically for award to motorised infantry.

THE PANZER ASSAULT BADGE (*PANZER KAMPFABZEICHEN*)

Introduced in December 1939, this badge consisted of a vertical wreath of oakleaves topped by the *Wehrmacht*-style eagle and swastika. In the centre was depicted a tank, breaking through the wreath from left to right. Silver in colour, it was issued after the recipient had participated in three individual tank actions against the enemy. In June 1940, an additional version, identical to the first but in a bronzed finish, was introduced for award to those such as Panzer Grenadiers and crews of armoured reconnaissance vehicles.

By 1943 it had become clear that so many panzer crews had taken part in countless additional actions since receiving their Panzer Assault Badge that the basic badge was no longer sufficient, and a new series of badges was created. Two specific patterns were manufactured, one to reflect 25 or 50 tank actions, and another for 75 or 100 actions. The first consisted of the usual oval wreath of oakleaves with the *Wehrmacht* eagle at the top, but in this case the tank motif was in a chemically darkened finish and was separately attached by small rivets. The 75/100 pattern had a redesigned wreath, less oval in form and much wider at the base. The wreath was finished in gold

colour and the tank in silver. At the base of each badge was a small box bearing the number 25, 50, 75 or 100, as appropriate.

The bronze version was also made in the same form, with the 25/50 badge being entirely in bronze, whereas the 75/100 was bronze but with a gold-coloured tank.

These new grades were made retrospective, so that if at the date of introduction an individual had completed fifteen months' combat service, this would qualify him automatically for the 25 Badge, twelve months would count as fifteen engagements and eight months as ten engagements towards the total needed. The number of engagements could be reduced slightly for those who had been severely wounded in action. The 25 Badge, for instance, could be awarded after eighteen engagements if the recipient was seriously wounded.

THE FLAK BADGE (*FLAK ABZEICHEN*)

The anti-aircraft badge awarded to *Flak* units of the *Waffen-SS* was introduced in July 1941, and consisted of the usual vertical oval wreath of oakleaves topped by a *Wehrmacht* eagle. In its centre was a representation of a heavy flak gun, its raised barrel breaking through the wreath at top right. It was silver-coloured and worn on the left breast pocket.

This badge was awarded on a points basis, various points (the exact criteria changed through the war) being given for aircraft shot down, depending on whether the kill was solo or shared with another gun. A unit commander would qualify once more than half of his crews had earned the badge.

THE GENERAL ASSAULT BADGE (*ALLGEMEINES STURMABZEICHEN*)

As this name implies, this 'general' badge was issued for troops who did not have their

The General Assault Badge, basic level for three engagements with the enemy, for 50 engagements and for 75 engagements.

own specific war badge, and although even in period documentation it is often referred to as the *Pioniersturmabzeichen*, it was by no means restricted to issue for combat engineers. Introduced in June 1940, the badge consisted of a vertical oval wreath of oakleaves with in its centre a *Wehrmacht*-style eagle and swastika sitting atop a crossed bayonet and stick grenade. Silver in colour, it was issued after three separate engagements with the enemy and was worn on the left breast pocket.

In June 1943, as with the Panzer Assault Badge, additional grades were created for 25, 50, 75 and 100 engagements with the enemy. The 25/50 badge was broadly similar to the original design but with the central motif in a chemically darkened contrasting finish and made as a separate piece, which was then attached by rivets. At the base was a box with the number 25 or 50. The 75/100 badge was an altogether more impressive design, much larger and with a very imposing eagle. Again of two-piece construction, the central motif was

darkened but the wreath was gilded. This time, at the base was a small box with the number 75 or 100.

THE CLOSE-COMBAT CLASP (*NAHKAMPFSPANGE*)

This highly regarded award was created in November 1942 to recognise those who had taken part in bitter hand-to-hand fighting against enemy troops. It was so highly regarded that Adolf Hitler in fact reserved the right to personally award its highest grade, and indeed on occasion did so.

The badge consisted of a horizontal clasp, in the centre of which was a small square 'frame' of oakleaves enclosing a crossed bayonet and hand grenade, with an eagle and swastika with outspread wings above. Emerging from each side of this central motif was a spray of oakleaves backed by radiant sunburst rays. A small blackened-metal backing plate was placed behind the pierced-out central motif to give a contrasting effect. On the reverse

The Panzer Assault Badge, basic level for 3 engagements with the enemy, for 25 engagements and for 75 engagements.

was affixed a long horizontal hinged-pin fitting.

The Clasp in Bronze was awarded after participation in a total of 15 days of hand-to-hand fighting (reduced to 10 if during this fighting the soldier was seriously wounded so as to render him unfit for future close-combat action), in Silver for a total of 30 days (20 if wounded) and in Gold for a total of 50 days (40 if wounded). A total of 114 of the rare Gold grade were awarded to members of the *Waffen-SS*.

THE TANK DESTRUCTION BADGE (*PANZERVERNICHTUNGSABZEICHEN*)

This small but highly regarded award will be seen on many photographs of *Waffen-SS* combat soldiers. Introduced in March 1942, the award was for soldiers who had single-handedly knocked out an enemy tank using only individual weapons such as satchel charges, magnetic mines and grenades (the crews of anti-tank guns did not qualify).

The insignia consisted of a strip of woven aluminium braid with black edging, and in the centre a small metal tank motif. It was sewn to the upper right sleeve.

An example of this award was issued for the first four tanks destroyed. On destroying a fifth tank, the soldier would remove the four 'silver' versions and replace them with a single example on gold braid. Using various combinations of gold and silver braid versions, any combination of numbers could be represented.

CAMPAIGN AWARDS

Prior to the outbreak of war, SS-VT units were involved in the so-called 'Flower Wars', the bloodless occupations of Austria and the Sudetenland, and the retaking of the port of Memel. Medals were issued to those who took part. Only the ribbons were worn on military uniform, and these were in the form of small ones on the ribbon bar above the breast pocket, rather than full-size ones in the tunic buttonhole. They will thus be very difficult if not impossible to detect on anything but large studio portrait photographs.

SS-RELATED AWARDS

The East Front Medal (*Ostmedaille*, or more correctly *Medaille 'Winterschlacht im Osten'*), the principal Campaign award worn by members of the *Waffen-SS*, was in fact designed by a serving *Waffen-SS* front-line combat soldier, *SS-Unterscharführer* Krause, and his sketches were brought to fruition in May 1942.

This rather attractive award consists of a circular medal with, at its top, a stick grenade on which is balanced a steel helmet. The helmet and edge of the medal are finished in a matt silver colour. The grenade and central field are chemically blackened and have a deep lustre, the obverse centre field showing a *Wehrmacht*-style eagle grasping a swastika, with a sprig of laurel running behind the swastika. The reverse field has the inscription *'Winterschlacht im Osten 1941/42'* over a small Iron Cross motif. Attached to the apex of the helmet is a ribbon suspension ring. The ribbon for the award has a red field with a narrow white central strip, in the centre of which is a thin black line. As with most medals, the award itself was generally only worn on the day of the award, and thereafter the ribbon only was worn, usually in the tunic buttonhole.

The medal was bestowed upon all soldiers who had honourably served on the Eastern Front during the first winter of the Campaign against the Soviet Union, between 15 November 1941 and 15 April 1942. The minimum requirement for combat troops was to have taken part during this period in at least fourteen days of combat operations, to have been wounded, or to have suffered from frostbite.

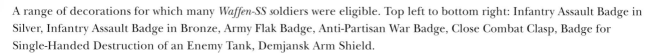

A range of decorations for which many *Waffen-SS* soldiers were eligible. Top left to bottom right: Infantry Assault Badge in Silver, Infantry Assault Badge in Bronze, Army Flak Badge, Anti-Partisan War Badge, Close Combat Clasp, Badge for Single-Handed Destruction of an Enemy Tank, Demjansk Arm Shield.

The Campaign decoration for service on the Eastern Front during the winter of 1941–2, designed by a serving *Waffen-SS* NCO.

The last criterion was no doubt due to the huge number of cases of frostbite suffered by German troops during the first winter of the war in the East. Indeed, over this winter it is often claimed that casualties through frostbite were greater than casualties caused by enemy action. This resulted in the award being dubbed by the troops as the *'Gefrierfleischorden'*, or the 'Order of the Frozen Meat'.

The Demjansk Shield

This was but one of a range of commemorative arm shields recognising the wearer's

participation in key battles. This was the only such award, however, which commemorated a battle where SS units played a major part in the fighting. A few individual SS soldiers may have qualified for other shields, sometimes having served in other branches of the armed forces before transferring to the *Waffen-SS*, but in the case of the battle for the Demjansk pocket, the *3 SS-Panzer Division Totenkopf* played a pivotal role.

The shield itself is made from stamped sheet metal and has a silvered finish. It shows on its central field two large crossed swords over the date 1942. In the upper part of the field is a head-on view of an aircraft (recognising the part played by the *Luftwaffe* in keeping the beleaguered troops supplied). Above the main field is a large eagle and swastika, flanked either side by a bunker with a distinctive firing slit. For *Waffen-SS* troops, the shield was worn on a field-grey cloth backing, which allowed it to be stitched to the sleeve of the tunic just above the SS-pattern national emblem.

The shield was instituted on 25 April 1943, and was awarded to all who had participated in the successful defence of the Demjansk pocket against overwhelming enemy forces from February 1941 to April 1942.

The Anti-Partisan Badge (*Bandenkampf abzeichen*)

This rare award was instituted by Heinrich Himmler as *Reichsführer-SS* and *Chef der deutschen Polizei*, on 30 January 1944. It consisted of a vertical oval wreath of oak-leaves with at its base a skull and crossbones. In the centre field is a hydra (the mythical many-headed serpent) representing the partisan menace. Plunging through the centre of the hydra is a broad-bladed sword in the style of the Roman gladius, with, as its crosspiece, a circular *'Sonnenrad'*, or sunwheel-type swastika.

The award was manufactured in three grades, bronze, silver and gold, and was to be worn on the left breast pocket. The grades were awarded as follows: Bronze – for 20 days' combat in anti-partisan operations, Silver – for 50 days' combat in anti-partisan operations, and Gold – for 100 days' combat in anti-partisan operations.

A special version in gold with the *Sonnenrad* set with small diamonds was projected, but although many copies circulate it is uncertain whether any such pieces were ever made before the end of the war.

Although an SS-instituted piece, this award was also widely bestowed on police troops, as well as numbers of Army, airforce and even naval shore forces who had taken part in anti-partisan operations.

CHAPTER TEN

WEAPONS

RIFLES

GEWEHR GEW 98

This weapon was a rather elderly rifle, first used during the First World War. A simple, but accurate and effective piece, it was of basic single-shot bolt-action design, with an internal five-shot box-magazine and weighing around 4.2 kg. The Gew 98 had a barrel length of 740 mm and fired a standard 7.92 mm bullet with a muzzle velocity of 870 m per second and an accurate range of up to 2,000 metres.

It was used to a considerable degree by SS-VT units prior to the Second World War, and although it remained in use in large numbers, particularly by lower-grade formations and security units, by the outbreak of war in September 1939 it had been largely replaced by the Kar 98k. Apart from its greater length, it can be readily identified on photographs by the attachment of the sling to a metal loop on the butt rather than through a slot in the butt. A hole through the butt allowed for a retaining pin to pass through several rifles to secure them when crated up for transport.

KARABINER KAR 98K

This excellent weapon was basically a shortened carbine version of the *Gewehr* 98, weighing 3.9 kg and with a barrel length of 600 mm. The bolt on the Kar 98k was turned down against the stock to prevent snagging, and its wooden stock had a slot cut through it to accept the leather sling. It still fired the basic 7.92 mm cartridge and retained the five-shot box-magazine. Its muzzle velocity was 755 m per second and effective range was around 800 m.

As the war progressed, necessary cost-saving measures saw the wooden stock replaced by cheaper plywood furniture and the fine blueing to the barrel give way to a cheaper chemical greying. It remained an effective firearm, however, and was never fully replaced by any other weapon, remaining the principal armament of the German soldier throughout the war.

The Kar 98k was also manufactured under licence in Czechoslovakia, and after the German occupation these Czech-made carbines were used by the Germans as the Kar M33/40, being widely used by several of the *Waffen-SS* mountain troop units.

GEWEHR G41 AND G43

This rather disappointing effort saw only limited issue. It was an attempt to provide the German soldier with a semi-automatic rifle roughly equivalent to the US M1 carbine. The initial version, the G41, weighed in at 5.03 kg and had a 546 mm barrel. It was provided with a larger, detachable ten-round

Waffen-SS troops train with a captured Czech heavy machine-gun.

box-magazine mounted just in front of the trigger guard. It fired the standard 7.92 mm cartridge with a muzzle velocity of 776 m per second and an effective range of around 800 m. The operating system used a gas-blowback method, with the gases from the firing of the cartridge being forced back down the barrel to operate a piston which then forced a connecting rod to feed a new round into the chamber.

The G41 was highly unpopular with those troops using it during trials. Subsequent modifications produced the G43, a lighter weapon at 4.4 kg. This weapon used a much more efficient automatic loading system, though still gas-operated. It was much more

popular with the troops but never came close to replacing the trusted Kar 98k.

PISTOLS

P.08 (LUGER)

This most famous of all automatic pistols was still in large-scale volume production at the outbreak of the Second World War. Firing a 9 mm parabellum round, it featured an eight-shot box-magazine in the hand grip and utilised a distinctive toggle action to eject used cartridges and chamber fresh shells before effectively locking the movement. Having previously been manu-

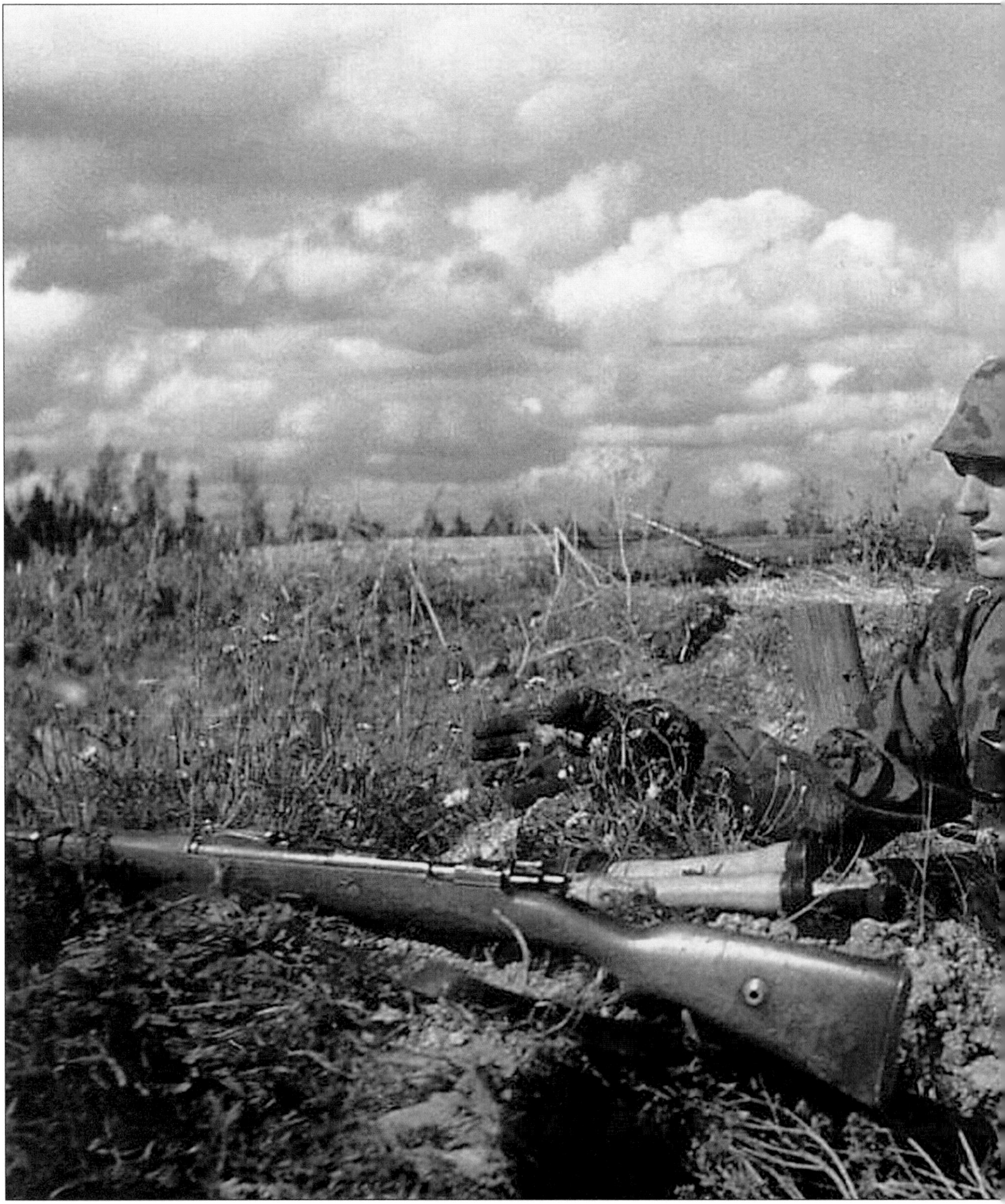

factured in 4 in, 6 in and 8 in barrel models, by the Second World War it was only produced in the standard 4 in pattern. It was, unfortunately, of rather complex construction, extremely expensive to manufacture and prone to jamming under combat conditions due to the exposed nature of the working parts. Although widely replaced by the P.38, it remained a firm favourite with any soldier fortunate enough to lay hands on one.

P.38

Developed by the Walther firm, the P.38 was a fine double-action semi-automatic pistol, firing a standard 9 mm parabellum round. It featured an eight-shot box-magazine in the hand grip. It was cocked using a more conventional slide. When fired, the slide moved backwards, cocking the hammer before moving forward to chamber another round. The barrel also moved backwards slightly during the recoil movement. It was a highly successful and robust pistol, which was so highly regarded that at one stage the SS tried to procure the entire production of this weapon for itself. It went into service again in the postwar German Army as the P.1.

MAUSER C96 ('BROOMHANDLE')

This fine but rather antiquated weapon, dating from 1896, was still in use by *Waffen-SS* troops during the Campaigns in

An *SS-Oberscharführer*, or squad leader, in full camouflage gear. The tunic collar with its rank insignia was worn outside the neck of the smock which allowed instant identification of the soldier's rank. The rifle by his side is the *Gewehr* Gew 98. Note also the *Stielhandgranate*, or 'stick grenades'.

Probably the most important of all the variety of German and captured enemy handguns are shown here. Top left to bottom right: the 'Broomhandle' Mauser C96, Walther P.38, the Mauser HSc, the P.08 'Luger', and the Walther PP. The Mauser C96 was still being used by SS units during the 1940 Campaign in the West, if not beyond.

Poland in 1939 and the Western Campaign of 1940.

Known as the 'Broomhandle' because of its solid, rounded grip, it featured a small internal box-magazine mounted, not in the handle, but in front of the trigger guard. Initially chambered to fire a 7.63 mm round, many were also reworked to take heavier 9 mm ammunition. Its muzzle velocity was almost three times that of the P.08 and P.38, making it a very effective weapon. This large pistol was accompanied by a solid wooden holster which could be clipped to the rear of the handle to provide a shoulder stock, thus allowing its accurate range to extend to up to a theoretical 1,000 m. A version known as the *Schnellfeuer'* was also produced, with a 20-round magazine and the facility for rapid fire. Even when used with an extended extra-capacity magazine, however, its rate of fire would quickly exhaust the available

ammunition and its kick when fired on automatic meant that accuracy was woeful in this mode. It was rarely seen in front-line use after the opening months of the war.

THE WALTHER PP

This excellent, compact semi-automatic pistol with a 99 mm barrel (just 3 mm shorter than the P.08) was much favoured by officers and senior NCOs. Though available in 9 mm calibre, most were chambered for the 7.65 mm cartridge. Its poor stopping power and short effective range of just 25 m meant that it was not particularly suitable as a combat weapon. Indeed, its designation PP is an abbreviation of *Polizei Pistole*, or police pistol, having been intended for use by the civil police, a purpose for which it was far better suited.

THE WALTHER PPK

This pistol was visually very similar to the PP, but slightly smaller, with a barrel length of just 86 mm. The designation PPK indicated *Polizei Pistole Kurz*, or short police pistol. Ideal for use by plain-clothes police officers because of its easy concealability, it was also favoured by some officers, though its effectiveness in combat would be minimal.

THE MAUSER HSC

Broadly similar to the Walther PP, this pistol fired standard 7.65 mm ammunition, with an eight-shot magazine inside the handle. A fine pistol, it suffered, however, from the same disadvantages as the PPK, its short barrel of just 86 mm, small-calibre rounds and short effective range making it a less than effective combat weapon. It was, nevertheless, favoured by many officers.

THE BROWNING 9MM AUTOMATIC

On overrunning France and the Low Countries, the Germans found themselves in control of the Belgian armaments concern FN (Fabrique Nationale), which manufactured the Browning automatic pistol under licence.

The Germans continued to manufacture this excellent weapon, and many may be found with German proof marks. This rugged and reliable pistol was highly popular, having a useful 13-round magazine capacity.

MACHINE-PISTOLS AND ASSAULT RIFLES

THE MP38/40

The most commonly used sub-machine-gun in the German forces was without doubt the ubiquitous MP38/40, commonly referred to by Allied troops as the *'Schmeisser'*, though this particular weapon was not designed by Hugo Schmeisser. However, his name seems set to be for ever linked with this excellent weapon.

The initial version was the MP38. This weapon made heavy use of machined parts and was very expensive to make. It was, however, a first-class firearm, rugged and robust, yet simple and easy to maintain. It featured a 32-round box-magazine, a pistol grip, and a folding skeleton stock (some early examples were also manufactured with a solid wooden stock). In order to cut costs, a number of parts were subsequently stamped rather than machined from solid metal, resulting in the MP40. This weapon remained almost identical in appearance to its predecessor, the only easy way to tell from old wartime photographs being that the housing for the magazine on the MP38 is ribbed and that on the MP40 is smooth.

The MP38/40 had a muzzle velocity of 365 m per second, a rate of fire of 500 rpm and an effective range of between 100 and 200 m.

THE MP28/II

The MP28/II, manufactured by the Erma firm, is rarely seen in use by elite front-line *Waffen-SS* units, but may be seen frequently in photographs of lesser units, especially those used on anti-partisan duties, which often made use of obsolescent German and captured foreign weapons. It was also widely used by police and security units. The Erma MP28 is instantly recognisable by its solid wooden stock, the perforated cooling jacket over the barrel, and the 32-round box-magazine emerging horizontally from the left side of the receiver rather than vertically below it as in the MP38/40. A robust and reliable weapon, it was too expensive to manufacture in the numbers required for a large Army in wartime and

The same senior NCO as seen on pages 134–5. Laid down by his side is an MP28, with its distinctive sidewards-protruding magazine and wooden stock.

was replaced by the MP38/40. Thereafter all MP28 production went to the SS.

THE *STURMGEWEHR* STG44

This superb assault rifle was designed by Hugo Schmeisser and originally appeared as the MP43, its designation as a machine-pistol being a subterfuge as Hitler had opposed the development of such a weapon. Once the concept had been proved, however, it was redesignated in 1944 as an assault rifle. Making use predominantly of stampings, castings and plastic components rather than machined

parts made the weapon cheap to fabricate and resulted in this rather large weapon weighing in at just 5.2 kg. It featured a fixed solid wooden stock and a 420 mm barrel. It had a muzzle velocity of 650 m per second and could achieve a rate of fire of some 500 rpm with an effective range of 800 m. Its forward-curving magazine contained 30 rounds of 7.92 mm 'short'-calibre ammunition.

The gas-operated system was robust and dependable, and this weapon was extremely popular with troops fortunate enough to be issued with it. Its physical appearance leaves no doubt that Andrei

Kalashnikov took note of its many excellent qualities when designing his own famous assault rifle.

Many of the photographs of SS troops taken during the Ardennes Offensive show the StG44 in use. Owing to its late date of introduction and the difficulties in production because of the reversal of Germany's military fortunes, it was never available in sufficient numbers to meet demand.

MACHINE-GUNS
THE *MASCHINENGEWEHR* MG34

This superb multi-purpose machine-gun was one of the most devastating weapons at the disposal of the German soldier. Fitted with a folding bipod just to the rear of the muzzle, and weighing in at 11.5 kg, it was belt fed and could achieve a rate of fire of some 900 rpm at a muzzle velocity of 755 m per second. It used standard 7.92 mm

In this cold winter scene (note the padded hood worn by the gunner), the 'Number 2' fits a fresh belt of ammunition into the breech of this MG34, fitted to a tripod mount for use in the sustained-fire role.

The MG34 set up on its anti-aircraft tripod mount. Note the large circular anti-aircraft sight.

ammunition. The rate of fire, though devastating to the enemy, was difficult to sustain, firstly because of the danger of the barrel overheating (though the weapon, cleverly designed, allowed for extremely fast barrel replacement), but more importantly because of the sheer consumption of ammunition. It is instantly recognisable in photographs by its round, pierced cooling sleeve to the barrel.

As well as the standard bipod mount for infantry use, a large collapsible tripod was manufactured to allow this weapon to be used in the sustained-fire role as a heavy support weapon. Although a robust, accurate and effective weapon, being made prominently from machined parts it was expensive and time consuming to make.

Fortunately its replacement, though quicker, easier and cheaper to make, lost none of its devastating effectiveness.

THE *MASCHINENGEWEHR* MG42

The replacement for the MG34 made heavy use of machine-stamped parts for ease and cheapness of manufacture. It also saw the replacement of the wooden stock with plastic components. The weapon can be readily recognised on wartime photographs by the square, pierced cooling sleeve over the barrel, exposed along one side to allow for quick barrel changes. Weighing the same as the MG34, the MG42 had the same effective range and muzzle velocity. It used the same 7.92 mm ammunition as the

The MG42, a much-improved version of the MG34, being far cheaper to manufacture, set up on its tripod mount for sustained-fire use.

These SS recruits are undergoing weapons training. The weapon being stripped appears to be an example of the Czech ZB 1926, known to the Germans as the MG 26(t), large numbers of which fell into German hands after the annexation of the Sudetenland and subsequent occupation of Czechoslovakia. Many of these were used by the SS.

MG34, but achieved the phenomenal rate of fire of 1,550 rpm.

So efficient and effective was this weapon that it went into production again after the war virtually unchanged, and is still used in the German Army today, designated the MG1.

THE *MASCHINENGEWEHR* ZB.VZ 26 AND 30

This excellent light machine-gun was of Czechoslovakian manufacture, and after that country was overrun by Germany continued in production for the German Army. It was widely used in second-line units, particularly those engaged in anti-partisan duties.

Bearing a passing resemblance to the British bren-gun, also of course of Czech origin, it had a bipod mount just behind the muzzle, a wooden shoulder stock, pistol grip, and a top-loading, 30-round box-

magazine. The muzzle velocity was 762 m per second, cyclic rate 500 rpm and effective range 2,000 m.

THE *PANZERFAUST*

Introduced in 1942, the *Panzerfaust* (literally 'armoured fist') gave the German soldier a very simple but highly effective anti-tank weapon. Initially designated the *Faustpatrone 30*, it consisted of a hollow steel tube just 500 mm in length. At one end was fitted a shaped hollow-charge projectile, the gases from the firing of which simply vented through the rear end of the hollow tube. The single-shot disposable weapon, with its charge, weighed just 5.2 kg, yet was capable of penetrating up to 140 mm of armour plate. The main drawback was that its effective range was only 30 m.

To increase effectiveness, a more powerful propellant charge was designed,

SS troops on training exercises use yet another example of foreign-manufactured weaponry, this time the Czech MG37(t).

An interesting shot of an SS NCO candidate on practice exercises with a heavy machine-gun set up for the anti-aircraft role. The weapon appears to be a Czech design.

doubling the effective range to 60 m and resulting in the *Faustpatrone 60*. The most powerful *Panzerfaust* appeared in 1944, when the *Faustpatrone 100*, with a fin-stabilised charge and an effective range on 100 m, was introduced.

THE *PANZERSCHRECK*

This weapon, officially entitled the *Racketenpanzerbusche RPzB 54*, was modelled on examples of the American 'Bazooka' captured in North Africa. It consisted of a hollow pipe with a sheet-metal shoulder stock and simple pistol grip. A small blast shield with perspex viewing screen was also provided.

An electrically fired 88 mm projectile, weighing some 3.3 kg and stabilised by spring-loaded fins which opened as the projectile emerged from the tube, was launched with a muzzle velocity of some 105 m per second. Its range was around 100 m, and the charge was capable of penetrating 100 mm of armour plate. The main advantages of this weapon were that, unlike the *Panzerfaust*, which had to be fired from a standing or kneeling position, the *Panzerschreck* could be fired lying down, thus making the user less of a target, and that the weapon itself was re-usable.

MORTARS (*GRANATEWERFER GRW*)

A very cheap and effective weapon, the mortar consists of a simple metal pipe mounted on a baseplate, usually with an adjustable bipod which regulates the angle of the tube and thus the effective range. At the base of the pipe is a simple firing-pin. When the mortar bomb is dropped into the pipe, the firing-pin strikes the detonator in its base, igniting the propellant charge and throwing the bomb back out of the tube.

The *Waffen-SS* used the same three basic mortars as the German Army. These were the light GrW 36 at 5 cm, the medium GrW 34 at 8 cm and the heavy GrW 42 at 12 cm 'calibre'.

The short range and relatively ineffective charge of the GrW 36 led to it being virtually defunct by the invasion of the Soviet Union in 1941. The medium GrW 34 fired a much more useful 3.4 kg charge to a range of up to 2,400 m and the heavy GrW 42 a 15.8 kg charge for just over 6,000 m.

ARTILLERY

Artillery can be divided into six basic categories: infantry guns, medium field artillery, heavy artillery, mountain artillery, anti-tank guns and anti-aircraft artillery. The borders between these categories were rather indistinct, some anti-aircraft weapons being used in the ground role as anti-tank guns (the famous 8.8 being the classic example of such adaptability) while some weapons in the infantry support role were of the same calibre as some heavy artillery pieces. For the purposes of this handbook, however, these weapons will be considered under the above categories.

INFANTRY GUNS (*INFANTERIE GESCHÜTZE*)

The principal infantry guns used by the *Waffen-SS* were the IG 34, IG 37 and IG 42. All were of 7.5 cm calibre.

The IG 34, developed as its title suggests in 1934, fired a 6.4 kg shell with a muzzle velocity of 225 m per second, to a range of 3,840 m. Both of the later weapons that superseded it, in 1944, fired a lighter, 5.5 kg shell, but with a higher muzzle velocity of 280 m per second. The main differences between the two were that the IG 37 had a lighter carriage, making the weapon some 80 kg less in overall weight than the IG 42, and also had a greater maximum elevation, at 40 degrees as opposed to 32 degrees. This gave the earlier weapon a greater range, at 5,150 m as opposed to 4,600 m with the IG 42. All of these weapons were generally issued to infantry regiments.

Also designated an infantry weapon, but of much larger calibre, was the sIG 33 (*schwere Infanterie Geschütze*, heavy infantry gun). This gun, only two of which were normally issued to the heavy support section

A Waffen-SS soldier in his foxhole fires a 5 cm *leichte Granatewerfer 36*. Note the ammunition case with four rounds remaining.

The effectiveness of SS camouflage clothing is clear from this shot of two mortar men in their slit trench. The SS were one of the main pioneers of the use of camouflage clothing.

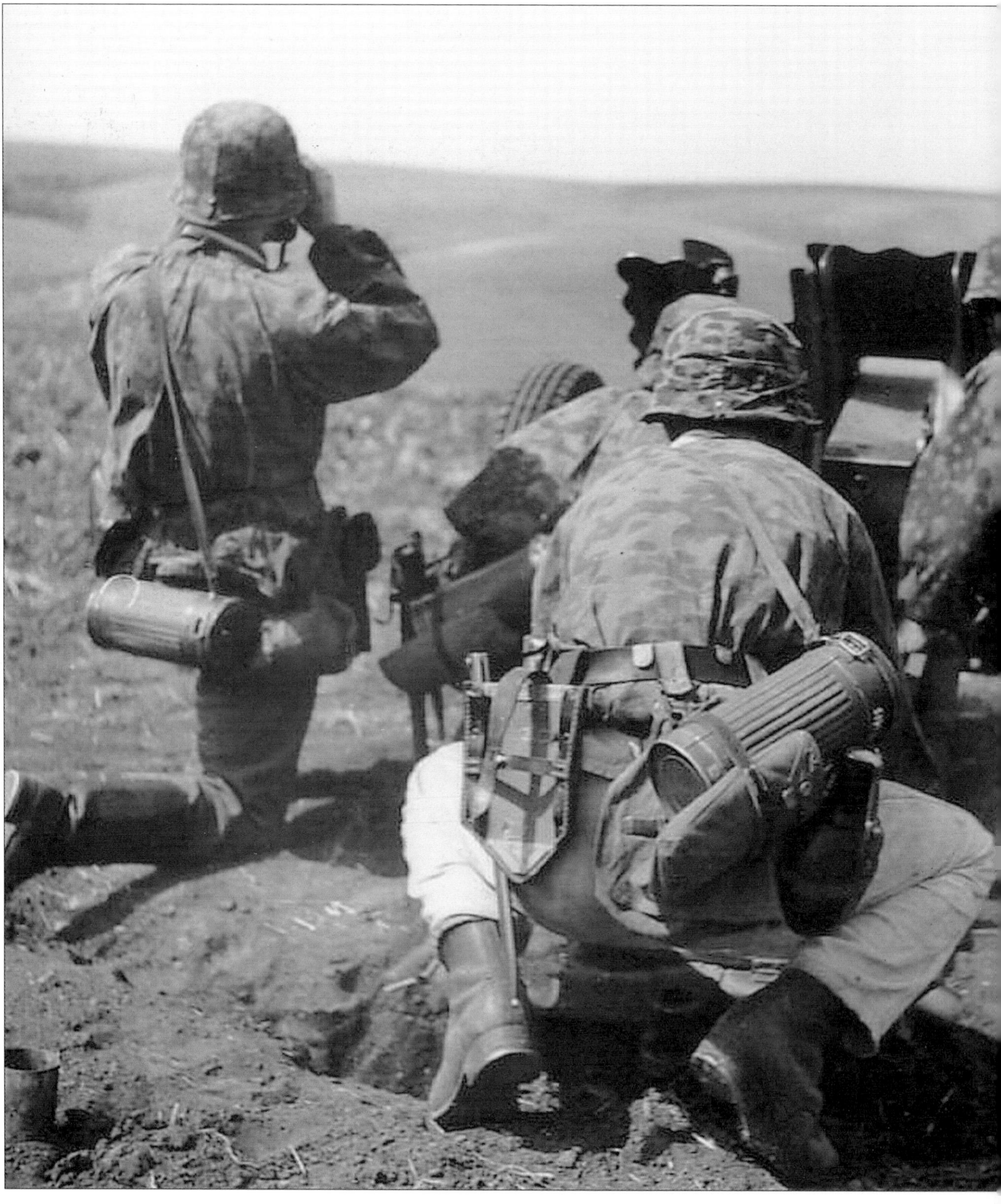

of an infantry regiment, fired a 38 kg shell with a muzzle velocity of 240 m per second, to a range of 4,700 m.

FIELD ARTILLERY

Also in use by infantry units, but at divisional level, was the 7.5 cm leFK 18 (*leichte Feld Kanone*, or light field cannon). This weapon fired a 5.8 kg shell with a muzzle velocity of 485 m per second, for a range of 9,425 m. The improved leFK 38, which was introduced in 1942, fired the same-size shell, but with an increased muzzle velocity of 605 m per second, giving a range of 11,500 m.

HEAVY ARTILLERY

In 1935, the first of the heavy-calibre artillery pieces to be used by the *Wehrmacht*, and later the *Waffen-SS*, was brought into service. This was the 10.5 cm leFH 18 (*leichte Feld Haubitze* or light field howitzer). This gun, with a traditional split trail, fired a 14.8 kg shell, with a muzzle velocity of some 470 m per second, to a range of 10,675 m.

In 1943, a major new weapon, the leFH 43, joined its predecessor with artillery units. This new weapon also fired a 14.8 kg shell, but with a higher muzzle velocity at 610 m per second and a range of 15,000 m. This new design featured a carriage with four outriggers. These were not in the traditional cruciform layout as found with the 8.8 cm flak, but two in the normal position of the standard trails, and two in

Waffen-SS artillerymen with the 7.5 cm *leichte Infanterie Geschütze*. Though the initial appearance may be of an action shot, the fact that the crewman nearest the camera is wearing drill trousers suggests this may have been taken on the training range.

The 'business-end' of the 7.5 cm *leichte Infanterie Geschütze*. The small stubby barrel of this infantry support weapon is instantly recognisable.

front, under the barrel. This set-up allowed the gun a useful full 360-degree traverse.

The heaviest-calibre artillery in general use was the 15 cm gun. As used by heavy artillery units, this calibre was found on the sFH 18 (*schwere Feld Haubitze*, or heavy field howitzer), a typical split-trail wheeled weapon firing a 43.5 kg shell with a muzzle velocity of up to 495 m per second and maximum range of 13,250 m.

An improved version, the sFH 36, was introduced in 1938, though it remained in production only until 1942. This modification used lightweight alloys in the design wherever possible, and had a muzzle brake added to its shortened barrel. Its muzzle velocity and range were both lower than the sFH 18.

MOUNTAIN ARTILLERY

The basic mountain artillery gun had one very important capability – it could be easily disassembled to allow its components to be transported high into the mountain peaks, usually by mule power.

Two particular weapons were widely used by mountain units of the *Waffen-SS*, these being the 7.5 cm GebG 36 (*Gebirgs Geschütze*, or mountain gun), and the 10.5 cm GebH 40 (*Gebirgs Haubitze*, or mountain howitzer).

Both were traditional split-trail wheeled guns, the GebG 36 being instantly recognisable by its distinctive muzzle brake. The GebG 36 fired a 5.75 kg shell with a muzzle velocity of 475 m per second to a range of 9,150 m, and the GebH 40 a 14.5 kg shell with a muzzle velocity of 565 m per second to a range of 16,740 m. In addition to these two modern guns, considerable numbers of the older 7.5 cm GebK 15 (*Gebirgs Kanone*, or mountain cannon) were still in use. This weapon had a single trail and solid, spoked wheels. It fired a 5.47 kg shell with a muzzle velocity of 386 m per second to a range of 6,625 m.

ANTI-TANK GUNS

On the outbreak of war in 1939, *Waffen-SS* anti-tank gunners were equipped with the 3.7 cm Pak 35/36 (*Panzerabwehrkanone*, or anti-tank cannon). This split-trail, wheeled gun was small, light and easily manhandled. It was, however, totally ineffective against the armour of most of the heavier British and French tanks of the day. Firing a 0.7 kg armour-piercing round with a muzzle velocity of 762 m per second and a range of some 4,000 m, it was capable of penetrating only 48 mm of vertical or 36 mm of sloped armour.

A tungsten-carbide-cored projectile was developed which increased its maximum penetration to 55 mm, but it was not until 1942, when a hollow charge armour-piercing round was developed, that this weapon became capable of taking on any known enemy tank in existence, as the new hollow charge, fin-stabilised projectile was capable of piercing up to 180 mm of armour plate.

Unfortunately, this projectile had a range of just 300 m, which meant that enemy

The low weight of the 7.5 cm *leichte Infanterie Geschütze* allowed it to be easily manhandled and towed by a small field car such as the Horch shown here.

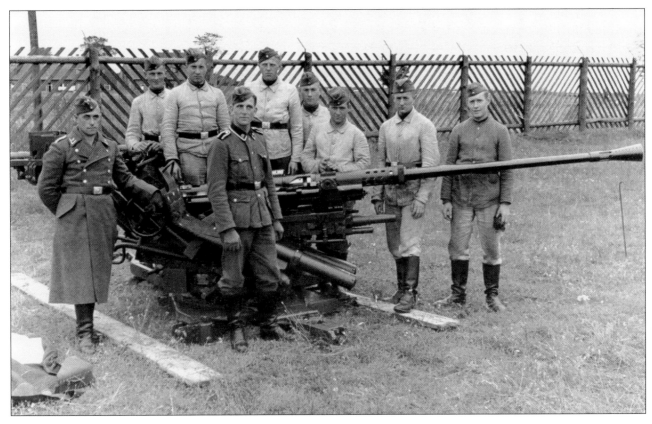

Flak troops from the *Totenkopf Division* are given training on the 3.7 cm *Flak* by comrades from the *Luftwaffe*. Many *Waffen-SS* units had their *Flak Abteilung* equipped with the 3.7 cm *Flak* mounted on the 8-ton SdKfz 7 half-track.

tanks could only be destroyed at dangerously close ranges, making this weapon suitable only in ambush.

The need for a more powerful anti-tank weapon saw the introduction of the 50 cm Pak 38 in 1940. This gun fired a 2.25 kg projectile with a muzzle velocity of 823 m per second and a range of 2,650 m. It was at its maximum effectiveness, however, at a range of just 1,000 m, when it could penetrate up to 50 mm of sloped armour, a capability halved when used at its maximum range. As with its predecessor, its capabilities were improved by the introduction of a tungsten-carbide-cored projectile.

In November 1941, German anti-tank troops finally received a top-class weapon

on the introduction of the 7.5 cm Pak 40. This excellent weapon, visually similar to the 5 cm version, but larger, fired a 6.6 kg projectile with a muzzle velocity of 792 m per second to a range of 7,680 m. It could penetrate 94 mm of sloped armour at 1,000 m.

Probably the most effective of all the anti-tank guns in general use with the German armed forces was the 8.8 cm Flak 41. This weapon had evolved from the famed 8.8 cm Flak 18/36. Mounted on a cruciform base with detachable wheeled bogies, it was, however, a very 'tall' weapon and not so easy to conceal as the 3.7 cm, 5 cm or 7.5 cm Pak. But it was an extremely effective weapon, firing a 9.4 kg projectile at a

SS anti-tank troops with the 3.7 cm Pak 35/36 light anti-tank gun. Like the *leichte Infanterie Geschütze*, it was light and easily manhandled, though its low calibre meant that its stopping power was rather limited.

A further example of the 3.7 cm Pak is shown here manned by *Waffen-SS* troops, though the officer with binoculars standing next to the weapon is from the Army.

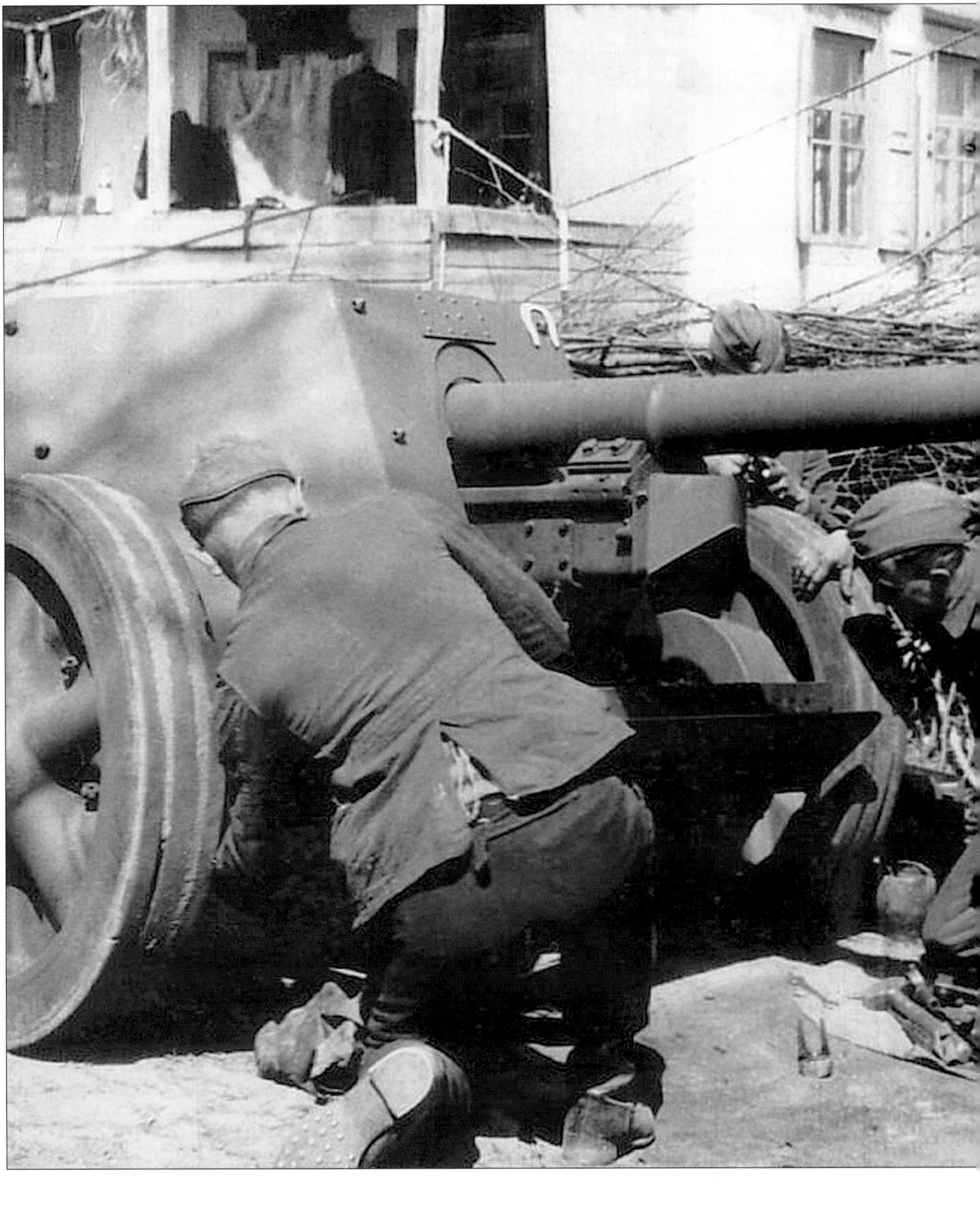

muzzle velocity of 980 m per second to a maximum range of 20,000 m. Its normal effective range in the anti-tank role was around 2,000 m, and at this range it could penetrate 132 mm of armour plate.

This fine weapon saw its prime in the Pak 43, using the same basic gun but on a lowered carriage, with sloped shield. This version fired a heavier, 10.4 kg projectile with a muzzle velocity of 1,000 m per second, which could penetrate 167 mm of sloped armour plate at 1,000 m.

As well as these major weapons, a number of smaller-calibre weapons were also produced, the most successful of which was the 2.8 cm *Panzerbüsche 41*, a very small, wheeled, taper-bored weapon capable of penetrating 52 mm of sloped armour at 500 m.

EDGED WEAPONS

BAYONET

The standard edged weapon issued to soldiers of the *Waffen-SS* was the *Seitengewehr s84/98*, designed to be used with the Mauser *Gewehr* 98 or *Karabiner* 98k. The bayonet had a single edged blade, with the point double edged, and with a single fuller. The metal fittings were blued and the grip plates were black or dark brown plastic. Some earlier issues with wooden grip plates were also still in use. The handle was slotted to allow the bayonet to be fitted to a securing lug on the rifle, and it was fastened by a spring-loaded button stud. The bayonet was contained in a plain blued-steel scabbard with a metal lug on the

Not until the arrival of the larger 7.5 cm Pak 40 were Germany's anti-tank troops presented with a top-quality weapon which could take out virtually any enemy tank at long range.

The 5 cm Pak 38 brought a far greater level of power to German anti-tank troops but still lacked the ability to penetrate the frontal armour of some of the heavier enemy tanks.

Close-up of a 2 cm *Flakvierling* from a *Waffen-SS* unit. These weapons could lay down a devastating rate of fire.

face, which passed through a slot on the black leather belt frog.

The weapon was manufactured and issued in vast numbers, at least 15 million having been produced.

THE DAGGER

The SS dress dagger was introduced in December 1933, and was based on a famous sixteenth-century dagger which had an intricately fretted scabbard crafted to represent the painting *The Dance of Death* by Holbein, court painter to Henry VIII.

The dagger featured a wide spearpoint-style blade with a pronounced ridge down its centre. Engraved on the face of the blade was the motto of the SS, *'Mein Ehre Heisst Treue'*. Top and bottom crossguards were nickel plated and the handle itself made from ebony or black-stained wood. The centre of the handle featured an inset silvered eagle and swastika, while just below the top crossguard was an inlaid, enamelled SS runic symbol.

The dagger was provided with a sheet-metal scabbard with silvered top and bottom mounts, the former being fitted with a single suspension ring. The body of the scabbard was either anodised or painted in gloss black. A single short leather strap served to suspend the dagger from a loop on the wearer's waist-belt.

The dagger was presented to the prospective member when he attained full membership, during a special ceremony held on 9 November each year (the anniversary of the Munich Putsch in 1923). In 1940, production of the dagger was suspended for the duration of the war.

THE 1936-PATTERN DAGGER

This revised pattern was introduced on 21 June 1936, and was intended for wear by SS officers and by NCOs who had joined the

SS prior to 30 January 1933, the date on which the Nazis took power. The actual dagger itself was identical in its basic form to the 1933 pattern, but featured an additional central scabbard band with a pattern of raised, linked, swastikas. An ornate chain, attached to lugs on the upper and central scabbard bands, replaced the simple leather strap of the 1933 pattern. The upper portion of chain had two links and the lower four. The links had alternating designs of the SS deathshead and the SS runes.

From 15 February 1943, officers of the *Waffen-SS* who possessed this dagger were permitted to wear it in walking-out dress with their field-grey uniform. In such cases an aluminium porte-epée was tied around the handle in the same manner as those

The SS M36-pattern dagger with chain suspension hangers. This was briefly authorised for wear with *Waffen-SS* walking-out uniform.

worn on the handle of the dress dagger of the Army. Only four months later, however, the production of the SS dagger ceased and authority for its wear was rescinded.

In addition to the 1933- and 1936-pattern daggers, numerous special honour daggers were produced. These ranged from privately commissioned presentation pieces to be awarded at local unit level to official patterns awarded as a token of esteem by the *Reichsführer-SS* personally. The first such examples were made in 1934 and consisted of the basic dagger but with the reverse of the blade featuring an engraved dedication, *'In herzlicher Kameradschaft, H. Himmler'* (In heartfelt comradeship, H. Himmler). A further honour dagger, introduced in 1936, had ornate oakleaf decorations to the upper and lower scabbard fittings and had the scabbard covered in black leather. Both the upper and lower crossguards were similarly decorated and the blade was hand-crafted from Damascus steel. The SS motto, this time flanked by oakleaf motifs, was gilded. These were not *Waffen-SS* weapons *per se*, but it is known that several *Waffen-SS* officers received such honours.

THE SWORD

The dagger was, for a short time at least, the official sidearm for walking-out dress for *Waffen-SS* officers. The sword, however, was the official dress weapon for the SS and was used on a wide variety of formal occasions.

The SS-pattern sword was introduced in 1936 and was of the style known as the *'Degen'*. This had a long, plain, straight blade, which was distinctively different from the curved sabre used by Army officers, and different blade lengths were produced to allow for the height of the wearer.

It featured a simple 'D'-shaped knuckle-bow for the handle, which featured a ribbed black wooden grip, bound with silver wire and featuring an inset disc with the SS runes. The scabbard was painted in black enamel and had a decorative silvered top mount (locket) and bottom mount (chape).

The sword was officially awarded to individually selected officers of the *SS-Verfügungstruppe* and *SS-Totenkopfverbände* in recognition of special merit and also to all those who graduated through the *SS-Junkerschulen* at Bad Tölz and Brunswick. As well as being carried by *Waffen-SS* officers as a formal dress weapon, it was often used for ceremonial purposes, such as the swearing of the official oath by SS recruits. It was worn with an aluminium braid sword knot embellished with the SS runic symbol in black on the stem.

An NCO-pattern sword was also produced. This was similar to the officer version but differed in several points of detail. The scabbard had a plain un-adorned chape, the handle lacked the silver wire wrap found on officer swords and the SS runes insignia were moved from the handle to the pommel.

CHAPTER ELEVEN

SOFT-SKINNED VEHICLES

CARS AND FIELD CARS

VOLKSWAGEN VW TYPE 82 *'KÜBELWAGEN'*

Although the term *Kübelwagen* immediately conjures up images of the ubiquitous Volkswagen field car, the term was in fact widely used to describe a range of light general-purpose field cars made by numerous manufacturers.

Volkswagen's Type 82 appeared in December 1939, and rapidly became the most popular vehicle of its type, being made in large numbers for all branches of the armed forces. The term *Kübelwagen*, or 'Bucket Car', aptly describes the extremely simplistic and utilitarian nature of the vehicle. It weighed 1.17 tons, had a seating capacity for four, and its rear engine was the famous VW air-cooled 'Boxer' 4-cylinder 985 cc engine developing just 22 bhp, though the later 1.13-litre version increased this to 25 bhp. It carried up to 40 litres of fuel, giving it a maximum road range of 500 km. Length was just 3.7 m and width 1.6 m. With the canvas roof folded it measured just 1.1 m in height. Although generally unarmed, a 7.92 mm machine-gun could be fitted to a pedestal mount just behind the front seats.

Its light weight, excellent cross-country performance, rugged construction, ease of repair and maintenance and long operational range made it a firm favourite. Many still survive to this day.

VOLKSWAGEN VW TYPE 166 *'SCHWIMMWAGEN'*

The Type 166 was an amphibious field car developed by Volkswagen. It weighed 1.3 tons and was powered by a VW 1.13-litre 4-cylinder 'Boxer' engine developing 25 bhp. In water it was driven by a small propeller on a hinged mount, which could be swung up over the rear of the vehicle when on land.

The *Schwimmwagen* could carry four persons, and had a top speed of 80 kph on roads, and had a road range of 520 km. In water, the *Schwimmwagen* could make 10 kph. Although generally unarmed, it could be fitted with a 7.92 mm machine-gun.

PKW *(PERSONENKRAFTWAGEN)* STEYR 1500A

This extremely hardy four-wheeled-drive field car was built in substantial numbers, at least 18,000 being produced. Weighing 2.5 tons, it was powered by a Steyr 3.5-litre V8 petrol engine developing 85 bhp. It had a high maximum road speed of 90 kph and a respectable 45 kph across country. It could carry up to 1.6 tons in payload and had a

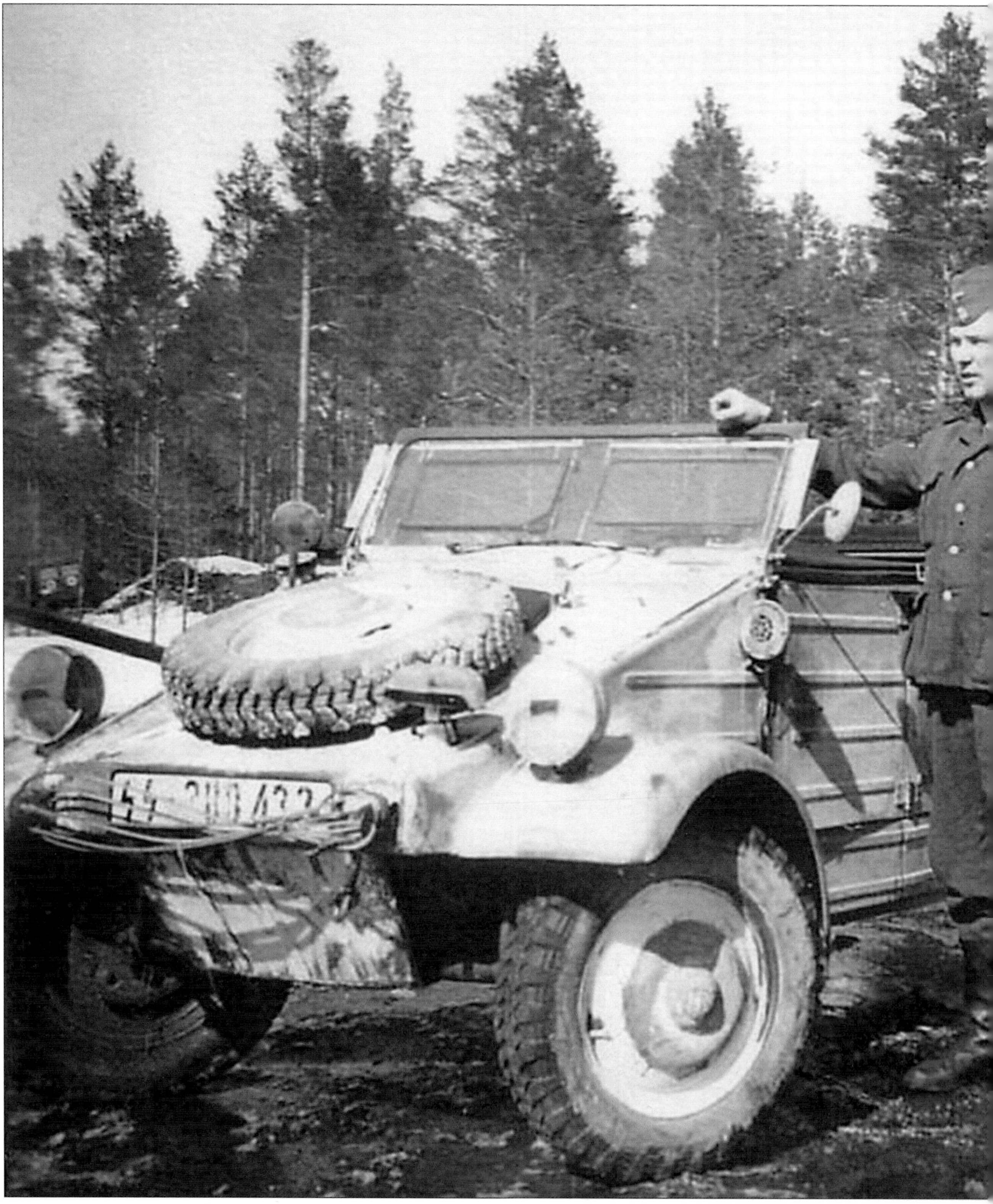

range of some 400 km on road and 280 km across country.

Two versions were made – a standard troop carrier, and a variant known as the 'Kommandeurwagen' which was effectively an officer's staff car.

PKW (*PERSONENKRAFTWAGEN*) STOEWER R200 TYPE 40

This light four-wheeled-drive field car was built by the Stoewer firm in Stettin, around 4,700 being constructed between 1940 and 1943. It weighed 1.77 tons and was powered by a Stoewer 2-litre, 4-cylinder, water-cooled engine developing 50 bhp. Top speed was 80 kph and operational range around 350 km. The same chassis was used for a number of special vehicles, including radio cars.

MERCEDES BENZ 1500A

The Mercedes Benz 1500A was a direct equivalent of the Steyr 1500A. Based on a standard 1.5-ton truck chassis, it was given a standard field car body which allowed it to carry up to seven passengers in addition to the two-man crew. The vehicle weighed 2.4 tons, just a little less than its Steyr equivalent, and had a top speed of 84 kph. Powered by a Daimler Benz 2.6-litre V6 petrol engine developing 60 bhp, it had an operational range of 370 km.

TRUCKS
LKW (*LASTKRAFTWAGEN*) OPEL *BLITZ*

Probably the most widely used German truck in the Second World War was the Opel *Blitz*.

The Volkswagen *'Kübelwagen'*, Germany's answer to the Jeep. This vehicle was built in great numbers, and many survive in working condition even today.

A Volkswagen *'Schwimmwagen'* amphibious field car crewed by *Waffen-SS* reconnaissance troops emerges from a river. The SS made widespread use of this excellent little vehicle.

Another example of a civilian-specification automobile pressed into military service. This staff car belongs to the *Leibstandarte SS Adolf Hitler*.

A Horch 1A field car from *2 SS-Panzer Division Das Reich*. This was one of a large range of such vehicles produced for the military, some even featuring provision for a light flak gun mount.

Based on a civilian pre-war design, this vehicle gave sterling service to all branches of the armed forces throughout the war. It was produced in several variants, including ambulances, buses and command trucks. Some were even fitted with light 2 cm or 3.7 cm flak weapons on their rear platforms. Late in the war as an economy measure, these trucks were manufactured with an 'ersatz' wooden cabin in place of the formed metal cabin of earlier models. The Opel *Blitz* weighed 2.5 tons and had a top speed of 85 kph. It could carry troops or cargo of up to 3.3 tons. The basic engine used was a 3.6-litre 6-cylinder four-stroke developing 68 bhp. Some 92 litres of fuel were carried, giving it an operational range of around 320 km.

A light field car from the *Wiking Division*, as indicated by the 'sun wheel' swastika in yellow, below which is a white K showing that this division was acting as part of *Panzergruppe Kleist*.

LKW (*LASTKRAFTWAGEN*) MERCEDES L3000A

As well as manufacturing the Opel *Blitz* truck under licence, Mercedes manufactured a range of trucks of its own. The Mercedes L3000A light truck was very similar in specification to the Opel. It weighed 3.02 tons and had a similar load/troop-carrying capacity as its Opel equivalent. Like the Opel, it was also

manufactured with an 'ersatz' wooden cabin in the late part of the war. It was fitted with a 75 bhp diesel engine.

LKW (*LASTKRAFTWAGEN*) BÜSSING-NAG 4500

Büssing-NAG manufactured some of the German armed forces' heavier trucks. The basic 4500S-1 was a 4.5-ton vehicle with typical rear-wheel drive, powered by a 6-

The workhorse of the German military where transport was concerned was without a doubt the Opel *Blitz*. Here, a standard truck-bodied example is inspected by an *SS-Unterscharführer*.

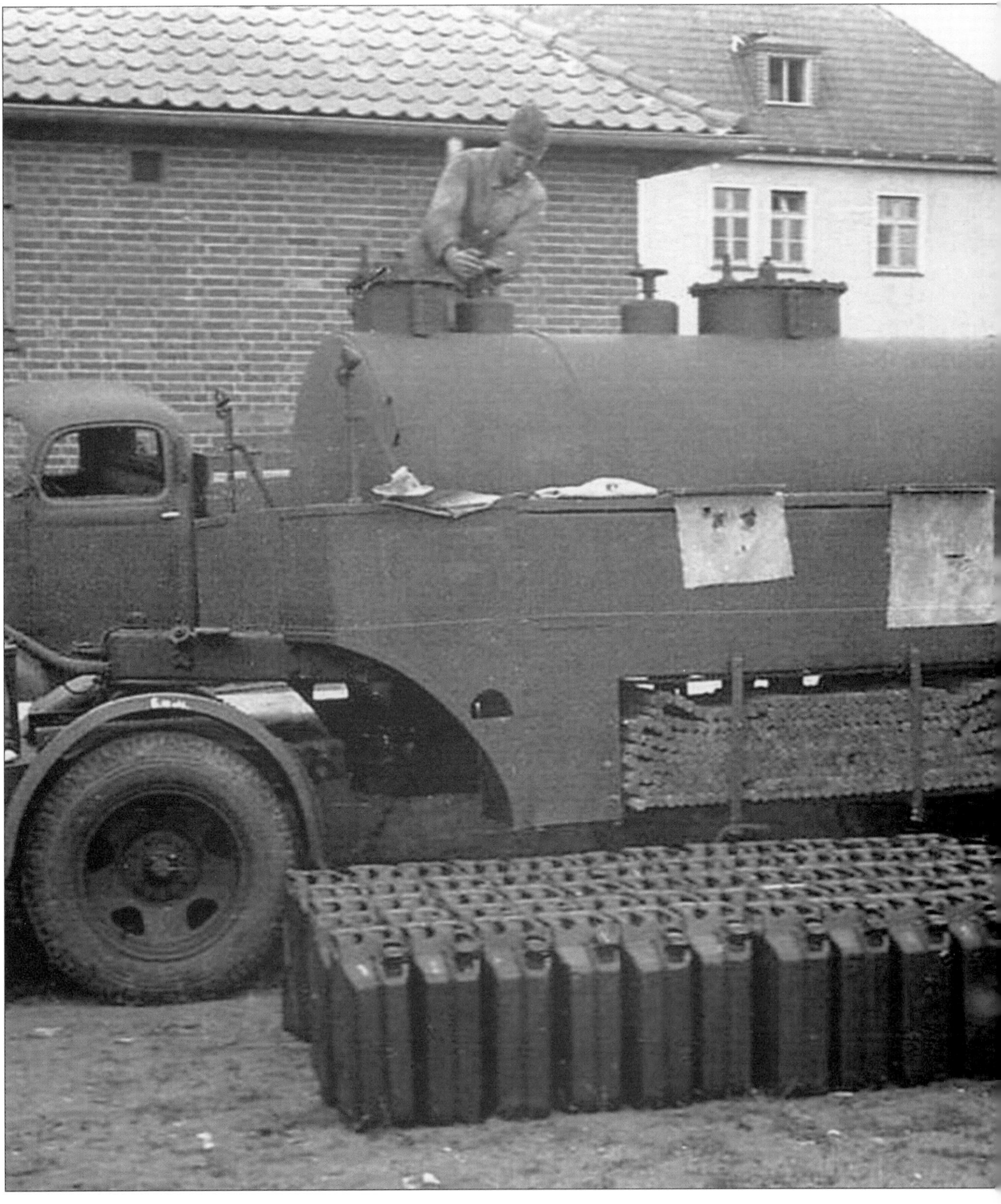

cylinder diesel engine developing 105 bhp. The 4500A-1 variant had a very similar specification, but with four-wheel drive. Around 15,000 were built.

LKW (*LASTKRAFTWAGEN*) KFZ 70, KRUPP *PROTZE*

Around 7,000 examples of this light truck were manufactured by Krupp between 1933 and 1936. Weighing 2.45 tons, it was a six-wheeled vehicle with open cab, powered by a 4-cylinder Krupp M-304 'Boxer' engine developing 60 bhp. It could carry loads of up to 1 ton and had a top speed of 70 kph. Its range on roads was up to 400 km.

This vehicle was widely used within the *Waffen-SS*. As well as the standard truck version, it was used to tow the 3.7 cm flak gun, or could have a 2 cm flak gun mounted on its rear platform. Radio car versions were also built, and even a version mounting a small searchlight.

EINHEITSDIESEL

The *Einheitsdiesel* programme was introduced in 1933 in order to develop a range of standard generic diesel trucks that would be produced by a wide range of manufacturers. The design took the form of a six-wheeled truck with open and closed cab variants being produced. Manufacture was undertaken by firms such as Krupp, MAN, Magirus, Faun, Borgward and

The vast distances covered by the German military on the Eastern Front necessitated the availability of huge amounts of fuel. On the right is a truck manufactured by Ford of Germany, and in the centre a supply of fuel jerricans and a petrol bowser trailer.

One of the most enduring images to come from the first part of the war was that of the speed of the German advance. While much of the German transport remained horse-drawn, spearhead units were fully motorised, with motorcycles playing an important role.

Vehicle maintenance during the rainy season on the Russian Front was no fun. Here a *Waffen-SS* mechanic works on the wheel of an *Einheitsdiesel.*

Büssing-NAG, the last producing the greatest number. The truck, powered by a 6-cylinder diesel engine developing 80 bhp, was manufactured in a number of forms, to include even field kitchen trucks and mobile cranes.

Production ceased in 1940 but the vehicle continued to see front-line service for some considerable time.

MOTORCYCLES
BMW R75

The R75 was one of the best known of Germany's heavy motorcycles, being manufactured in huge numbers between 1940 and 1945. It is estimated that as many as 17,500 may have been produced, and indeed many restored specimens are still active today.

The BMW R35 motorcycle in combination with a sidecar was widely used by the military, particularly by reconnaissance units and military police. It could also have a machine-gun mount fitted to the forward part of the sidecar.

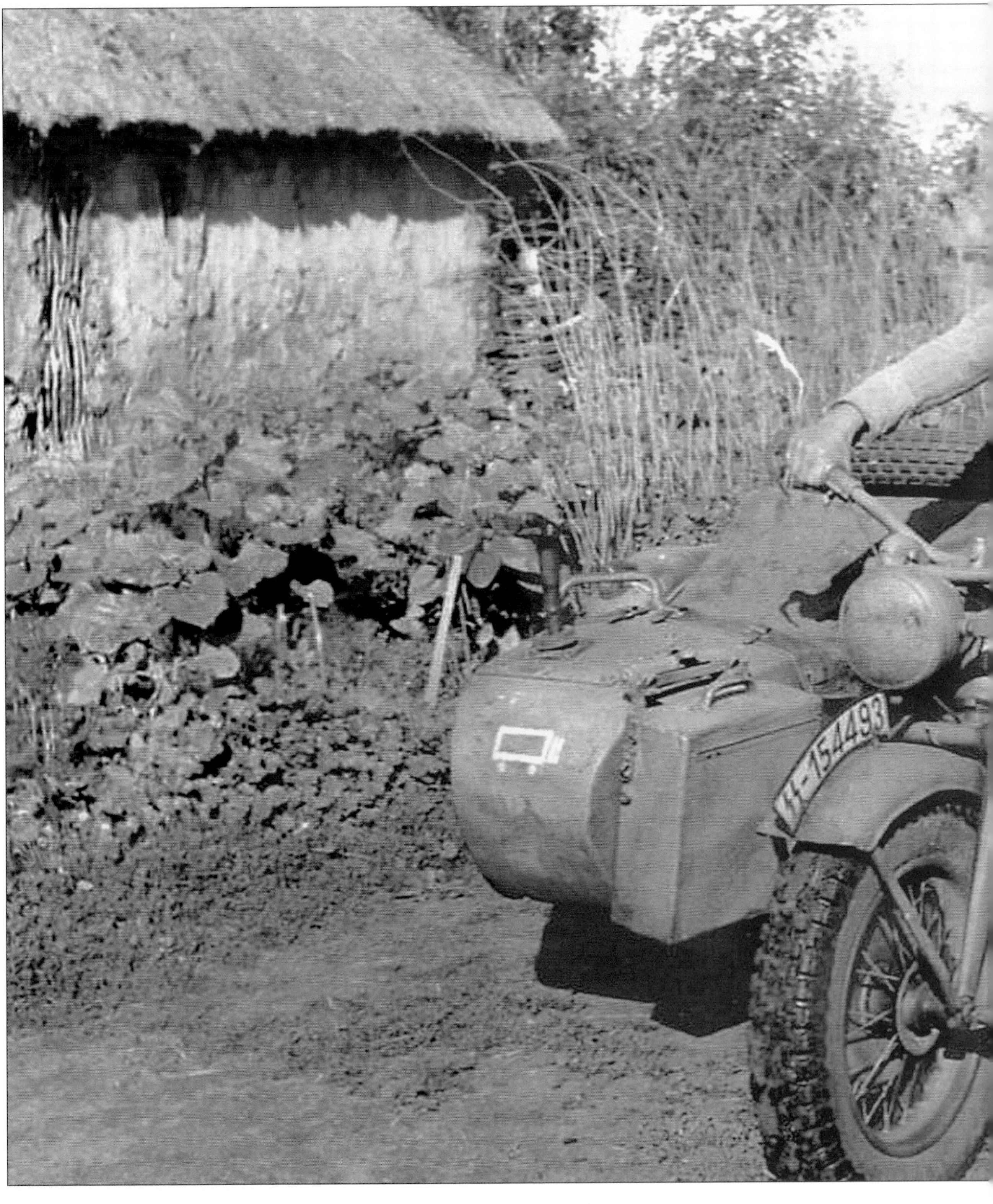
SS-154493

This motorcycle was developed for the *Wehrmacht* to meet military specifications, and was driven by a 745 cc, 2-cylinder, 4-stroke engine, developing 26 bhp. It had a maximum on-road speed of around 92 kph. The fuel tank held 24 litres of petrol, giving it a range of some 400 km. The cycle, with sidecar, weighed around 410 kg. The R75 was widely used with a sidecar attached, this having a 7.92 mm MG34 or MG42 attached to a pintle mount. This motorcycle was widely used by reconnaissance troops and by military police.

ZUNDAPP KS750

The KS750 was a direct equivalent of the R75 and was made by another of Germany's great motorcycle manufacturers. It first went into major volume production in 1941, and well over 18,500 were eventually produced. It was powered by a 751 cc, 2-cylinder, 4-stroke petrol engine developing 26 bhp. Top speed on the road was 95 kph, and a 23-litre fuel tank gave it a range of just over 300 km. Its weight was around 420 kg.

DKW-NZ350

This medium motorcycle was produced in large numbers between 1939 and 1945, estimates of total production being in excess of 45,000 units pre-war and 12,000 of the military contract model. It was powered by a 350 cc, single-cylinder, 2-stroke petrol engine. It weighed 145 kg. Top speed was 105 kph and a 14-litre fuel tank on the military version gave it a range of some 425

A Zundapp KS750 motorcycle combination. Just visible in front of the grab-handle on the sidecar is the pintle mount for the provision of a machine-gun. This and the BMW R75 were the mainstay of the German reconnaissance forces.

An exhausted *Waffen-SS* dispatch rider grabs some much-valued rest beside his motorcycle.

The range of vehicles used by the military was immense. Not only regular trucks, but mobile offices, mobile kitchens and, as here, ambulances, were constructed on basic truck and bus chassis.

km. This lighter-weight machine was used by communications units, reconnaissance units and dispatch riders, for instance.

SPECIAL EQUIPMENT

TRIPPEL AMPHIBIOUS FIELD CAR

Hans Trippel was a pioneer of amphibious vehicles and developed his own 'Schwimmwagen' alongside the better-known amphibian manufactured by Volkswagen. The Trippel version was a bizarre-looking beast with protruding headlights and bath-shaped hull. It was manufactured in much smaller numbers than the VW version, but a few have survived still in running order today. It is known that *Waffen-SS* units were among the few that used this vehicle.

CHAPTER TWELVE

ARMOURED FIGHTING VEHICLES

ARMOURED CARS AND RECONNAISANCE VEHICLES

From the beginning of the Second World War, and before the first SS panzer units were formed, light armoured vehicles such as armoured cars were serving with the reconnaissance (*Spähtruppe*) platoons of SS regiments. The first types to go into service in significant numbers were the four-wheeled SdKfz 221 and SdKfz 222. The earlier 5-ton six-wheeled SdKfz 231 series, which boasted a top speed of 65 kph and a range of 300 km, a crew of four and a 2 cm cannon in a rotating closed turret, saw little use by the SS.

SDKFZ 221

This was a small 3.7-ton vehicle powered by a Horch 8-cylinder petrol engine developing just 75 bhp. Nevertheless it was capable of speeds up to 80 kph, and a 100-litre fuel capacity gave it an operational range of 280 km. It was crewed by two men and carried a single 7.92 mm machine gun in a small revolving turret.

SDKFZ 222

This vehicle utilised the same chassis and bodywork as the SdKfz 221, but featured a larger turret mounting a 2 cm cannon, as well as a coaxial 7.92 mm machine-gun. It was heavier, at 4.8 tons. The open-topped turret was provided with a two-part hinged frame-top covered in wire mesh, the purpose of which was to prevent grenades being thrown into the turret.

SDKFZ 231

The early SdKfz 231 was replaced by a larger eight-wheeled model, which retained the same designation and was somewhat similar in appearance. This vehicle featured two driving positions – one facing forward and one to the rear. In an emergency the driver could simply switch to the rear seat and drive the vehicle out of danger in reverse gear as fast as it could be driven forwards. The SdKfz 231 was armed with a 2 cm cannon in a closed, rotating turret, with a 7.92 mm coaxial machine-gun. The allocation of these vehicles was slow and somewhat niggardly. Only after the invasion of the Soviet Union did *Waffen-SS* units begin to receive these heavy armoured cars in significant numbers. A radio vehicle, virtually identical, but with a large frame antenna, was designated the SdKfz 232.

SDKFZ 233

The SdKfz chassis also provided the basis for an infantry-support vehicle. This version

SdKfz 222 armoured cars from the *Aufklärungs Abteilung* of the *Leibstandarte SS Adolf Hitler.*

An SdKfz 221 armoured car, with swastika flag draped over the engine compartment as a simple aerial recognition measure.

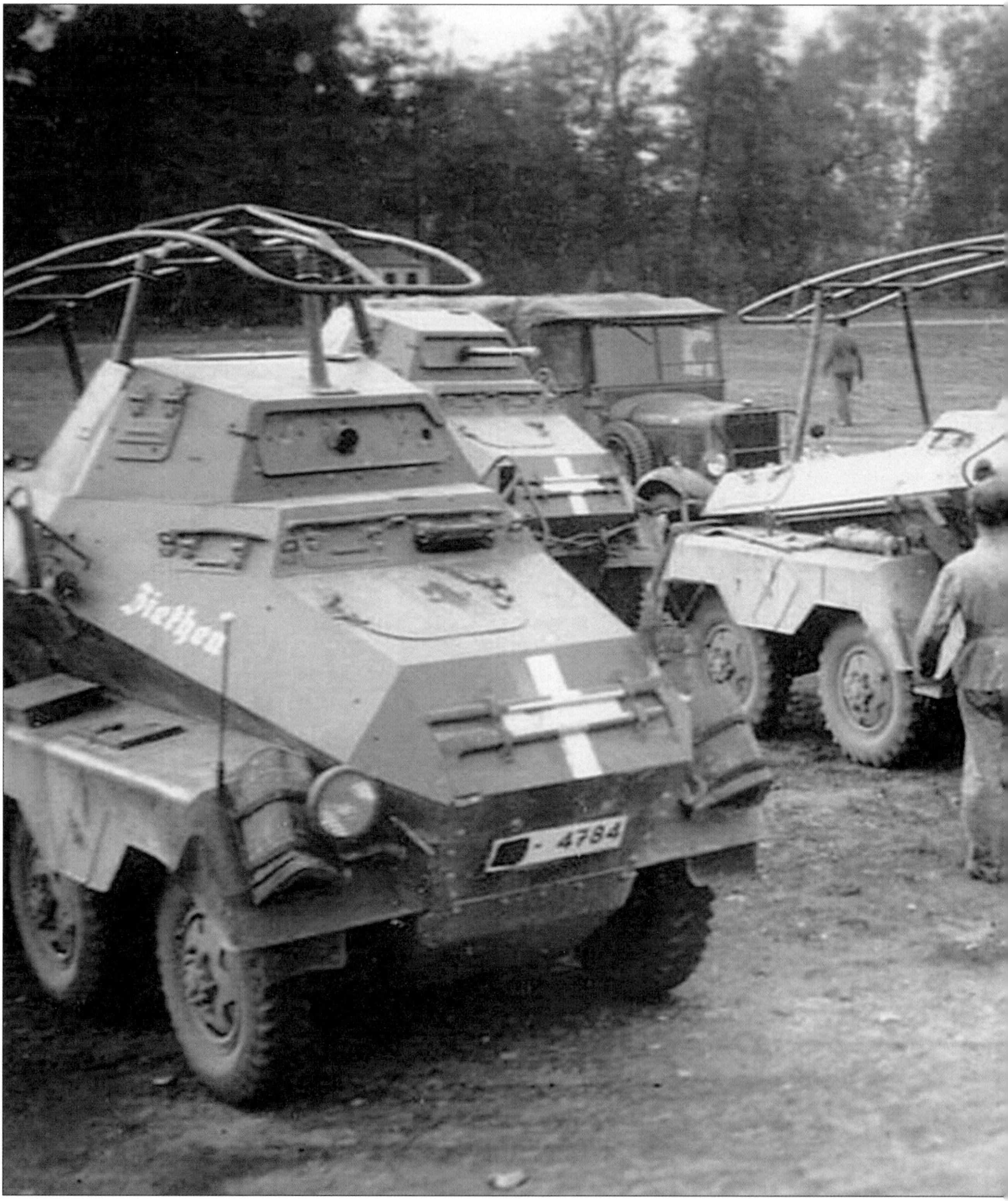
- 4784

had the turret removed and featured an open-topped fighting compartment. In this compartment was mounted a short-barrelled 7.5 cm howitzer.

SDKFZ 234/2 PUMA

The eight-wheeled heavy armoured car design reached its zenith in the SdKfz 234 series. These were a great improvement over the original design, though the basic shape of the chassis and superstructure remained very similar. They were powered, however, by a Tatra 12-cylinder diesel engine developing 220 bhp, providing an excellent top speed of 85 kph, and a fuel capacity of 405 litres, giving it a range of 1,000 km on the road and 805 km across country. This excellent body provided the basis for one of the war's finest armoured cars, the SdKfz 234/2 Puma. This heavy reconnaissance armoured car mounted a 5 cm cannon in a closed, fully rotating turret. The Puma had a crew of four and weighed in at 11.7 tons. The Puma began to be issued to *Waffen-SS* units in 1943.

SDKFZ 234/4

One other version of the 234 series which deserves mention is the SdKfz 234/4. This vehicle featured an open-topped fighting compartment into which was mounted a 7.5

SdKfz 232 eight-wheeled armoured cars. The large tubular frame above the turret is a radio antenna. It is presumed these vehicles have been returned from the front line for repair as their main armament seems to have been dismounted. This photograph dates from the time of the Polish Campaign; the white crosses were changed to black after this period as they provided a perfect aiming point for enemy gunners.

The large eight-wheeled armoured cars remained in use throughout the war. These SS vehicles are pictured in Normandy during the invasion battles in 1944.

cm high-velocity anti-tank gun, providing the Germans with a first-class weapon which could be rapidly moved around the battlefield.

As was the position with tanks, a number of foreign 'booty' armoured cars were pressed into service with the *Waffen-SS*, particularly with units engaged in anti-partisan duties in the Balkans. One notable example was the French Panhard 178 armoured car, the wheelbase of which (as was the case with many German armoured cars) was the same

as the standard German railway gauge and could be made to run on rails as well as on the roads.

ARMOURED HALF-TRACKS

SDKFZ 250 *LEICHTE SCHUTZENPANZERWAGEN*

This rather diminutive armoured half-track weighed just 5.3 tons and had a top speed of 60 kph. It featured a 7.92 mm machine-gun with an armoured shield mounted above the driver compartment and another on a pivoting mount on the rear hull above the entrance door. Because of its limited capacity (only six men could be carried), initially it was used principally as a commander's vehicle. A large range of variants was later produced, including radio vehicles (SdKfz 250/3), support vehicles carrying the short-barrelled 7.5 cm howitzer (SdKfz 250/8) or a mortar and its crew (SdKfz 250/7), a 3.7 cm anti-tank gun (SdKfz 250/10) and even the turret from the SdKfz 222 armoured car (SdKfz 250/9). A total of fourteen variants of the SdKfz 250 were produced.

An improved version was introduced in 1943 (termed the SdKfz 250 *neuer Art*, or n.A.), with built-in storage lockers along the side of the fighting compartment above the track guards, a redesigned nose and a redesigned rear panel.

SDKFZ 251 *MITTLERER SCHUTZENPANZERWAGEN*

The SdKfz 251 was the 'big brother' of the SdKfz 250, looking remarkably similar to its smaller sibling. The larger vehicle weighed 7.8 tons and had a top speed of 52.5 kph, thanks to its Maybach NL42 6-cylinder

The SdKfz 250 half-track personnel carrier was widely used within the *Waffen-SS Panzer* and *Panzergrenadier* Divisions. Shown here is one of the later models (*neuer Art*) with revised bodywork, but retaining the same chassis and running gear as the earlier models.

It is sometimes difficult to determine whether what is seen is an SdKfz 250, or its larger, but visually similar brother, the SdKfz 251. Both vehicles carried two dismountable MG34 or MG42, one at the front of the crew compartment with an armoured shield and another at the rear, firing over the entry doors.

Waffen-SS PzKpfw III tanks, supported by armoured infantry in SdKfz 251 half tracks, advance across the vast Russian plain.

An SdKfz 251 of the *Leibstandarte* advance over the Russian steppe. This is one of the earlier models.

engine developing 100 bhp. Its armament was identical to that on the SdKfz 250, but the larger vehicle, essentially a lightly armoured personnel carrier, with simple bench seating along each side of the interior, was capable of carrying a full ten-man squad of infantry. Entry was by way of hinged double doors at the rear of the fighting compartment. Large-scale issue of these half-tracks to the *Waffen-SS* only began in 1942. As with the SdKfz 250, this half-track was built in a bewildering range of variants. The standard armoured personnel carrier version was designated the SdKfz 251/1. Other variants included the combat engineer version 251/5, command version 251/6, the 251/9 with a short-barrelled 7.5 cm infantry support gun, the 251/10 with a 3.7 cm anti-tank gun mounted in place of the forward machine-gun, the flame-thrower-equipped 251/16, the 251/17 with 2 cm flak gun and 251/21 with triple barrel *'Drilling'* 2 cm flak gun, the 'UHU' with its huge infra-red searchlight designed to operate alongside tanks equipped with infra-red sights, and the 251/22 with the

The medium-calibre anti-tank weapons were typically towed by light half-tracks such as the 5.5-ton SdKfz 10 Demag shown here. Over 17,000 of these vehicles were built.

superb 7.5 cm high-velocity Pak 40 anti-tank gun.

One particularly interesting variant was the standard troop carrier model but with framing along each side to accommodate racks, set at a fixed angle of 45 degrees, which held 28 cm rocket projectiles. The entire half-track was simply aimed in the direction of the enemy and the projectiles launched in sequence (a salvo was not possible as the vehicle was not a robust enough launch platform to cope with all six projectiles being fired off at the same time). This version was generally known to the troops as the 'Stuka zu Fuss'.

Like the 250 series, the 251s were improved in the second half of the war, with a single flat nose-plate replacing the

original angled plates, storage lockers fitted along the hull side just above the track guard, and the rear plate and doors modified from a faceted angled assembly to a single large sloping plate.

SOFT-SKINNED HALF-TRACKS

A number of unarmoured prime movers were used by the *Waffen-SS* throughout the war, some of these being subsequently modified as special-purpose vehicles.

SDKFZ 6

Built by the firm of Büssing-NAG, this half-track weighed 9 tons and was given a top speed of some 50 kph by its 6-cylinder Maybach HL54 petrol engine, developing 115 bhp. Operational range was 300 km provided by a 190-litre fuel tank. As well as the standard prime-mover version, generally used for towing medium howitzers, it was produced with a 3.7 cm flak gun on a platform replacing the seating area. As a basic prime mover it could carry up to fifteen men.

SDKFZ 7

This vehicle, produced principally by the Kraus-Maffei firm, weighed in at 9.7 tons and was powered by a 6-cylinder Maybach HL64 petrol engine developing 140 bhp and giving it a top speed of around 50 kph.

Operational range of the vehicle was 250 km on its 215-litre fuel tank.

This vehicle was used principally for towing large artillery pieces, such as the 10.5 cm or 15 cm howitzers, and of course the famous 8.8 cm flak gun. The vehicle, as well as being able to tow up to 8 tons, could accommodate a twelve-man gun crew.

A number, however, were modified with a flat deck replacing the seating area, and had a 3.7 cm or four-barrelled 2 cm *Flakvierling* fitted. Some of these flak variants had an armoured cab fitted to replace the earlier simple open cab with canvas tilt. Volume production of the SdKfz 7 began in 1939, and by 1945 over 12,000 of these medium half-tracks were produced. Predominantly

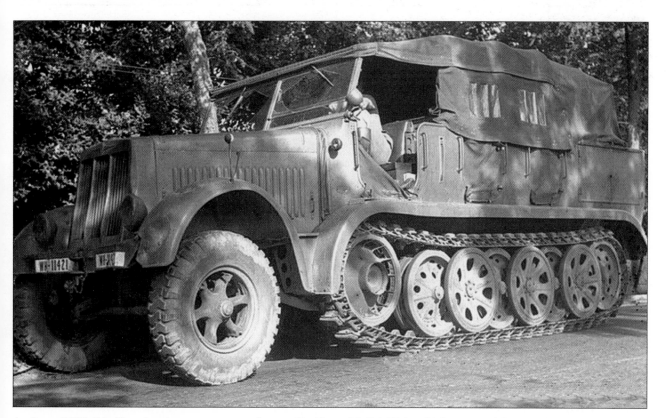

An 8-ton SdKfz 7 half-track prime mover manufactured by Kraus-Maffei. This vehicle was used for a multitude of purposes, the version shown being widely used for towing the famed 8.8 cm flak gun, often used against ground targets and developed into a deadly tank killer.

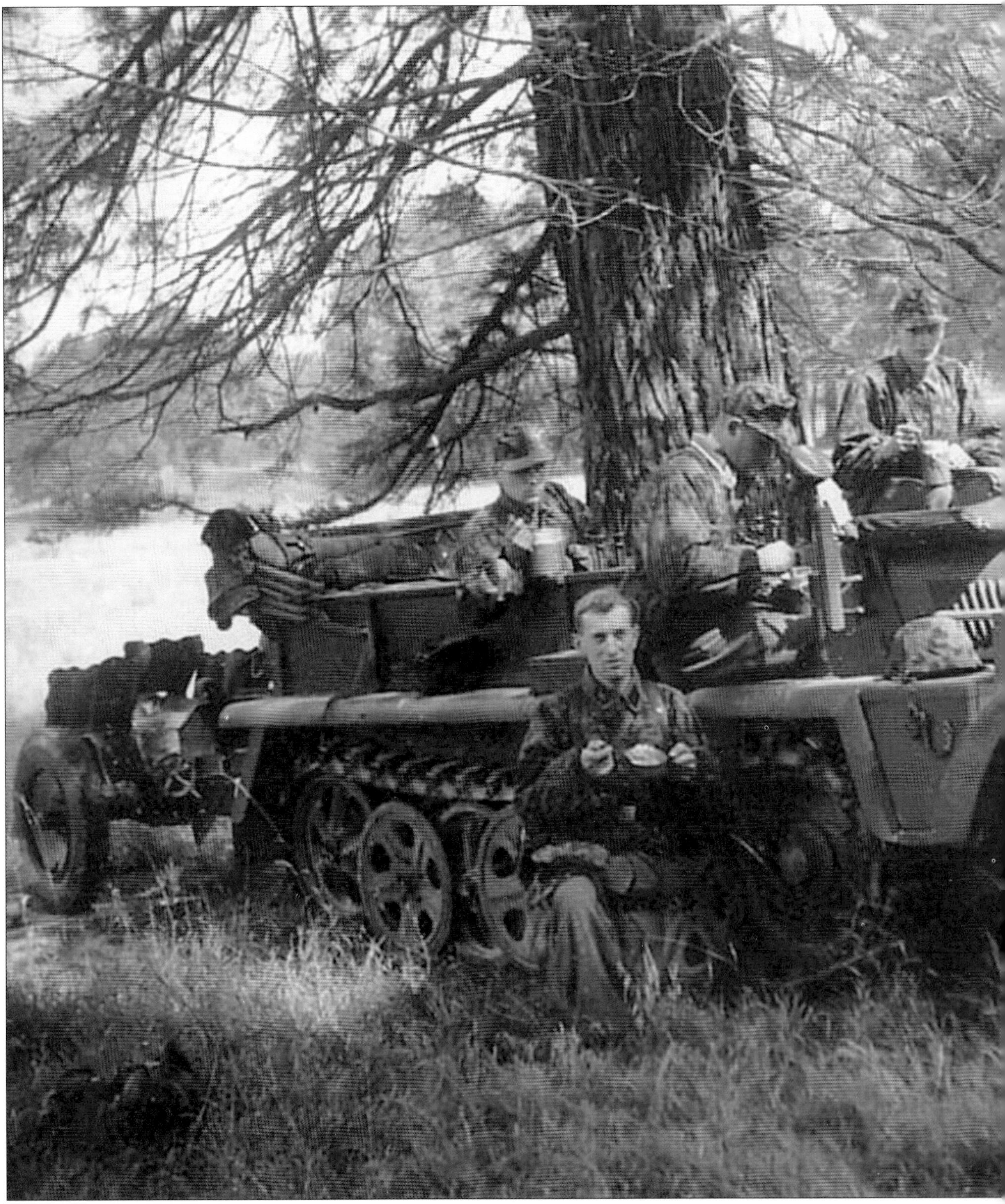

manufactured by Kraus-Maffei, the SdKfz 7 was also made by Borgward, Büssing-NAG, Daimler-Benz and Saurer Werke AG.

SDKFZ 9

This huge half-track, manufactured by FAMO, weighed 15 tons and was generally issued to engineer units, either as a general prime mover, used for towing tank-transporter trailers, or with a crane fitted to its platform for use in lifting heavy weights, such as when removing the engines or turrets from tanks under repair. It was almost identical visually to the SdKfz 7, but much larger. The FAMO was also used for towing exceptionally large field artillery, such as the 17 cm *Kanone.*

SDKFZ 10

This early half-track, first produced in 1937, was manufactured through to 1945, with over 25,000 units being made. It weighed only 4.9 tons and could be used as a personnel carrier, transporting up to ten men, as well as pulling up to 1 ton of towed load – usually small artillery pieces, wheeled *'Nebelwerfer'* mortars or anti-tank guns. Both 2 cm and 3.7 cm flak guns were fitted to many of these light half-tracks. Its top speed was some 65 kph, with a range on roads of 300 km. One of the most common of the smaller half-tracks, the SdKfz 10 was principally manufactured by Demag, but was also produced by Adler, Saurer, Phaenomen and Büssing-NAG. Armour plate 'shields' were sometimes added around the bonnet and cab on flak versions.

A 5.5-ton SdKfz 10 Demag half-track from an SS infantry unit has stopped during a meal break for its crew. It is towing a 7.5 cm *leichte Infanterie Geschütze.*

185

An SdKfz 7 of the *Flakabteilung* of the *Leibstandarte SS Adolf Hitler*, whose tactical sign of a skeleton key can be seen on the right mudguard, carries a single-barrelled 3.7 cm flak gun with armoured shield. These were just as effective against ground targets as enemy aircraft.

This overhead aspect gives an excellent view of the 3.7 cm gun carried on the *Flak* half-tracks. Other variants carried a quadruple 2 cm *Flakvierling*.

An interesting adaption of the standard Opel *Blitz* truck, with a tracked rear drive replacing the wheels, it became known as the *'Maultier'*. These vehicles belong to *1 SS-Panzer Division*.

SCHWERE WEHRMACHT SCHLEPPER (BÜSSING-NAG)

This vehicle, first produced in 1943, was used as a general transporter and towing vehicle. It weighed 4 tons and could carry/tow up to 8 tons. Produced predominantly by Büssing-NAG, it is reported that some were also made by Tatra under licence towards the end of the war. Power was supplied by a Maybach HL42 6-cylinder engine developing 100 bhp and giving the vehicle a top on-road speed of 27.4 kph. A fuel capacity of 240 litres gave it a range of 300 km on-road or 150 km off-

road. It was manufactured in a number of variants, including a flatbed 'truck'-type platform on the rear, with a 3.7 cm flak gun fitted, as an engineer vehicle with a crane fitted to the platform, and with a fully armoured cab and body mounting a revolving *Nebelwerfer* projectile launcher on the roof.

OPEL *MAULTIER*

The chassis of the mass-produced Opel *Blitz* truck was also manufactured in a half-tracked version with the rear wheels replaced by treads, giving it far better cross-

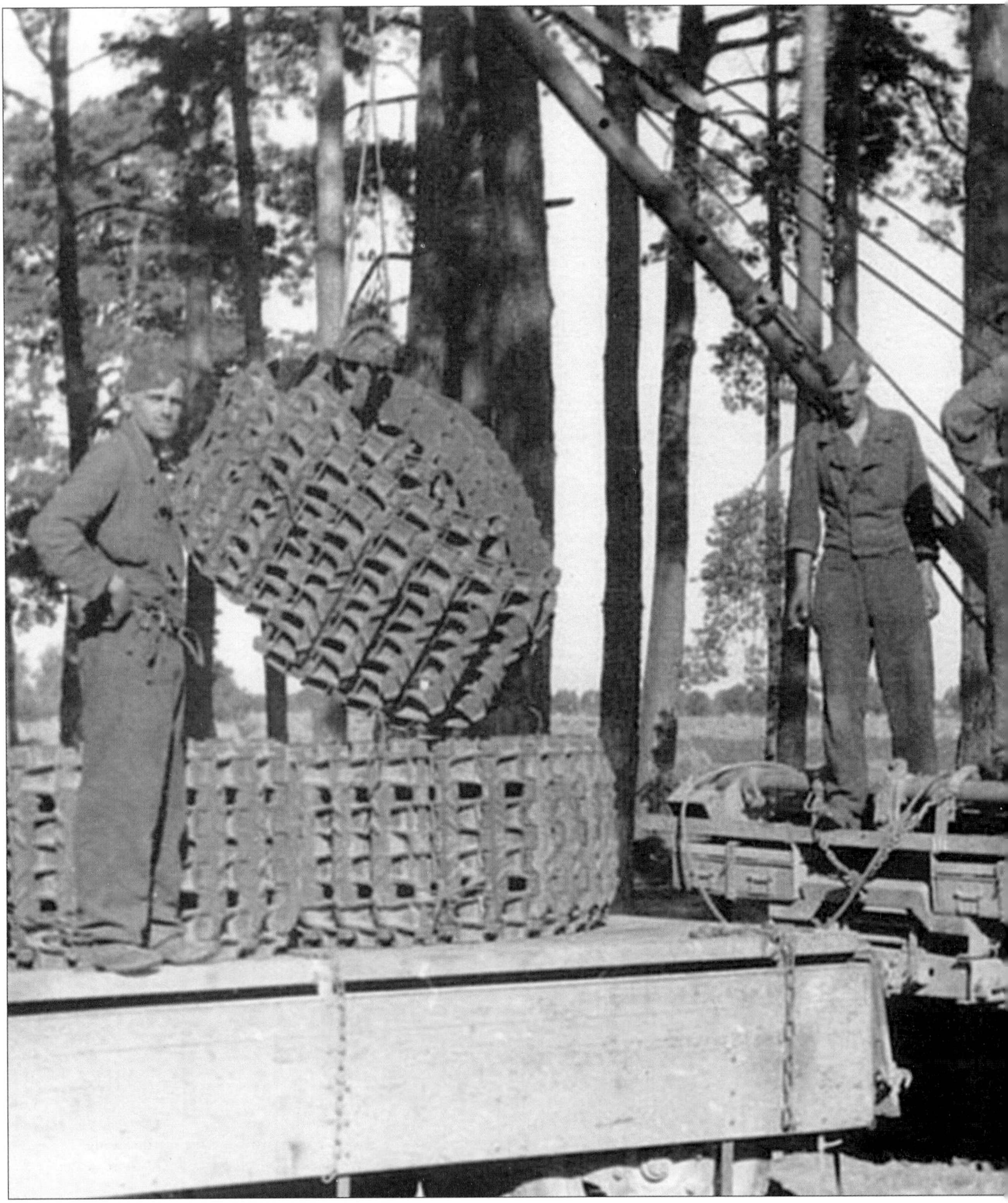

Waffen-SS troops of the *Instandsetzungsabteilung*, or workshop unit, unload a new set of tracks for a Panther tank. These troops were essential in keeping German tanks, prone to mechanical breakdown, in service.

country performance than a standard truck. This half-track version was known as the *Maultier* and was also produced in a special variant with a fully armoured body and cap. On the roof of the body was a revolving mount carrying an eight-barrelled *Nebelwerfer* 15 cm rocket projectile launcher.

TANKS

The first tank to be volume produced for the German Armed Forces after the end of the First World War was the PzKpfw (*Panzerkampfwagen*) I. This diminutive vehicle went into service in 1934, and by the outbreak of war was already obsolete, its armament of two 7.92 mm machine-guns being of no great offensive value in anything other than a light recon-naissance role. By the time the first *Waffen-SS* panzer units were being formed this vehicle was already being withdrawn from service.

PANZERKAMPFWAGEN PZKPFW II (SDKFZ 121)*

In 1937, a slightly larger light tank, the PzKpfw II, went into production, and this vehicle was indeed used widely within the early *Waffen-SS* panzer formations. This tank weighed a mere 8.9 tons and carried a crew

* The abbreviation SdKfz is for *Sonderkraftfahrzeug*, or 'Special Vehicle' – a term used to prefix the model number of all military vehicles, soft skinned or armoured.

A *Waffen-SS Panzer II*. By the time the first *Waffen-SS* panzer units were being formed the *Panzer II* was already obsolete, so this vehicle only saw limited use by the SS.

The *Panzer III* tanks on the left of this photograph were fairly small, as can be gauged by the scale of the crew-members. The three-man *Panzer II* tanks to the right were even smaller, and not suited for much other than a reconnaissance role.

A train-load of *Waffen-SS* tanks on the move. These railway flatcars carry a mixture of *Panzer II*, *Panzer III* and *Panzer IV*.

A *Waffen-SS Panzer III*. Note the spaced armour fitted to the face of the gun mantlet and also to brackets hung around the turret. These were intended to explode anti-tank projectiles before they hit the tank itself.

Two *Waffen-SS Panzer IV*. The vehicle at left has the short-barrelled 7.5 cm gun and was intended predominantly for the infantry support role. The example at right has the long-barrelled 7.5 cm gun, which also gave it excellent capabilities in the anti-tank role.

of three. Overall length was 4.8 m, width 2.28 m and height just 2 m. Its main armament was a 2 cm gun with a coaxial 7.92 mm machine-gun in the turret.

Its Maybach HL62 6-cylinder petrol engine gave it a maximum speed of 40 kph on roads and 19 kph across country. Its fuel tank capacity of just 170 litres, however, gave it a range of 200 km (130 km across country) without the need for refuelling.

The only version used by the *Waffen-SS* was the PzKpfw II F, with improved armoured protection, twelve of which saw service with *5 SS-Panzerregiment I* LSSAH.

Like the PzKpfw I, however, this tank was severely undergunned, making it worthless for anything other than a light reconnaissance role. It only served with *Waffen-SS* formations for a year or so before it was withdrawn, though many PzKpfw II hulls were reworked to produce extremely useful self-propelled tank destroyers.

PANZERKAMPFWAGEN PZKPFW III (SDKFZ 141)

The PzKpfw III first entered service in 1936 and was to form the mainstay of the armoured corps for several years. This medium tank weighed just over 22 tons and carried a crew of four. Overall length was 6.3 m, and width 2.95 m. By the time the first

Waffen-SS panzer units were being created, the model most prevalent was the PzKpfw III J, carrying a long-barrelled 5 cm gun. It was powered by a Maybach HL120 12-cylinder petrol engine developing 300 bhp, and was capable of top speeds of up to 40 kph on roads and 25 kph across country. It had an operational range of some 200 km (110 km across country) on its 320-litre fuel tank.

This version was followed in 1943 by the PzKpfw III L, carrying the same armament but with improved armour protection, and subsequently by the PzKpfw III M, again with improved armour protection, and finally the PzKpfw III N, which mounted a short-barrelled 7.5 cm gun, inadequate for tank *v* tank engagements but excellent in the close-support role for which it was intended. Production of the PzKpfw III ended in August 1943, though the basic chassis lived on in a series of excellent and highly successful self-propelled guns.

A *Panzer IV* of the *Leibstandarte* during the attack on the Kursk salient. Note that the dark grey colour scheme of the early part of the war has been replaced by a sand-yellow base with dull red-brown and green mottle patterns. As well as spaced armour around the turret, armoured skirts have also been fitted to brackets around the hull side.

A column of PzKpfz III tanks, painted in white as snow camouflage. Note the tank's call sign 555 painted on the turret stowage bin.

PANZERKAMPFWAGEN PZKPFW IV (SDKFZ 162)

The PzKpfw IV first went into service in 1936, and by the time it was first issued to *Waffen-SS* formations had reached the PzKpfw IV D, though this was issued only in very small numbers (probably no more than six) to the *Leibstandarte*. This tank weighed in at 17 tons and mounted a short-barrelled 7.5 cm gun. The tank was 2.9 m wide, 7 m in overall length and 2.7 m in height. It carried a crew of five and was powered by a Maybach HL120 12-cylinder petrol engine developing 300 bhp. This gave it a top speed of 30 kph on roads and 16 kph across country. Its 470-litre fuel capacity gave it a range of some 210 km (130 km across country).

By 1942, when the process of providing *Waffen-SS* divisions with their own panzer formations began in earnest, the principal model being used was the heavier PzKpfw IV F2, weighing 23.6 tons and mounting an excellent 7.5 cm long-barrelled gun, capable of destroying the highly effective Soviet T-34. In the years that followed, the PzKpfw IV F2 was joined by the later G, H and J models, each with enhanced armour protection and improved weaponry.

PANZERKAMPFWAGEN PZKPFW V (SDKFZ 171)

The PzKpfw V, better known as the Panther, is considered by many to have been the finest medium tank of the Second World War. It was developed as a direct result of the nasty shock experienced by German tankers when they encountered the Soviet T-34; its sloped armour proved impervious to the guns on most German tanks and its 76 mm and later 85 mm gun was capable of taking out most German tanks well before they could get close enough for their own inferior weapons to stand any chance of being effective. The Germans set about developing what was in many ways a copy of the basic design of the Soviet tank, with well-sloped front and side armour, and wide tracks to more effectively spread its ground load and allow it to cross soft ground or snow more easily.

Weighing 43 tons, the Panther was powered by a 12-cylinder Maybach HL230 petrol engine developing 700 bhp. This large tank was 3.3 m wide, and overall length was 8.9 m and height 3 m. Its fuel capacity of 730 litres gave it a range of 200 km on roads and 130 km across country, with a top speed of 46 kph on roads and an excellent cross-country top speed of 30 kph. The Panther was crewed by five and was armed with a superb high-velocity long-barrelled 7.5 cm gun, with a coaxial 7.92 mm machine-gun and a further 7.92 mm machine-gun in the hull.

Despite its huge potential, the Panther was not a total success. Desperate for an effective counter to the T-34, the Germans rushed through the developmental stages, giving insufficient time for debugging of the tank's numerous technical problems. The gearbox was barely robust enough for the Panther's heavy weight, and failures were common, as were collapsing suspensions and fires in the engine compartment because of inadequate cooling. Panthers first saw action during the great tank battle at Kursk in July 1943, where 80 per cent of those committed to action were lost within two days, most through mechanical failure. In late July *Leibstandarte*, *Totenkopf* and *Wiking* Divisions were each equipped with a small number of the first production model, the Panther 'D'. One month later *Das Reich*, which had been training in Germany, returned to the Eastern Front also equipped with the Panther 'D'.

The problems encountered with the first production model had already led to the development of an improved version, the Panther 'A', with improved transmission and gearbox and additional cooling for the engine. This model was highly successful, but although the problems were improved upon they were not entirely eradicated.

The last major production model of Panther and the versions produced in greatest numbers was the 'G', which featured improved armour protection, increasing its weight to 44.8 tons. It first appeared in February 1944.

PANZERKAMPFWAGEN PZKPFW VI (SDKFZ 181)

The PzKpfw VI, probably the most famous tank of all time, is better known simply as the Tiger.

Its development began as early as 1940, but it did not enter operational service until August 1942. This behemoth was 3.7 m wide, 8.2 m in overall length and 2.86 m in

A *Waffen-SS Panzer V* Panther undergoing maintenance under the cover of a copse of trees. As the war progressed, the danger from enemy aircraft became ever more acute. This vehicle is having its tracks replaced, rendering it temporarily immobile and thus vulnerable.

Another Panther undergoing routine maintenance. The crewman in the background is using the vehicle's large jack to raise one of the roadwheels for removal.

height. The Tiger, crewed by five, weighed 56 tons and was powered by a Maybach HL230 V12 petrol engine developing 700 bhp. This gave it a top speed of 38 kph on roads and 20 kph across country. Fuel capacity was 534 litres, allowing a maximum range on roads of 100 km and just 60 km across country.

Despite its monstrous weight, the Tiger's extremely wide tracks allowed it to operate reasonably efficiently across relatively soft ground, though many bridges were incapable of bearing its weight. Tigers were generally transported to the front on railway flatcars to reduce wear on its engine and drive train. To accomplish this, its great width was reduced by exchanging its wide battle tracks for narrow transport tracks. These then had to be changed again when it reached its destination. Recovery of damaged Tigers was also a problematic exercise. The only vehicle capable of towing a Tiger was another Tiger, but as this huge tank's powerplant was only just capable of handling its great weight, using one to tow another Tiger risked putting unbearable strain on the towing vehicle, and the use of Tigers as ad hoc recovery vehicles was expressly forbidden. To recover a single Tiger the authorised method was to use no fewer than three of the massive 18-ton Famo half-tracked prime movers.

Despite its obvious drawbacks, the Tiger possessed two distinct advantages – massive frontal armour protection, making it almost invulnerable unless an enemy was able to approach from the Tiger's more lightly armoured flanks or rear, and a superb 8.8 cm high-velocity cannon capable of taking out any tank in the world at that time.

Tigers were initially allocated to *Leibstandarte*, *Das Reich* and *Totenkopf* Divisions as heavy tank companies. These were later converted to heavy tank battalions

(*SS-schwere Panzer Abteilung 101, 102* and *103* – later renumbered as *501, 502* and *503*).

The Tiger achieved a truly awesome reputation and was greatly feared by Allied tank crews. So paranoid did some become that almost any enemy tank sighted would be reported as a 'Tiger'. The Tiger's armour was so thick that a frontal attack against one was all but suicidal. It was a common belief that if a Tiger was encountered at least five M4 Shermans would be required to tackle it, with an expectation that at least four of them would be lost.

PANZERKAMPFWAGEN PZKPFW VI B (SDKFZ 182)

Mighty as the Tiger was, it was not the largest German tank to see extensive combat service. That claim lay with its successor, the even larger *Königstiger*, or King Tiger. This massive beast weighed in at 69.4 tons. Despite carrying the Tiger name, it bore no resemblance to the boxy shape of its predecessor. Instead its design owed more to that of the Panther, with sloped front and side armour. Powered by a Maybach HL230 12-cylinder engine developing 700 bhp, its top speed was a creditable 38 kph on roads and 17 kph across country. Fuel capacity was 860 litres, giving it a range of 110 km on roads and 85 km across country.

A huge vehicle, at 3 m high, 3.75 m wide and 10.26 m in overall length, it was crewed by five and mounted an 8.8 cm high-velocity cannon, with a coaxial 7.92 mm machine-gun in the turret and another in the hull.

This gigantic vehicle, like its predecessor, was cumbersome, and had a very short operational range and a powerplant barely capable of handling its huge weight. It was unsuited to many types of terrain, but when well sited was a superlative defensive weapon, picking off enemy vehicles well

The huge bulk of the Panther is very apparent in this shot of '401', the steed of panzer ace Ernst Barkmann, who is seen here in the turret. It is assumed the tank is some way from possible enemy action as the protective dust cover is fitted over the muzzle of the gun barrel.

The mighty Tiger tank. This example is shown during test firing on the gunnery ranges. Many *Waffen-SS* panzer aces made their reputations with this awesome weapon.

Captured enemy armoured vehicles were put to good use. This Soviet armoured car has had large white SS runes painted on the side of the turret in the hope that this will prevent it from being shot at by other German troops.

before they came within the effective range of their own weapons. The *Königstiger* was capable of knocking out any existing tank in the world at that time, while its own frontal armour was virtually impervious to any known enemy anti-tank weapon. It was effectively a mobile pillbox.

The first *Königstiger* were manufactured by Henschel, the first examples going into service in January 1944. These early models used the Henschel hull, but were fitted with

a prototype turret manufactured by Porsche. These turrets had a curved frontal plate, which it was found could deflect an incoming enemy shell down on to the roof of the more thinly armoured fighting compartment. The Panther in fact suffered from a similar problem, which resulted in an angular 'chin' being fitted to the lower part of the curved gun mantlet. In the case of the *Königstiger*, Henschel produced its own version of the turret, the face of which

Another captured Soviet armoured car is put to use by the *Waffen-SS*. The small white sword emblem just visible on the rather crumpled mudguard is the tactical sign used by *Totenkopf Infanterie Regiment 4*.

was formed by an immense thick slab of flat armour.

Königstigers were allocated to all three of the *Waffen-SS* heavy tank battalions and saw action on both the Eastern and Western Fronts. Although their use in the Ardennes Offensive, through terrain (wooded hills and narrow roads) for which they were entirely unsuitable, led to less than favourable results, records of actions on the Eastern Front are replete with examples of small numbers, or even lone *Königstiger* halting, albeit temporarily, Soviet armoured advances.

MISCELLANEOUS OTHER TANKS

As well as the above standard models, a number of other vehicles are known to have been used by *Waffen-SS* units. Following the

successful end to the Campaign in the West in 1940, large numbers of French tanks fell into German hands. These were in the main not considered suitable for front-line combat use by the *Wehrmacht* or *Waffen-SS*, but a number were used by units employed on policing and security duties, in particular those in action against lightly armed partisan units. The *7 SS-Freiwilligen Gebirgs Division Prinz Eugen* is one such example. Though tanks are not something one would particularly imagine being extensively used by a mountain unit, this division did field a small armoured detachment, equipped with captured French light tanks such as the Renault, in its struggle against Tito's partisans in Yugoslavia.

The Soviet T-34 had earned the respect and admiration of *Waffen-SS* tankers for its robust, if often crude, construction coupled with excellent armour, cross-country performance and effective armament. German units lost no opportunity to turn captured T-34s on their former owners, and in one case, within *Panzer Regiment 2 Das Reich* a whole section of captured T-34s was formed, its commander Emil Seibold being decorated with the Knight's Cross for his achievements. These T-34s were of course boldly emblazoned with German markings to avoid them being taken out by over-anxious German troops, who had every reason to fear the approach of a T-34.

TANK DESTROYERS AND SELF-PROPELLED GUNS

SCHWERES INFANTERIEGESCHÜTZ (SIG) 33

Although the *Panzerkampfwagen* PzKpfw I light tank had been withdrawn from service before the first *Waffen-SS* panzer units were formed, this obsolete vehicle did see service in the form of the sIG33, which mounted a 15 cm infantry gun on the chassis of the PzKpfw I. The huge box-shaped fighting compartment gave this otherwise diminutive vehicle an ungainly look, and its armour protection was inadequate in a vehicle which made such a conspicuous target. Nevertheless, as a stop-gap it provided useful heavy-gun support to *Waffen-SS* infantry units in the early part of the war.

STURMGESCHÜTZ III (SDKFZ 142)

The German armaments industry lost no opportunity to extract the best possible use from each vehicle design, and in the case of the PzKpfw III, the self-propelled assault guns which were developed around the basic tank chassis were so effective and successful that they remained in service and indeed in production long after the basic

tank had ceased to be manufactured. The design of the *Sturmgeschütz* (usually abbreviated to StuG) III retained the basic hull, running gear and engine compartment of the tank version, but had the turret replaced by a fixed super-structure with forward-facing gun capable of only limited traverse. If more than this was required, the whole vehicle had to be turned.

Early-model StuG IIIAs were first used by the *Waffen-SS* in 1940. This vehicle weighed some 21.3 tons and measured 5.4 m in length, 2.9 m in width and just 1.95 m in height. This low silhouette made it a difficult target to hit and aided concealment.

The StuG III was powered by a Maybach HL120 12-cylinder petrol engine developing 300 bhp. This gave it a top speed of 45 kph on the road and 19 kph across country. Its 320-litre fuel capacity allowed it an operational range of some 161 km on roads and 97 km across country. This vehicle had a crew of four and mounted a short-barrelled 7.5 cm gun.

Subsequent improved models saw an increase in armour protection and greatly improved weaponry, allowing its use as a support weapon with a howitzer fitted and as an equally effective tank killer with a high-velocity 7.5 cm long-barrelled gun.

This extremely versatile weapon was widely used throughout the *Waffen-SS*, and not just in panzer divisions. In general it was found, not in the panzer regiments and detachments, but with the artillery regiments due to its original role as mobile assault artillery.

STURMGESCHÜTZ IV (SDKFZ 167)

The StuG IV, or assault gun version of the PzKpfw IV, was to all intents and purposes a slightly larger twin of the StuG III, to which

A *Waffen-SS Sturmgeschütz*. This is one of many variants of StuG III built on the chassis of the *Panzer III*. Production of the *Sturmgeschütz* continued long after the basic tank version was discontinued.

it bore a remarkable resemblance. In fact only the eight road wheels each side of the hull, as opposed to the six carried by the StuG III, helps to instantly identify the larger of the two. The StuG IV began to be manufactured in December 1943, but was only used in very limited numbers by *Waffen-SS* units.

PANZERJÄGER MARDER II (SDKFZ 131)

When the useful life of the PzKpfw II came to an end, the remaining hulls were principally used as the bases for a new tank destroyer, the *Marder* (Marten), by the simple expedient of removing the turret and superstructure and bolting a 7.63-calibre long-barrelled anti-tank gun, a weapon which in fact came from captured Russian stocks. Thus, by making efficient

use of an obsolete tank and captured Russian guns, a highly effective tank destroyer was created. This vehicle began to see service in 1942, and was very popular with the *Waffen-SS*. It was light-weight, around 10.8 tons, and had a crew of four. Powered by a Maybach HL62 6-cylinder petrol engine developing 140 bhp, it was relatively fast with a top speed of 45 kph on the road and 19 kph across country. A 200-litre fuel capacity gave it a range of 185 km on the road and 121 km across country. The *Marder* packed a powerful punch, but its open fighting compartment meant that the crew were somewhat vulnerable. Later examples of the *Marder II*, of which numerous variants were made in terms of the exact configuration of the fighting compartment, were fitted with German 7.5 cm anti-tank guns.

STURMHAUBITZE WESPE (SDKFZ 124)

The *Wespe*, or Wasp, was yet another modification of the elderly PzKpfw II chassis. An open fighting compartment was built on the rear of the chassis, mounting a 10.5 cm field howitzer. The original PzKpfw II engine, a Maybach HL62 6-cylinder, was retained, giving a top speed of 40 kph on roads and 20 kph across country. These vehicles went into service with *Waffen-SS* units in 1942, and were fielded in the divisional *Panzerartillerie Abteilung* of the *Leibstandarte*, *Das Reich* and *Totenkopf* Divisions.

HUMMEL (SDKFZ 165)

Another effort to provide mobile heavy artillery resulted in the *Hummel*, or Bumble Bee. This utilised a hull made from various components from both the PzKpfw III and PzKpfw IV. On to this hybrid was built an open fighting compartment to accommodate a 15 cm field howitzer. One battery of *Hummels* was allocated to the artillery regiment of *Waffen-SS* panzer divisions.

PANZERJÄGER MARDER III (SDKFZ 138)

As well as the chassis of the obsolete PzKpfw II, a large number of older Czech-made PzKpfw 38(t)s were converted in a similar fashion to become the *Marder III*. This vehicle mounted a German 7.5 cm anti-tank gun, though a version with a captured Soviet 7.62 mm anti-tank gun was also produced, as the SdKfz 139. Weighing 10.5 tons, it had a maximum speed of 42 kph on the road and 24 kph across country. Powered by a Praga EPA 6-cylinder petrol engine developing 125 bhp, its 218-litre fuel capacity gave it a range of 185 km on roads and 140 km across country. Like the *Marder*

II, this version had an open fighting compartment which left its crew somewhat exposed. Both versions of the *Marder* were used extensively by *Waffen-SS* units.

JAGDPANZER 38(T) HETZER

Without a doubt the finest armoured fighting vehicle to be based on the Czech 38(t) chassis was the diminutive *Hetzer*, or Baiter. Just 6.3 m in length, 2.6 m in width and 2.1 m in height, the *Hetzer* weighed 16 tons. Within its fixed superstructure was mounted a 7.5 cm anti-tank gun, and on its roof was mounted a 7.92 mm machine-gun with armoured shield, which could be controlled from within the vehicle to discourage the approach of enemy infantry.

Entering service with the *Waffen-SS* in 1944, the *Hetzer* weighed 16 tons and was powered by a Praga EPA TZJ 6-cylinder petrol engine developing 158 bhp. This gave it a top speed of 26 kph on the road and 15 kph across country. Its 386-litre fuel capacity allowed it a range of 161 km on the road and 80 km across country. The *Hetzer* was an excellent design, and was highly popular but never available in sufficient numbers to satisfy demand. It entered service first with the *Sturmgeschütz Abteilung* of *8 SS-Kavallerie Division Florian Geyer* and subsequently with numerous other units.

JAGDPANZER IV (SDKFZ 162)

This excellent tank destroyer was based on the chassis of the PzKpfw IV and was intended as a replacement for the StuG III, an excellent weapon but one which had reached the limits of its design. Its manufacture was approved by Hitler, but the *Generalinspekteur der Panzertruppe*, Heinz Guderian, felt that its introduction would endanger the manufacture of the standard PzKpfw IV battle tank which was still

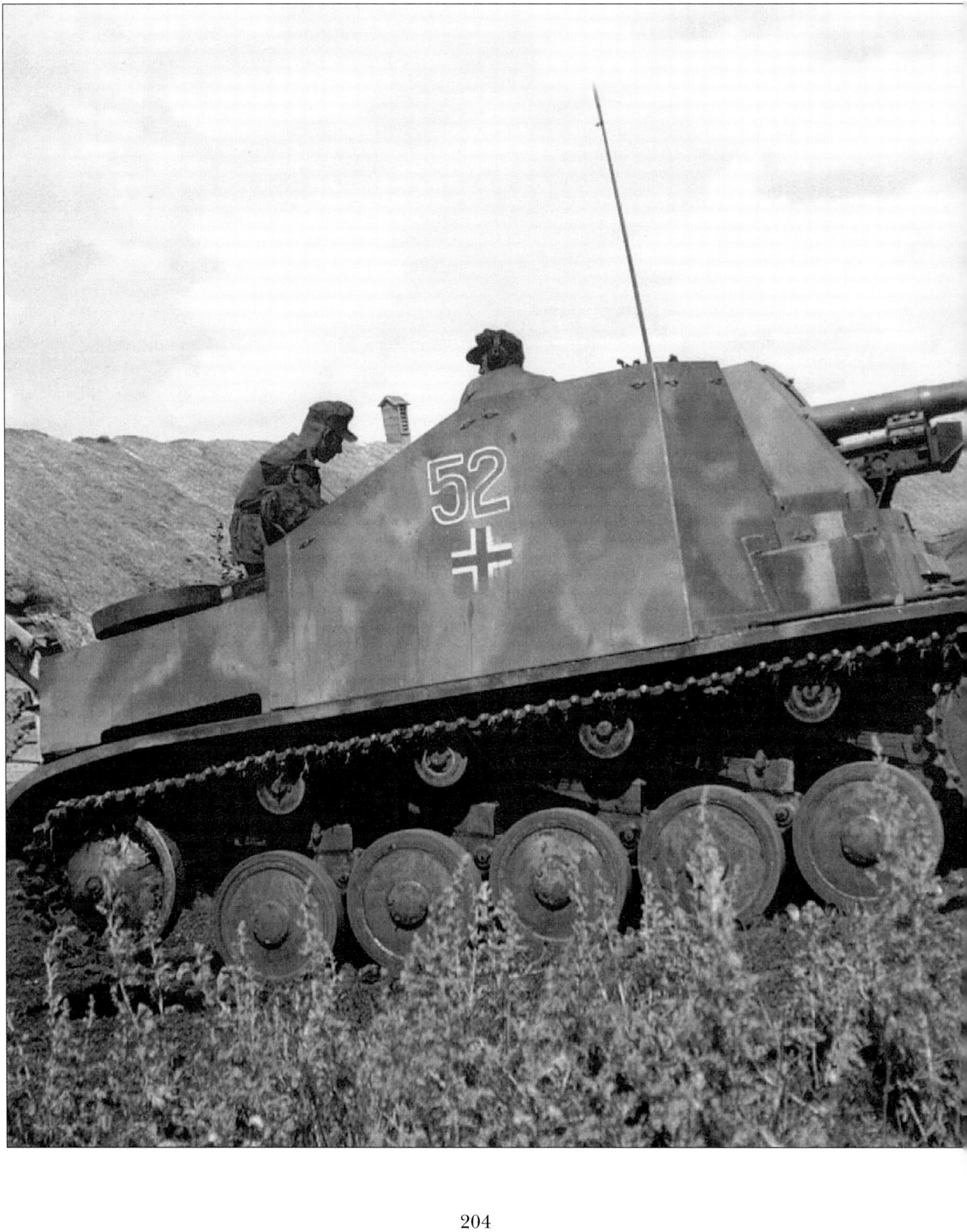
52

desperately needed. Guderian managed to delay but not prevent the introduction of the new vehicle, though his fears were somewhat allayed by the granting of manufacturing contracts to Vomag of Planen, not heavily involved in the production of the PzKpfw IV battle tank, so that existing production of the latter was not much affected.

The order for volume production was given in December 1943 after successful testing of the prototype, and the *Jagdpanzer IV F* went into service in early 1944. The vehicle weighed 24 tons and measured 6 m in length, 3.3 m in width and just 1.96 m in height, making its profile much smaller than the PzKpfw IV battle tank. It mounted a 7.5 cm anti-tank gun and a 7.92 mm machine-gun. It was powered by a Maybach HL120 12-cylinder petrol engine developing 300 bhp. Fuel capacity was some 470 litres, giving it a range of 210 km on roads and 130 km across country. The first examples of this vehicle to be issued to the *Waffen-SS* went to the newly formed *12 SS-Panzer Division Hitlerjugend*, though it also saw service in the *Das Reich*, *Polizei* and *Frundsberg* Divisions.

An improved model mounting the same long-barrelled 7.5 cm gun as in the Panther tank followed in August 1944, and these were also issued to the *Leibstandarte*, *Totenkopf*, *Wiking* and *Hohenstaufen Division*s.

JAGDPANZER V JAGDPANTHER (SDKFZ 173)

Generally recognised as the best tank destroyer of the war, the *Jagdpanther* was

A *Marder* tank destroyer from the *Leibstandarte*. This vehicle mounted the excellent 7.5 cm Pak 40 on the chassis of the Czech-built *Panzer* Pz38(t).

produced by mounting a fixed super-structure on to the chassis of the PzKpfw V Panther tank. A powerful 8.8 cm anti-tank gun was mounted, along with a 7.92 mm machine-gun. A relatively low profile, sloped armour providing excellent protection, an impressive top speed for a vehicle of its size and excellent cross-country performance made this an all-round first-class weapon.

The *Jagdpanther* weighed in at 45 tons and was powered by a Maybach HL230 12-cylinder engine developing 700 bhp. This gave it a top speed of 45 kph on roads and 24 kph across country. A 700-litre fuel capacity gave it a range of 210 km on roads or 140 km across country. Length was 6.9 m, width 3.3 m and overall height 2.7 m.

Unfortunately for the *Waffen-SS*, only a small number of *Jagdpanther* were available to it, fourteen examples being allocated to each of the *Das Reich*, *Hohenstaufen* and *Frundsberg* Divisions. Most of these were lost in the battle in Hungary and the defence of Vienna in the closing stages of the war.

MISCELLANEOUS

Among the other interesting armoured fighting vehicles which saw service, albeit limited, with *Waffen-SS* units were the special anti-aircraft tanks. These consisted of a chassis from the Pzkpfw IV, on to which was mounted a variety of different anti-aircraft weapons. The two most commonly encountered in *Waffen-SS* units were the 'Möbelwagen' and the 'Wirbelwind'.

FLAKPANZER IV MÖBELWAGEN

In this vehicle, the original central section of the fighting compartment was removed and a flat floor fitted. On to this was fitted either a single-barrelled 3.7 cm flak gun or a four-barrelled 2 cm *Flakvierling*, which could be equally effective in a ground-combat role. Armoured side-plates protected the weapon until it was ready for use, at which point these hinged plates could be dropped to give the weapon a clear field of fire. This vehicle's nickname, *Möbelwagen* (furniture van), was a clear reference to its boxy structure. It weighed 25 tons and was manned by a crew of seven. Only 240 of these vehicles were ever produced, making it a fairly rare piece of equipment.

FLAKPANZER IV WIRBELWIND

This vehicle retained the basic PzKpfw IV chassis and superstructure, but had the standard tank turret replaced by an octagonal open top turret in which was mounted a quadruple 2 cm *Flakvierling*. This was an even rarer beast than the *Möbelwagen*, only 86 being built. An alternative version, with a single 3.7 cm *Flak* in place of the *Flakvierling*, was known as the *Ostwind*.

A number of *Flakpanzer 38(t)s* were also produced, some 162 in total, and were used predominantly by the *Waffen-SS*. These were built in Prague, on the PzKpfw 38(t) chassis, and carried a single 2 cm flak gun.

CHAPTER THIRTEEN

COMBAT TACTICS

The basic tactics adopted by the Germany military during the Second World War, at least during the first part of the war, have become universally known as the *Blitzkrieg* or lightning war.

This depended on well-coordinated and well-integrated use of all available branches of the armed forces, and in particular, close cooperation between ground and air forces. The German Army, though powerful, was not huge and was well outnumbered by its opponents on many occasions, for instance by the French during the Campaign in the West.

By concentrating its forces at the focal point of the attack, the *Schwerpunkt*, the Germans would smash through the enemy defences, and most importantly, keep moving thereafter, leaving secondary units to mop up. Despite the impression given by the newsreels of the day, the German Army was not made up predominantly of well-equipped fully motorised panzer divisions. In fact many units were still horse-drawn, and the bulk of the infantry still had to move to their destinations by marching.

Rather than wait for such slower units to catch up, the spearhead units would press on, leaving those that followed to take care of the fragmented and demoralised enemy defenders. This often left the flanks of the spearhead units dangerously exposed, but fortunately for the Germans, the sheer speed and momentum of their advance often left the enemy unable to respond adequately.

The *Waffen-SS* was no different from other units in the basic tactics used. Where it did often differ, however, was in the degree of risk that its members were prepared to take to achieve their objectives.

The concept of *Härte*, or toughness, was of extreme importance. This did not merely relate to physical fitness, although this did feature strongly in SS training, but to mental and psychological toughness too. The loyalty of the average *Waffen-SS* soldier to his parent unit cannot be over-stated. Those, for instance, who had served with a particular elite unit would often continue to wear the insignia of their parent unit even after transferring to another. Total loyalty, not only to the unit, but to the soldier's immediate comrades in the squad, platoon, company or regiment, was an essential requirement. With this loyalty, tested in battle, came a degree of trust in the soldier's comrades, NCOs and officers which, though not unknown in other branches, rarely seems as strong as it was in the *Waffen-SS* (the probable exception being elite units or formations of the *Wehrmacht*, such as the *Grossdeutschland* Division, the *Fallschirmjäger* and the *Gebirgsjäger*).

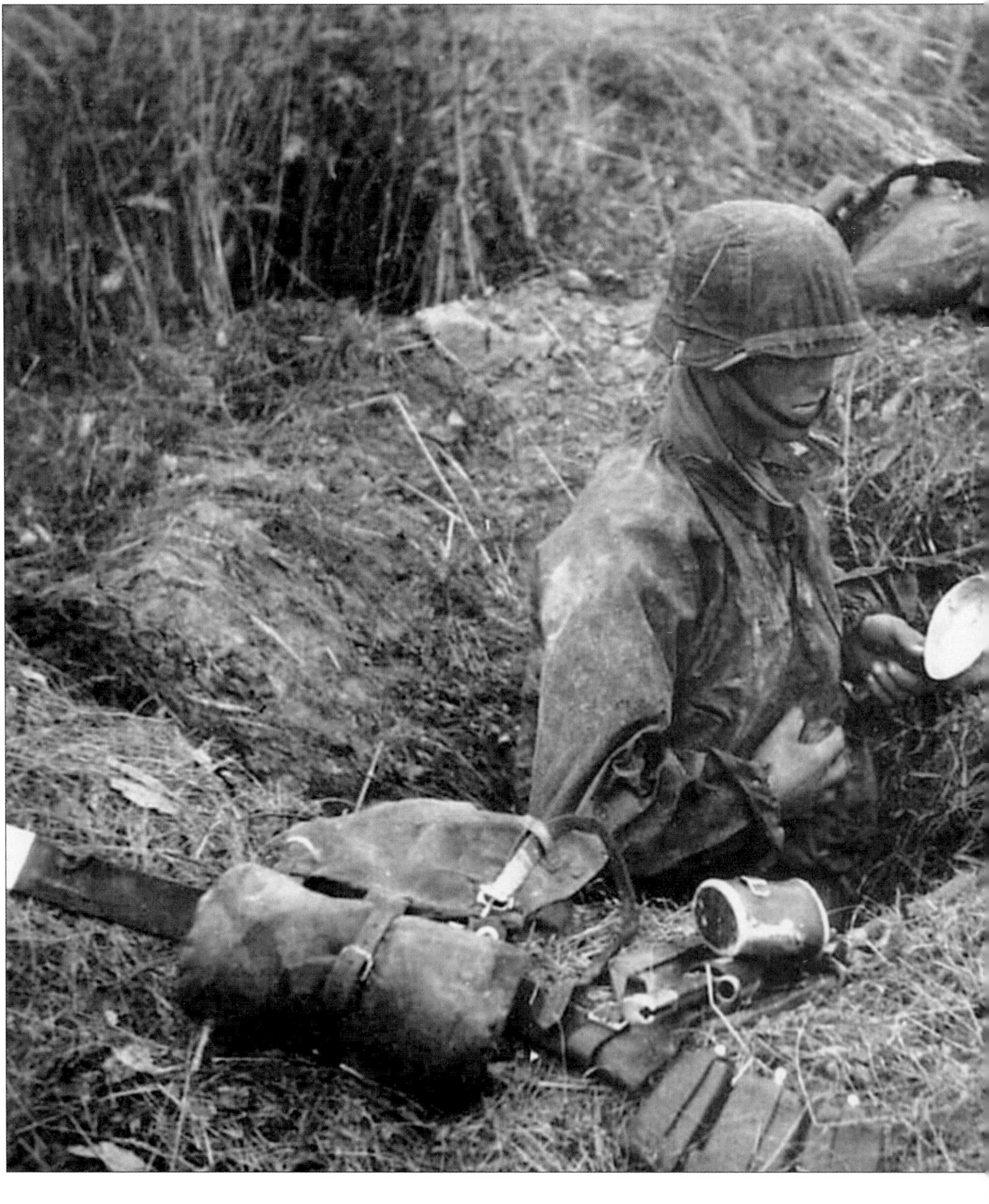

Waffen-SS officers were very much expected to lead from the front, providing their men with an example to follow. Consequently, battlefield casualties among officer ranks were rather high. Generally speaking, however, the average soldier was trained to show initiative, and there is no shortage of examples of junior ranks successfully taking over a squad where the NCO had been killed or wounded, or NCOs taking over a platoon or even a company from an officer. Unlike the situation in the German Army, where officers and junior ranks rarely if ever mixed off duty, in the *Waffen-SS* such social mixing was strongly encouraged. Officers were expected to partake in sporting activities with the men, and to mix with them in whatever free time was available. In addition, the prefix *'Herr'* before a rank was not used, but simply the rank itself, or the term *'Kamerad'* when off duty. All of this was part of the policy of fostering the type of comradeship between officers, NCOs and men which is still a hallmark of many elite military units today, but was very much a rarity then.

Waffen-SS soldiers were expected to leave their lockers containing their personal effects unlocked, as to secure them suggested mistrust of one's comrades. On the rare occasions when soldiers did dishonour themselves by stealing from their comrades, punishment would be far more draconian than would have been the case in the Army.

Much has been said about the high level of casualties suffered by *Waffen-SS* troops in

A *Waffen-SS* soldier in his foxhole at the front. It seems he is preparing to have his rations. Although his ammunition pouches are to hand there is no sign of his weapon, so it can be assumed that action is not imminent.

A mixture of Army and *Waffen-SS* troops at a defensive position in the field. Note the scissors-style trench periscope and the heavy machine-gun. The Army officer is clearly from a panzer unit, so it would seem that these troops have some armoured support.

The transport and supply unit of an *SS-Totenkopf* Regiment during the Campaign in the West in 1940. The trucks are lined up ready for departure with their motorcycle escorts.

the early part of the war, and derogatory comments made about this fact by the Army. The counter-argument, however, often put forward as the *Waffen-SS* viewpoint, was that suffering a high initial rate of casualties to quickly secure an objective could in many cases result in an overall lower rate of losses that would be the case if a more cautious approach was taken. The assertion was that the cautious approach could result in gradual attrition over a longer period. The German Army in fact lost approximately one third of its total strength in combat attrition, while the *Waffen-SS* lost approximately one quarter, so there are indeed grounds for arguing that the aggressive tactics employed by the *Waffen-SS* were ultimately less costly than those of the Army.

Just how much of a role political indoctrination played in the aggression shown by *Waffen-SS* troops in battle is

Here we see a late war version of the SdKfz 7 *Flak* half-track. Still mounting the 3.7 cm gun, it now has an armoured cab, and an armoured shield protecting the radiator and front of the engine.

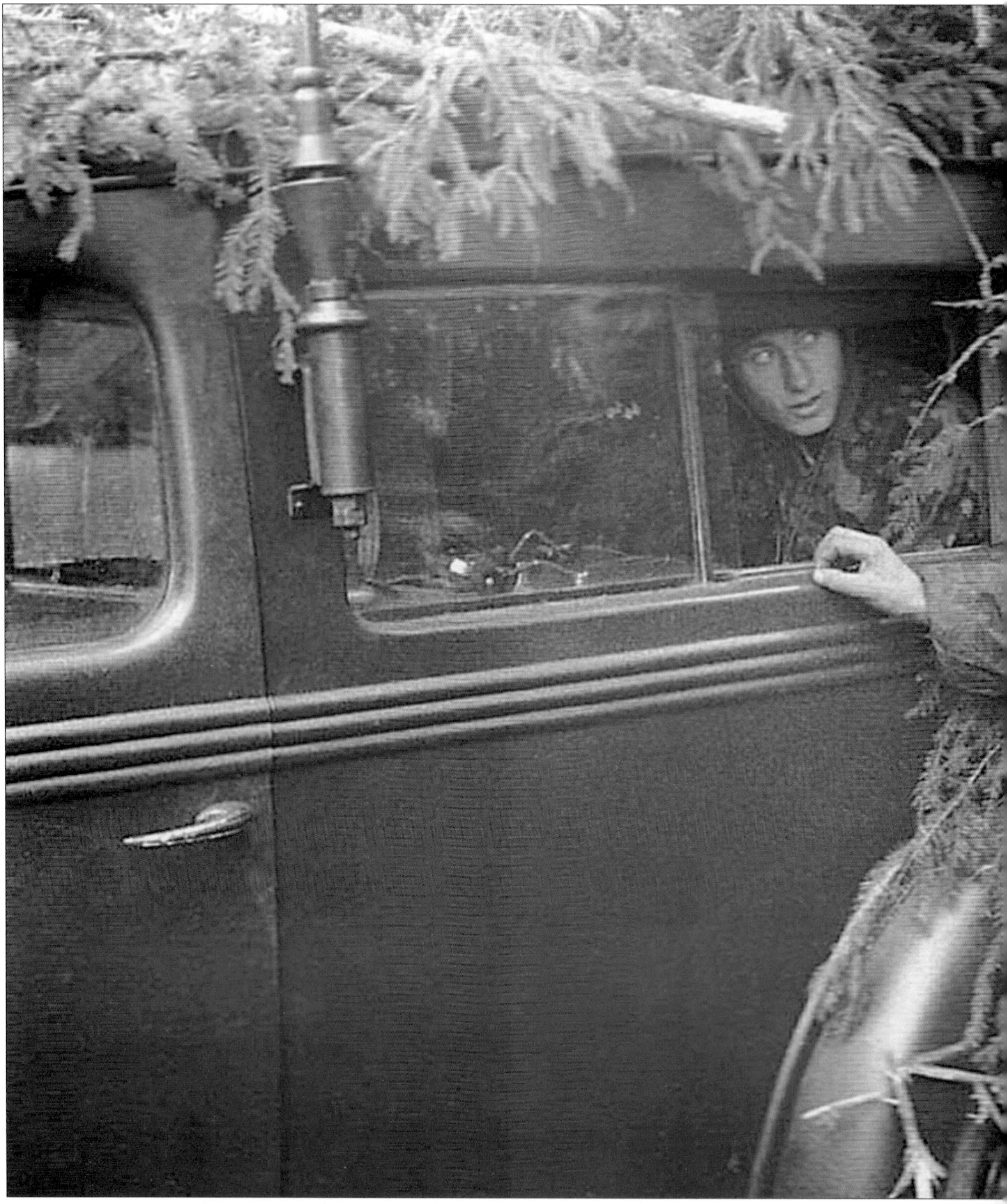

debatable. Certainly no effort seems to have been spared to build up a hatred for Bolshevism, and so it may be assumed that a hatred of the ideological enemy would play a part in the attitudes of some *Waffen-SS* men during the Campaign in the East. On the other hand, however, there was no shortage of often fanatical levels of aggression shown by *Waffen-SS* troops during the Campaign in the West, where nowhere near so much hate propaganda had been generated against Anglo-French forces. It simply seems that in many cases the risk of a high level of battlefield casualties was seen as secondary to the achievement of the mission goals.

Although the Army often berated this apparent reckless disdain for danger in the early part of the war, many *Wehrmacht* troops had occasion to be grateful for it when the fortunes of war turned against Germany in the East. It was, in the main, *Waffen-SS* units which formed the so-called 'fire brigades' that rushed from one danger spot to another where an enemy breakthrough seemed possible. The arrival of an elite *Waffen-SS* unit in their midst was often sufficient to revive flagging spirits among worn-out Army units. *Waffen-SS* units were noted for their steadfastness in defence, and often provided rearguard formations to protect the withdrawal of regular units.

Of course, such was the reputation of *Waffen-SS* troops that few wished to risk being captured by the enemy, particularly the Soviets (though the shooting of *Waffen-SS* soldiers taken prisoner was by no means unknown on the Western Front). A greater

This close-up of a radio car (which appears to be a civil vehicle pressed into military service) is interesting in that it gives a particularly clear view of the camouflage smock worn by the soldier in the foreground.

This Soviet soldier, who has just been taken prisoner on the Eastern Front, has been offered a cigarette by his captors before he has even been disarmed.

An Opel truck from a *Waffen-SS* unit negotiates a temporary wooden causeway on the Eastern Front. Supplies were obliged to be transported huge distances in Russia, making a large fleet of transport trucks an absolute essential.

The fate of many *Waffen-SS* soldiers. Here members of a *Waffen-SS* panzer unit bury their dead.

tendency to fight to the last man among *Waffen-SS* troops might therefore be, to some degree, expected. Indeed it has been said that SS troops on the Eastern Front would keep their last bullet for themselves rather than be taken alive.

As already stated in the Introduction, in the closing stages of the war, with the exception of a few fanatics, *Waffen-SS* men had long since lost any faith in their political leadership or the regime they served. They did, however, retain an intense loyalty to the *Waffen-SS* itself, and to their unit comrades, and their own commanders, and when asked to do so, even in the closing hours of the war, were usually willing to fight with considerable tenacity against overwhelming odds.

CHAPTER FOURTEEN

MAJOR PERSONALITIES

SS-OBERSTGRUPPENFÜHRER JOSEF 'SEPP' DIETRICH

Josef Dietrich was born on 28 May 1892. This tough Bavarian served in the Imperial German Army during the First World War. After seeing combat service in the artillery, he transferred to the nascent German armoured corps as an NCO and was one of a small number of German soldiers to win the Tank Assault Badge.

Dietrich took part in the abortive Munich Putsch of 1923 and joined the Nazi Party in 1928. By 1932 he had reached the rank of *SS-Hauptsturmführer*. In June of that year, he was appointed to command Hitler's new bodyguard unit. His loyalty to his *Führer* was unquestioned, and indeed Dietrich was heavily involved in the arrest and execution of *SA-Stabschef* Ernst Röhm.

Dietrich has often been described as coarse and uneducated. It is true that he was very much a soldier's soldier and probably felt a greater kinship to his men than to other senior-ranking officers. He was seen as a father figure to his men and showed great concern for their welfare. Although the *Leibstandarte* was one of the most highly disciplined military formations in existence, Dietrich was known on many occasions to intervene and reduce or quash sentences passed on young soldiers for disciplinary offences if the individual was felt to be of previously good conduct. Dietrich was awarded the Knight's Cross of the Iron Cross on 4 July 1940 for his command of the *Leibstandarte* during the Campaign in the West. The Oakleaves were added to Dietrich's Knight's Cross on 31 December 1941, with the *Leibstandarte* fighting on the Russian Front. Dietrich's men fought with great distinction. Dietrich earned the Swords to his Oakleaves on 16 March 1943, and on 6 August 1944 was awarded the coveted Oakleaves with Swords and Diamonds Clasp in recognition of the steadfast defence offered by troops under his command after the Allied invasion of Normandy.

Dietrich's troops took part in the ill-fated Ardennes Offensive in December 1944 before returning to the Eastern Front once again, where they counter-attacked Soviet forces around Lake Balaton in Hungary. When this offensive failed, Hitler, in a rage, is reputed to have accused the *Waffen-SS* of cowardice and ordered them to remove their unit cuffbands. There is an apocryphal story that Dietrich removed his cuffbands and sent them to Hitler in a chamber pot along with all his military decorations. This, the stuff of legend, is almost certainly untrue. In any case, none of those around Hitler would have dared to pass Dietrich's insult on to Hitler. It is also the case that many SS units had already removed their

Josef 'Sepp' Dietrich, seen here as an *SS-Obergruppenführer*. He wears the Knight's Cross with Oakleaves and Swords. Dietrich was one of the highest decorated soldiers of the *Waffen-SS*, being one of only two SS soldiers to win the Oakleaves with Swords and Diamonds.

This earlier photograph shows Dietrich as an *SS-Gruppenführer*. At this time he wears only the Knight's Cross. On the pocket flap of his right breast pocket is the ribbon of the Nazi Party's 'Blood Order', bestowed on those who accompanied Hitler during the Munich Putsch of 1923.

SS-Obergruppenführer Paul 'Papa' Hausser. Hausser was one of the most accomplished soldiers in the *Waffen-SS.* He was also one of the few willing to ignore or disobey direct orders from Hitler.

Though he had been decorated with Germany's highest military decorations for his leadership of *Waffen-SS* units, and in particular his beloved *Leibstandarte*, Dietrich is often referred to in less than glowing terms where military leadership is concerned, it being claimed that he was promoted well above his abilities. There can be no doubt, however, that this charismatic figure, whatever his failings, was greatly admired by the men he led.

SS-OBERSTGRUPPENFÜHRER PAUL 'PAPA' HAUSSER

Paul Hausser was born on 7 October 1880. He served in the Imperial German Army, being commissioned to officer rank before the outbreak of the First World War. He was decorated with both Second and First Class Iron Crosses, and by the end of hostilities was serving as a *Major* with the General Staff of the Bavarian Army. Unlike many of his contemporaries who were paid off after the end of the war, he remained in military service, rising through the ranks to eventually retire in 1932 as a *Generalleutnant.*

He was persuaded to join the *SS-Verfügungstruppe* in 1934, bringing his considerable military experience as first commander of the *SS-Junkerschule* at Bad Tölz in Bavaria. In 1936 he was appointed Inspector-General of the *SS-Verfügungstruppe.* Hausser was instrumental in ensuring top-quality military training for the soldiers of the SS-VT, using his good relations with the Army to arrange joint training exercises and an exchange of officers between the two for training purposes.

Shortly after the invasion of the Soviet Union, Hausser was in command of the *SS-Panzer Division 'Das Reich'*, a duty which he fulfilled skilfully enough to earn the Knight's Cross of the Iron Cross on 8 August

cuffbands for security reasons, to avoid the enemy becoming aware of the identity of the units that faced them.

Dietrich was arrested and charged with complicity in the murder of US prisoners of war by SS troops at Malmedy during the Ardennes Offensive, and was sentenced to twenty-five years in prison. He was released after ten years, but was immediately re-arrested and prosecuted for his part in the execution of Ernst Röhm, during the 'Night of the Long Knives'. He served only eighteen months in prison on these charges before finally being released. Josef 'Sepp' Dietrich died in April 1966, his funeral being attended by thousands of former *Waffen-SS* soldiers.

1941. In October, he was seriously wounded, losing his right eye. Thereafter he adopted the eye-patch that was to become a virtual 'trademark' of this first-class officer.

In March 1943, Hausser infuriated Hitler by disobeying his orders to hold the city of Kharkov against overwhelming enemy forces. Instead, Hausser withdrew, avoiding the encirclement and almost certain destruction of the three elite SS divisions of the *SS-Panzerkorps*, *Leibstandarte*, *Das Reich* and *Totenkopf*, then turned and in a brilliantly executed counter-attack drove the Soviets out of the city, a victory which earned him the Oakleaves to his Knight's Cross, the award being bestowed in July. The delay was almost certainly Hitler's way of expressing his displeasure at Hausser's disobedience, even though the outcome was a resounding success.

Hausser commanded the 7th Army on the Western Front following the Allied invasion of Normandy, and once again was seriously wounded when leading the breakout through the Falaise Gap. His personal bravery and leadership earned him the Swords to his Oakleaves on 26 August 1944. For the remainder of the war, he commanded *Heeresgruppe G*.

After the war, Hausser worked tirelessly for the 'rehabilitation' of the soldiers of the *Waffen-SS*, insisting that they were 'soldiers just like any others' (*Soldaten wie andere auch*), the title of the book written by Hausser as a tribute to those he commanded.

Paul Hausser died on 21 December 1972 at the ripe old age of ninety-two, his funeral being attended by thousands of his former soldiers. In contrast with Dietrich, Paul Hausser was a highly cultured, professional Army officer who had come to the SS only after retiring from the *Wehrmacht*, having already reached high rank. Hausser gained universal respect, conducting himself with dignity throughout and after his military career.

SS-OBERGRUPPENFÜHRER THEODOR EICKE

An Alsatian, born in Hudingen on 17 October 1892, Theodor Eicke served during the First World War, but in a non-combatant role, as an Army paymaster. Following the end of the war, he volunteered to serve with the *Freikorps* units, which were active in Silesia and on Germany's disputed eastern borders. After his adventures with the

SS-Obergruppenführer Theodor Eicke, bearer of the Oakleaves to the Knight's Cross of the Iron Cross. Despite his brutal and unpleasant nature, Eicke did manage to turn members of the *SS-Totenkopfverbände* into one of the most powerful and effective panzer divisions of the *Waffen-SS*.

Theodor Eicke receives his Oakleaves personally from Hitler. He still wears the old original cuffband of *SS-Totenkopfstandarte 1 Oberbayern.*

Freikorps, Eicke became a security official in the chemicals industry, and eventually, in 1927, joined the police but was sacked from his job in 1928.

He drifted into the SA, like many of his *Freikorps* contemporaries, and from there transferred to the SS. In 1933 he was involved in the formation of the *SS 'Hilfspolizei'*, or auxiliary police, who were also used to guard enemies of the State who had been arrested. From these guards emerged the so-called *SS-Hundertschaften*, and ultimately the *SS-Totenkopfverbände*. Eicke took command of the concentration camp guard units in June 1933. He was a brutal taskmaster and gradually turned the unruly and undisciplined guards, who were generally regarded as the 'dregs' of the SS, into well-trained soldiers, though the treatment they meted out to the inmates of the camps scarcely improved. Gradually, using his own 'sources', Eicke secured weapons and equipment for his men (the Army had refused to train or equip the *Totenkopf* units). In recognition of his efforts to improve the quality and morale of his troops, Himmler appointed Eicke to the post of Inspector of Concentration Camps.

By the outbreak of war, all of Eicke's troops had received full military training and had been formed into a division, the *Totenkopf Division*, organised along traditional military lines. The division performed moderately well during the Campaign in France, despite being equipped with second-rate weapons and transport, but was involved in a serious war crime when *Totenkopf* troops murdered a number of surrendered British soldiers in a farmhouse at Le Paradis.

On the invasion of the Soviet Union, Eicke's troops operated on the northern sector of the front, earning considerable respect for its part in the defence of the Demjansk pocket during the winter of 1941/2. Eicke was decorated with the Knight's Cross of the Iron Cross on 26 December 1941 for his leadership of the *Totenkopf Division*. The division was constantly thrown into critical sectors of the front where the fighting was heaviest, and although it considerably enhanced its fighting reputation during this period, it suffered horrendous losses in doing so. When finally withdrawn from the front for refitting, it had been reduced to just over 6,000 men.

In recognition of the achievements and sacrifices made by his men, Eicke was decorated with the Oakleaves to his Knight's Cross on 20 April 1942.

On 26 February 1943, Eicke was airborne in a Fieseler Storch light aircraft carrying out an inspection flight when his plane was attacked and shot down by Soviet fighter aircraft. Eicke was killed, but thanks to the determined efforts of his men, his body was recovered from behind enemy lines and interred in a military cemetery near Orelka.

SS-Panzergrenadier Regiment 6 was given the title 'Theodor Eicke' in honour of their former divisional commander.

SS-OBERGRUPPENFÜHRER ARTUR PHLEPS

Artur Phleps was born on 29 November 1881 in Siebenburgen, part of the old Austro-Hungarian Empire that after 1919 became part of Romania. He was a career soldier who served with distinction in the First World War, and after his homeland was ceded to Romania, he played a prominent part in the modernisation of the Romanian Army, becoming an instructor at the Military Academy in Bucharest. He was promoted to the rank of *General* and given command of a division. His true loyalty, however, lay not with his new Romanian masters but with his Germanic roots.

SS-Obergruppenführer Artur Phleps, first commander of 7 SS-Gebirgs Division Prinz Eugen. Phleps was a career soldier who had previously served in the Army of the Austro-Hungarian Empire.

Disturbed by the Romanian treatment of the ethnic German minority, once the Balkans came under German influence in 1941, he resigned his commission and moved to Germany.

Phleps was readily accepted into the *Waffen-SS* and initially joined the *Wiking Division* as a supernumerary officer on the divisional staff. He was eventually given command of the *Westland* Regiment within the division. His performance was such that

he soon came to the attention of the commander of the Army division to which his regiment was attached, *General* von Mackensen. Mackensen attempted to persuade Phleps to transfer to the Army, where he was assured of a divisional command. In the event, however, Himmler was to promote Phleps to *SS-Gruppenführer* and entrust him with the task of forming a new division for the *Waffen-SS*. This unit, to become the *7 SS-Freiwilligen Gebirgs Division Prinz Eugen*, was to be manned by volunteers from among the ethnic German or 'Volksdeutsche' communities in Hungary, Romania and Yugoslavia. The unit was to be tasked principally with combating the menace in Yugoslavia coming from both the Communist partisans under Tito and the Royalist partisans under Mihailovic. Phleps was to be decorated with the Knight's Cross on 4 July 1943 for his leadership of the division. He was subsequently promoted to *Obergruppenführer* and relinquished command of the *Prinz Eugen* to form *V SS-Gebirgskorps*.

By September 1944, the situation in the Balkans had significantly worsened. Although the Royalist partisans were no longer a major threat, Tito's partisans had not been vanquished and still posed a serious threat, to say nothing of the rapidly approaching Red Army.

With uncertainty as to the exact strength and disposition of approaching enemy troops, Phleps and his adjutant decided to carry out a forward reconnaissance. While passing through one village they were caught unawares by a Soviet armoured unit and captured. Unaware of the significance of their captives, the Soviets executed them during the course of a *Luftwaffe* attack on the advancing Russians.

Phleps was initially only posted as missing in action, but his Knight's Cross and some of his uniform insignia were eventually recovered and accepted as evidence of his death. On 24 November 1944, the Oakleaves to the Knight's Cross were posthumously bestowed upon Artur Phleps, and were accepted in his name by his son, who also served in the *Waffen-SS*. As a further honour, *SS-Freiwilligen Gebirgs Regiment* was named 'Artur Phleps' and granted the privilege of wearing a cuffband with his name.

SS-GRUPPENFÜHRER HERMANN-OTTO FEGELEIN

Born on 30 October 1906 in Ansbach, Hermann Fegelein entered the Army at the age of nineteen when he joined *Kavallerie Regiment 17*. As well as regular military service, he fought with the volunteer *Freikorps* units on Germany's eastern borders, and also served for a time in the Bavarian police.

In 1933, Fegelein joined the *Allgemeine-SS*, his cavalry roots leading him to join the *Reiter-SS*, or Mounted SS. Fegelein was an accomplished equestrian and in fact represented Germany during the 1936 Olympics. He also became commander of the *SS-Kavallerie Schule* in Munich. When it was decided to form the first organised cavalry units of the SS, their creation fell to Hermann Fegelein, the manpower being taken from elements of the *SS-Totenkopfverbände*.

On the outbreak of war against the Soviet Union, the SS Cavalry Brigade were considered ideal for the pursuit of the large numbers of Red Army stragglers and partisans cut off behind German lines. Many of these enemy troops had made their way into the forests and swamps where regular Army troops would have difficulty following and whence they could threaten German lines of communications and essential supplies. The SS cavalry, supported by two SS motorised infantry brigades, were ideally

Hermann Fegelein, seen here as an *SS-Oberführer*. Fegelein came to an ignominious end, executed by SS guards in the garden of the *Reichskanzlei* in the closing days of the war.

suited for this task. The fighting was extremely bitter, with quarter rarely given by either side, and losses were heavy, but eventually the German supply lines were made safe from the considerable threat posed by these enemy troops. For his leadership of the SS cavalry during these long and bitter battles Fegelein was awarded the Knight's Cross on 2 March 1942 and the Oakleaves on 25 December 1942.

liaison officer at Hitler's headquarters. He met and married Margarete Braun, the sister of Hitler's mistress, Eva Braun, and became a part of Hitler's entourage. Fegelein was ultimately given command of the newly formed *8 SS-Kavallerie Division Florian Geyer* and on 30 July 1944 received the Swords to his Oakleaves, before returning to serve as a liaison officer at the *Führerhauptquartier* once again.

As the war drew to a close, Fegelein became conspicuous by his absence from Hitler's bunker. A search team sent to locate him found him in civilian clothes, ready to escape the crumbling Reich with a large sum of Swiss francs and various pieces of jewellery. His marriage to Eva Braun's sister might yet have saved him, and indeed initial pleas for clemency on his behalf by Eva Braun were successful. Unfortunately for Fegelein, Himmler's own unauthorised peace feelers then became known to Hitler. This, plus the fact that he was about to abandon his pregnant wife and her sister while making good his own escape, and the fact that some of the jewellery he was making off with appeared to have been stolen from Eva Braun, meant that there was no longer anyone prepared to plead or intercede on his behalf. Hitler had him taken into the gardens of the garden of the *Reichskanzlei* (Reich Chancellery) in Berlin and shot by SS guards on 28 April 1945.

SS-Brigadeführer Heinz Harmel, one of the better divisional commanders of the *Waffen-SS*. Harmel commanded *10 SS-Panzer Division Frundsberg*. Greatly admired by his men, he maintained close contact with his former *Frundsberg* soldiers until the day he died.

Fegelein's younger brother Waldemar, also an accomplished equestrian, joined his elder sibling in the SS Cavalry and indeed became a regimental commander in the same division. Waldemar was also to become a recipient of the Knight's Cross, presented to him personally by Himmler on 21 December 1943.

Hermann Fegelein's true notoriety stemmed from his appointment as an SS

SS-BRIGADEFÜHRER HEINZ HARMEL

Heinz Harmel was yet another high-ranking SS officer who came from a military background. He was born on 29 June 1906 in Metz, his father a general in the Army Medical Corps. After working for some time as a farming administrator, he enlisted into the *SS-Verfügungstruppe* in 1938 and soon thereafter gained a commission in the *Der Führer* Regiment. During the Campaign in the West, Harmel commanded *II Bataillon* of the regiment, earning himself the Iron Cross in both Second and First Classes, and equally importantly, earning the trust and respect of his men. A true soldier's soldier, Harmel commanded the *Deutschland* Regiment on the Eastern Front and was always to be found at the front with his men.

He did not suffer fools gladly and equally despised unnecessary red tape. On one occasion one of his men discovered that his Dutch girlfriend was pregnant. At this time, each application from an SS man to marry had to be personally approved by Himmler. Harmel ignored the proper channels and gave his young soldier his personal permission to marry. On discovering what had happened, Himmler complained bitterly to Harmel's superior, Paul Hausser, about this unacceptable insubordination. Fortunately Hausser was too good a soldier himself to consider an infraction of a petty bureaucratic rule as being of significance, and Harmel's career did not suffer. He was decorated with the Knight's Cross of the Iron Cross on 31 March 1943, with the Oakleaves following on 7 September.

By April 1944, Harmel had been promoted to the rank of *SS-Brigadeführer* and given command of the newly formed *10 SS-Panzer Division Frundsberg*. Harmel commanded the division during the battle for Normandy, in which it was badly mauled. Ordered to Holland for rest and recuperation, *Frundsberg* found itself just outside the town of Arnhem and suddenly became embroiled in one of the most fiercely contested battles of the war, as Allied airborne units attempted to punch their way through the German lines and capture the strategically important bridge over the Rhine. Harmel's troops conducted themselves with a degree of chivalry during this hard-fought battle, granting a ceasefire to allow the recovery of the wounded and treating the British paratroopers who were captured with considerable respect.

Harmel was subsequently awarded the Swords to his Oakleaves on 28 November 1944. He commanded his division through many difficult defensive battles on the Eastern Front in the final phase of the war before being relieved of command in April 1945 by the fanatical Nazi *Generalfeldmarschall* Schörner for refusing to sacrifice his beloved *Frundsberg Division* in a suicidal last stand.

Sent to Carinthia, his final orders were to build a defence line to withstand the Allied advance. With a small number of second-rate, under-strength and badly equipped troops, he nevertheless fulfilled his task well enough to completely halt the British advance in this area until the end of the war.

Postwar, Harmel became a successful businessman, but never lost touch with the veterans of his division. It was said that no 'Frundsberger' turning up at Harmel's door would ever be turned away as unwelcome. He took a great interest in the welfare of all former members of his division and was said to keep a card index file with notes on every surviving *Frundsberger* he could trace. One of his former drivers, a mere private, was astonished when, after undergoing surgery many years after the war, he received a call from 'his' general asking if all had gone well.

Despite advancing age and infirmity, Harmel attended every reunion of former *Frundsbergers* that he could, and his arrival inevitably resulted in him being surrounded by swarms of his former soldiers eager to wish him well.

Heinz Harmel died peacefully in 2000 at the age of ninety-four.

SS-BRIGADEFÜHRER OTTO KUMM

Otto Kumm was born on 1 October 1909 in Hamburg, and served with the *Germania* Regiment prior to the outbreak of war. He was decorated with both the Second Class and First Class Iron Crosses during the Campaign in the West, and during the Campaign in Russia served first as a battalion, then as a regimental, commander with the *Der Führer* Regiment.

SS-Brigadeführer Otto Kumm, who succeeded Artur Phleps as commander of *7 SS-Gebirgs Division Prinz Eugen*. His successes earnt him the Oakleaves with Swords to the Knight's Cross. He ultimately commanded the elite *Leibstandarte* in the closing stages of the war.

He rapidly gained a reputation as a daring and resourceful officer and was highly respected by his men. On 16 February 1942, he was decorated with the Knight's Cross of the Iron Cross for his leadership of the regiment on the Eastern Front. The Oakleaves followed on 8 April 1943, being presented by Hitler personally. Shortly thereafter this accomplished officer was transferred to the divisional staff of the newly formed *7 SS-Freiwilligen Gebirgs Division Prinz Eugen*, and when the divisional commander Artur Phleps was promoted to command *V SS-Gebirgskorps*, Kumm was given command of the division, leading his troops in the war against Tito's partisans, for which he was awarded the Swords to his Oakleaves on 17 March 1945.

In the last few days of the war, Kumm was to become the last commander of the elite *Leibstandarte SS Adolf Hitler*, a testament to his abilities.

SS-BRIGADEFÜHRER KURT MEYER

Born in Jerxheim on 23 December 1910, Kurt Meyer was to become one of the most charismatic figures in the *Waffen-SS*. Originally a police officer, he joined the elite *Leibstandarte SS Adolf Hitler* in 1934 and participated in both the Polish Campaign, where he was decorated with the Iron Cross Second Class, and the Western Campaign, where he added the Iron Cross First Class to his awards. He quickly established a reputation for daring and élan and was very popular with the troops he commanded. His name came to prominence during the Campaign in the Balkans, where, as an *SS-Obersturmbannführer*, he commanded the *Panzeraufklärungs Abteilung* of the *Leibstandarte* and took part in the capture

Kurt Meyer, known to his men as 'Panzermeyer', shown here just after the investiture of his Oakleaves. Meyer was captured during the fighting in Normandy and survived the war, though he was imprisoned until 1954 because of allegations of atrocities committed by troops under his command.

of the Klidi Pass in Greece before pressing on towards Lake Castoria. The *Leibstandarte* faced stiff resistance when trying to traverse the Klissura Pass. The rapidly advancing infantry had outpaced their heavy support weapons, and their advance began to bog down in the face of heavy fire from Greek machine-gun nests. Meyer realised that the situation would rapidly become critical unless he could encourage his men to press home their attack. This he did by the rather extreme expedient of

lobbing hand grenades just behind his own troops. The startled SS infantry suddenly found the will to leave their positions behind cover and rushed forward towards the Greek positions. The enemy positions were overrun and passage through the Klissura Pass was secured. On 20 April 1941, the Greek III Army surrendered to the *Leibstandarte*'s commander, *SS-Obergruppenführer* Sepp Dietrich. For his part in the *Leibstandarte*'s success, Meyer was decorated with the Knight's Cross of the Iron Cross on 18 May 1941.

Following the invasion of the Soviet Union, Meyer continued his command of the *Panzeraufklärungs Abteilung* during the advance through southern Russia, by Uman, Cherson, Taganrog and at the crossing of the River Don at Rostov. On 23 May 1943, Meyer, now commonly known to his men as 'Panzermeyer', was decorated with the Oakleaves to his Knight's Cross.

Soon afterwards, Himmler having approved the formation of a new panzer division recruited from members of the Hitler Youth, it was decided to transfer a cadre of experienced combat veterans from the *Leibstandarte* to form the solid core around which this new division, *12 SS-Panzer Division Hitlerjugend*, would be built. Meyer was to be one of these veterans, and was given command of *SS-Panzergrenadier Regiment 25*. Meyer, though strict, was a very fair commander, and took great pains to ensure that the welfare of the teenage boys that formed the bulk of his regiment was given full consideration. He often interceded in disciplinary matters if he felt that the cause of the offence was a matter of the offender's immaturity rather than indiscipline.

Meyer's young grenadiers gave an excellent account of themselves during the battles following the allied invasion of Normandy, seriously delaying the Allied advance, though only at the cost of horrendous losses. The Divisional Commander, *SS-Brigadeführer* Fritz Witt, was killed on 16 June 1944 during a bombardment of the German positions by heavy artillery from Allied warships moored off the invasion beaches. Kurt Meyer was promoted to the rank of *SS-Brigadeführer* and given command of the *Hitlerjugend* Division. On 27 August 1944, he was decorated with the Swords to his Oakleaves. Meyer successfully led his division through the retreat from Normandy. On 6 September he was seriously wounded. Shortly afterwards he fell into the hands of Belgian partisans. Only the intervention of American troops prevented his immediate execution by the partisans. Handed over to the British, he was hospitalised and his wounds treated.

After the end of the war, Meyer was placed on trial before a Canadian court, charged with complicity in the murder of Canadian prisoners of war by soldiers under his command. Though both sides committed atrocities of this type, the charges laid against Meyer were certainly valid, as there is no doubt that Canadian soldiers were murdered by members of his division. Meyer was found guilty and sentenced to death. There was an element of unease about the sentence, however, especially as it was known that Canadian troops were also responsible for the execution of German prisoners. Many pleas for clemency were made on his behalf, and the sentence was finally reduced to life imprisonment. Some years later he was transferred to a prison in Werl, Germany, and thereafter, in poor health, he was finally released in September 1954.

Kurt Meyer died of a heart attack on 23 December 1960 while celebrating his fiftieth birthday at home.

SS-OBERFÜHRER WILHELM MOHNKE

Born on 15 March 1911 in Lübeck, Schleswig-Holstein, Wilhelm Mohnke was a fanatical supporter of the Nazis and was one of the very early members of the *Leibstandarte SS Adolf Hitler*. He was a stern disciplinarian who made no attempt to bond with his men, and he was not well liked.

Mohnke first gained notoriety during the Campaign in the West in 1940 when men under his command executed British prisoners, predominantly from the Royal

Wilhelm Mohnke, seen here as an *SS-Standartenführer*, was one of the more unpleasant characters in the *Waffen-SS*, with several allegations of atrocities made against him. Despite this he was never prosecuted after the war.

Warwickshires, at the small village of Wormhoudt near Dunkirk. The British prisoners were herded into a barn into which were thrown hand-grenades, and the survivors were machine-gunned. From the group of around ninety prisoners, fifteen survived to give testimony against the SS troops who carried out the atrocity.

Mohnke served with the *Leibstandarte* throughout the Balkan Campaign and the early Campaigns in Russia before being transferred as a regimental commander to the *12 SS-Panzer Division Hitlerjugend* in 1943. He was firmly implicated in the shooting of the Canadian prisoners of war which led to Panzermeyer's postwar trial. On 11 July 1944, Mohnke received the Knight's Cross in recognition of the achievements and sacrifices of his *Hitlerjugend* grenadiers during the battles in Normandy.

After the severe wounding of the commander of the *Leibstandarte*, *SS-Brigadeführer* Fritz Witt, Mohnke was given temporary command of the division. Once again, he was heavily implicated in war crimes, alleged to be the officer who gave the order to take no prisoners, which led to the execution of a number of American prisoners during the so-called Malmedy massacre.

In the closing days of the war, Mohnke commanded *Hitler's Reichskanzlei* guards and, a fanatical supporter of Hitler to the end, is reported to have wept openly when Hitler committed suicide. He was captured by the Russians while trying to escape Berlin and was held in captivity until October 1955. Released from prison, he returned to his native Schleswig-Holstein, where, despite the serious charges laid against him, no attempt seems to have been made to bring him to trial for the murder of British, Canadian and American troops by soldiers under his command, and reputedly on his specific orders. Despite several attempts by

British newspapers to regenerate interest in bringing him to justice, he was never prosecuted and lived in near Hamburg until his death in 2000. Unlike many of his peers who were held in high regard by their men, Mohnke was a thoroughly unpleasant man who seemed to have few friends.

SS-OBERFÜHRER KARL ULLRICH

Karl Ullrich was born on 1 December 1910 in Saargemünde. A highly intelligent and well-educated man, he was a graduate engineer and joined the *SS-Pioniersturmbann*

Karl Ullrich as an *SS-Oberführer*, the rank with which he commanded the elite *5 SS-Panzer Division Wiking* in the closing stages of the war.

Ullrich is shown here as an *SS-Obersturmbannführer* and commander of *III Bataillon, SS-Regiment Theodor Eicke*. He was promoted to *SS-Standartenführer* shortly after this photograph was taken.

of the *SS-Verfügungstruppe* in Dresden in 1934. Within a year, his potential was quickly realised by his superiors, and he was sent to the *SS-Junkerschule Braunschweig* for officer training and was commissioned as an *SS-Untersturmführer*.

On the outbreak of war, he served as commander of 3 Company of the *SS-Pionierbataillon* in the *SS-Verfügungs* Division, winning the Iron Cross in both Second and First Classes during the Campaign in the West. Promoted to *SS-Sturmbannführer*, he was given command of the *Pionierbataillon* of *3 SS-Panzer Division Totenkopf*. As commander of a small battle group serving on the northern sector of the Russian Front during the winter of 1941/2, he displayed outstanding qualities of leadership and personal gallantry, which brought him the award of the Knight's Cross of the Iron Cross on 19 February 1942. When informed of the award, the ever pragmatic Ullrich retorted, 'I would rather have some reinforcements!' Ullrich took part in the determined and successful defence of the Demjansk pocket in the face of over-whelming enemy numbers.

In 1943, he was given command of *III Bataillon, SS-Panzergrenadier Regiment 6 Theodor Eicke*, and shortly thereafter was promoted to *SS-Standartenführer* and given command of the whole regiment. On 14 May 1944 Ullrich received the Oakleaves to his Knight's Cross from Hitler personally, in recognition of the performance of the troops under his command.

In October 1944, promoted to the rank of *SS-Oberführer*, Ullrich was given command of *5 SS-Panzer Division Wiking*, and led this elite unit during the desperate defensive battles as the German were pushed out of Hungary and through Czechoslovakia. Ullrich and his unit surrendered to the Red Army on 8 May 1945. At the time of writing, he is still alive.

SS-STANDARTENFÜHRER JOACHIM PEIPER

One of the most controversial figures to emerge from the ranks of the *Waffen-SS*, Joachim 'Jochen' Peiper was born in Berlin on 30 January 1915, the son of an Army officer. At the age of just nineteen, he volunteered for service in the elite *Leibstandarte SS Adolf Hitler* and was commissioned as an *SS-Untersturmführer* after attending the *SS-Junkerschule Braunschweig*. From 1938 to 1939 he served as an adjutant on the personal staff of *Reichsführer-SS* Heinrich Himmler, and on the outbreak of war, he served with the *Leibstandarte* during the Campaign in the West, winning both Second and First Class Iron Crosses.

During the Campaign on the Russian Front, Peiper gained a considerable reputation for personal gallantry and almost reckless daring. On one occasion in 1943, serving as an *SS-Sturmbannführer* in command of *III Bataillon, SS-Panzergrenadier Regiment 2*, he led his unit, mounted in half-tracked armoured personnel carriers, deep behind enemy lines to rescue a stranded Army unit, and inflicted punishing losses on the Soviet units which tried to prevent the German escape. On 9 March 1943, he was decorated with the Knight's Cross of the Iron Cross for his actions.

Promoted to *SS-Standartenführer*, he was given command of *1 SS-Panzer Regiment* and led this armoured unit with the same élan as he had his *Panzergrenadiere*. Peiper became an extremely popular and respected commander, renowned for leading his men 'from the front' and never asking them to do something he would not do himself. On 27 January 1944 he was decorated with the Oakleaves to his Knight's Cross for his command of the panzer regiment.

Peiper's rise to notoriety came during the Ardennes Offensive, known as the Battle of

Joachim 'Jochen' Peiper, one of the most controversial of *Waffen-SS* officers. Even today, former soldiers who served under his command exhibit a fierce loyalty to *'Der Peiper'*. He was murdered at his home in France in 1976.

the Bulge. Peiper commanded a battlegroup, or *Kampfgruppe*, of the super-heavy *Königstiger* tanks. Awesome vehicles though they were, these monsters were not particularly suitable for movement through the densely forested Ardennes with its narrow winding roads. Nevertheless, Peiper initially made good progress, wreaking havoc wherever his *Königstiger* appeared. While Peiper and his battle group spearheaded the German attack, elements of *SS-Panzer Regiment 1* were passing through the road junction at Malmedy

when SS troops opened fire at a large group of disarmed US prisoners.

Peiper's initial progress soon slowed and finally ground to a halt as fuel supplies ran out and clearing weather allowed Allied fighter-bombers to launch highly effective attacks against the German armour. For his leadership of *Kampfgruppe Peiper* during the Ardennes Offensive, Peiper received the Swords to his Oakleaves on 11 January 1945.

In the aftermath of the Malmedy incident, however, investigations had already begun into the units responsible, and at the end of the war in Europe, the senior officers of the *Leibstandarte*, including Peiper, were arrested by the Americans. Trials were held at Dachau in 1946, and despite the fact that Peiper was many miles away from the scene when the Malmedy incident occurred, he was held responsible for the actions of those under his command and was sentenced to death. Afterwards, however, it became known that confessions and witness testimony had been obtained using both physical and psychological torture, and considerable controversy grew over the trials. Ultimately, the sentence on Peiper was commuted to life imprison-ment, and he was released in December 1956 having spent ten years in prison. After his release, Peiper lived in Germany for fourteen more years before moving to the quiet French town of Traves, where he undertook translating work for a publishing house.

But he began to receive death threats from French Communist groups, though initially he did not take these too seriously. He was, after all, living quite legally in France, having been granted a residence permit by the French authorities, who were perfectly well aware of his identity.

As things deteriorated, however, he decided to send his wife to safety in Germany. Determined that he himself would not be driven out of his home by such threats, he remained, with his shotgun for protection and with the company of his faithful dog. Then, on the night of 13 July 1976, armed intruders attacked his home. His dog was shot, Peiper was murdered and his home set on fire. No one has ever been charged in connection with his murder.

To this day, Peiper is held in the highest regard by his surviving comrades, many of whom still talk in awe of *'Der Peiper'*.

SS-STANDARTENFÜHRER OTTO SKORZENY

Once referred to as one of the world's most dangerous men, Otto Skorzeny was an Austrian, born in Vienna on 12 June 1908. A professional engineer, he had in fact first attempted to join the *Luftwaffe*, but this mountain of a man had great trouble manoeuvring himself in and out of an aircraft. He therefore joined the *Waffen-SS* and served on the Eastern Front with the *Leibstandarte* until he returned home, as he had picked up an illness and been seriously wounded. He was regraded fit for service on the home front only. Thanks to a fortuitous meeting with Dr Ernst Kaltenbrünner, a fellow Austrian and chief of the SD Security Police, Skorzeny was recommended as a suitable person to form a new SS commando unit for special operations, a job for which Skorzeny, as events would prove, was eminently suitable. Under Skorzeny's command, a special commando unit, with the code name Oranienburg, was formed under the auspices of the *Reichssicherheitshauptamt* in April of 1943.

The first major operation to be undertaken by this unit was the rescue mission to release the Italian dictator Mussolini from captivity. He was being held in a hotel on the Gran Sasso mountain some 100 miles north of Rome. All roads leading to the mountain were sealed by heavily armed Italian troops, and the mountain itself would take huge numbers of men to seize and almost certainly involve taking heavy losses. Skorzeny planned to land his troops by glider on a tiny flat patch on land among the rocky crags just by the hotel, and release Mussolini before his guards could eliminate him. He would then be taken off the mountain by funicular railway, the station at the base of the mountain having been seized by German paratroops. In the

Otto Skorzeny, here seen as an *SS-Sturmbannführer*, was a giant of a man, with an impressive duelling scar on his cheek. He gained notoriety as commander of numerous special-forces-type commando operations, the most famous of which was the rescue of Mussolini from the Grand Sasso in 1943.

dropped because of communication problems, and another, for a light aircraft to land in the valley below, went wrong when the light plane damaged its undercarriage on landing. In the end, it was decided to take the very risky option of actually landing a light plane on the mountain itself. Even though the Germans had a superb aircraft, capable of very short take-offs and landings, in the Fieseler Storch, putting this plane down on the mountain top would require extraordinary skill. Having landed, the pilot then faced an even bigger problem – taking off, with the combined weight of Mussolini and the giant Skorzeny! Hurtling over the edge of the plateau, the Storch nosedived, and was only brought up into level flight 200 feet from the valley floor. For his daring rescue of the Italian dictator, Otto Skorzeny was decorated with the Knight's Cross of the Iron Cross on 13 September 1943.

Skorzeny's subsequent exploits included an abortive attempt to snatch the Yugoslav partisan leader Tito, the snatching of Nicholas Horthy, son of the Hungarian regent, in a successful coup which prevented Hungary changing sides, leading a detachment of English-speaking German troops in American uniforms, used to spread chaos in the German advance through the Ardennes during the offensive of December 1944, and conducting a highly successful, if temporary, defence of Schwedt on the Oder against overwhelming Soviet forces. Skorzeny was decorated with the Oakleaves to his Knight's Cross on 8 March 1945.

Skorzeny's last orders were to join the forces which were intended to hold a last-ditch defence of the so-called 'Alpine Redoubt', a fantasy idea which never came to fruition. As soon as he received the news that the war had ended, Skorzeny presented himself to the nearest Allied soldiers and surrendered. In 1947, he was tried by a military court on a charge relating to his

event the Italian defenders were taken completely by surprise and Skorzeny's commandos soon had the mountain top in their control. Unfortunately, the original plan to leave the mountain by the funicular railway and then escape by road was now considered too risky. One alternative plan, to make for a local airfield in German hands and be evacuated by aircraft, was

men fighting in US uniforms during the Ardennes Offensive, but was acquitted. He subsequently moved to Spain and set up home in Madrid, where he became a highly successful businessman. He died in 1975.

SS-OBERSTURMBANNFÜHRER OTTO WEIDINGER

Otto Weidinger was born on 24 May 1914 in Würzburg. At the age of twenty, he enlisted in the *SS-Verfügungstruppe* and was commissioned as an *SS-Untersturmführer* after attending the *SS-Junkerschule Braunschweig.* He joined the *SS-Regiment Deutschland* in Ellwangen, serving as a platoon commander. He also attended training for combat pioneers, before returning to his regiment to participate in the occupation of Austria. He subsequently spent three months on attachment with an Army unit before being assigned to the *Kradschützen Abteilung* of the *Deutschland* Regiment. With this same unit, he served in the Polish Campaign, winning the Iron Cross Second Class. The First Class followed during the Campaign in the West, by the end of which he had been appointed divisional adjutant to the *SS-Verfügungsdivision.*

Promoted to *SS-Hauptsturmführer* in July 1940, he also served during the Balkan Campaign. In the summer of 1941, Weidinger was given command of the heavy company of the *Kradschützenbataillon* on the Eastern Front, following the invasion of the Soviet Union, before briefly returning to *SS-Junkerschule Braunschweig,* where he served as a tactics instructor.

Weidinger returned to the front in June 1943, having been promoted to the rank of *SS-Sturmbannführer,* and took command of *I Bataillon, SS-Regiment Deutschland* and found himself in the thick of the bitter fighting in the Kursk salient. During August he was severely wounded by grenade shrapnel during fierce hand-to-hand fighting. His personal gallantry and exemplary leadership brought him the award of the German Cross in Gold on 26 November 1943.

In late 1943, the *Das Reich* Division, of which Weidinger's regiment was part, was withdrawn from the front for conversion to a full panzer division. Weidinger, however, remained at the front with a *Das Reich Kampfgruppe,* in command of an *SS-Panzergrenadier* regiment. For distinguished achievements at the battles around Cherkassy

SS-Obersturmbannführer Otto Weidinger. He commanded the *Der Führer* Regiment and was decorated with the Oakleaves and Swords to the Knight's Cross.

and Tarnopol, Weidinger was decorated with the Knight's Cross on 21 April 1944.

Subsequently promoted to *SS-Obersturmbannführer*, on 14 June 1944 he was given command of *SS-Panzergrenadier Regiment 4 Der Führer*, which he commanded during the battles in Normandy, in particular the actions around Saint Lô, Coutances and Mortain, and the retreat through the Falaise Gap, earning himself the Oakleaves to his Knight's Cross. The award was bestowed on 26 December 1944.

After taking part in the ill-fated Ardennes Offensive, Weidinger and his regiment were once against sent eastwards, and took part in the defence of Hungary before being gradually pushed back into Austria. Commanding a *Kampfgruppe* on the Eastern Front in the closing stages of the war, Weidinger received the Swords to his Oakleaves on 6 May 1945.

Brought before a French court after the war for investigation into any involvement in the massacres at Tulle and Oradour, Otto Weidinger was acquitted of all charges. He subsequently wrote of his wartime experience in his book *Kameraden bis zum Ende* (Comrades to the End), and his definitive history, *Division Das Reich*, and he was elected President of the Division's Veterans' Organisation.

Always generous with his time in answering questions from students of military history, Weidinger died at his home in Aalen on 10 January 1990 at the age of seventy-five.

SS-OBERSTURMBANNFÜHRER MAX WÜNSCHE

Born on 20 April 1914 in Kittlitz, Saxony, Max Wünsche enlisted into the *SS-Verfügungstruppe* in 1934 and was commissioned to *SS-Untersturmführer* in 1936.

Max Wünsche, seen here as an *SS-Sturmbannführer*, was a veteran of the elite *Leibstandarte*. He was ultimately given command of the panzer regiment of the newly formed *12 SS-Panzer Division Hitlerjugend* in 1944, was captured in Normandy, and survived the war.

Wünsche had clearly made a good impression on his superiors, as from 1938 to 1940 he was assigned as a personal orderly to Hitler, and the photogenic young officer can be seen hovering in the background of many famous photographs taken during this period.

Returning to combat duty for the Campaign in the West, Wünsche took command of a company of motorised infantry of the elite *Leibstandarte SS Adolf Hitler*, earning himself the Iron Cross Second and First Classes within just five days of each other.

For the Campaign in the Balkans, Wünsche was posted as the divisional adjutant before being given command of the *Sturmgeschutz Abteilung*. After undergoing staff officer training, Wünsche was reassigned, this time to command *I Abteilung* of *SS-Panzer Regiment 1*, and he was to remain a 'tanker' for the rest of his career. He was greatly admired by his troops for his personal bravery, and was decorated with the Knight's Cross on 28 January 1943.

Wünsche was considered an ideal candidate for transfer to the new *12 SS-Panzer Division Hitlerjugend* when this was formed in 1943, and with the promoted rank of *SS-Obersturmbannführer*, he was given the task of forming and commanding the panzer regiment of the new division. His panzer troops fought exceptionally well in the hard-contested battles in Normandy, and in particular around Caen and at Hill 112. Wünsche and his men played a critical part in keeping open the Falaise Gap, and thus allowing vast numbers of German troops to escape encirclement and capture. He was decorated with the Oakleaves to his Knight's Cross on 11 August 1944 and promoted to *SS-Standartenführer*.

On 14 August 1944, Wünsche was captured and went into British captivity, remaining a prisoner of war until 1948. After a long illness, Max Wünsche died on 17 April 1995.

SS-STURMBANNFÜHRER HEINZ MACHER

Heinz Macher was a Saxon, born in Chemnitz on 31 December 1919. On completing his compulsory service in the *Reichs Arbeits Dienst* (Labour Corps), he enlisted in the *SS-Verfügungstruppe*, joining the *SS-Pionierbataillon* in Dresden. He served as an NCO during the Polish Campaign, and was selected for officer training. On completing training at the *SS-Junkerschule* at Bad Tölz he was commissioned as an *SS-Untersturmführer*.

In March 1943, Macher commanded an assault group from *16 (Pioniere) Kompanie* of the *Deutschland* Regiment during an attack on Kharkov. The Germans had been halted by a wide anti-tank ditch in front of the Soviet positions. Under cover of darkness, Macher's combat engineers attacked across the ditch and established a bridgehead some 300 m deep into enemy territory and killing or capturing over a hundred enemy troops as well as seizing a substantial number of enemy weapons. Not one single German soldier was lost during this audacious action. Macher was decorated with the Knight's Cross of the Iron Cross for his achievement.

On the Western Front, during the Normandy battles of summer 1944, Macher's men were responsible for repulsing over thirty enemy attacks in just eight days, and they launched almost as many counter-attacks of their own. On 19 August 1944, Macher became the 554th recipient of the Oakleaves.

Serious wounds Macher had received resulted in him being transferred from the front to a unit specialising in the testing of explosives. At the end of March 1945 Macher and his *Pioniere* were summoned to meet *Reichsführer-SS* Heinrich Himmler, who entrusted them with the destruction of his castle at Wewelsburg. This was a semi-derelict structure that Himmler had restored at great expense in an attempt to create a latter-day Germanic 'Camelot', complete with a round table for the SS 'Knights'.

Heinz Macher is seen here as an *SS-Obersturmführer*. He commanded the combat engineer detachment of the *Das Reich Division* and was Himmler's personal bodyguard in the closing days of the war.

Macher thereafter remained with Himmler's entourage, providing a bodyguard of tough battle-hardened SS combat engineers. Macher was with Himmler when the leader of the SS, disguised as a humble Army sergeant, was taken into British custody. Macher and his men were also taken prisoner.

SS-STURMBANNFÜHRER HEINRICH SPRINGER

Heinrich Springer was born on 3 November 1914 in Eckernförde, near Kiel. At the age of twenty-three, he volunteered for the *SS-Verfügungstruppe,* serving with the *SS-Standarten Germania* and *Der Führer.* He participated in the occupation of Austria and the Sudetenland before commencing officer training at the *SS-Junkerschule* at Bad Tölz in Bavaria. On completion of his training, in October 1939, he was commissioned as an *SS-Untersturmführer* in the elite *Leibstandarte SS Adolf Hitler.*

As a platoon commander during the French Campaign, Springer was decorated with the Iron Cross Second Class. By July of 1941, Springer was serving as adjutant to *I Bataillon* of the *Leibstandarte.* During this period, Springer was decorated with the Iron Cross First Class for leading a successful patrol deep behind enemy lines.

By November 1941, the *Leibstandarte* was involved in an assault on Rostov, on the River Don. On 20 November 1941, Springer, by now an *SS-Hauptsturmführer* and company commander, led an attack over the Don Bridge, which had already been prepared with demolition charges, fending off enemy counter-attacks until the bridge was secured. The capture of this bridge played a significant part in the successful capture of Rostov, and for his role in this action Springer was decorated with the Knight's

SS-Sturmbannführer Heinrich Springer. He was decorated with the Knight's Cross for the capture of a vital bridge over the River Don at Rostov. Thereafter he served on the staff of the *Hitlerjugend Division* and as an orderly officer on the staff of *Generalfeldmarschall* Model.

Cross. He had been seriously wounded in further combat actions on the day following the capture of the bridge, and received his Knight's Cross and its formal award document personally from the *Leibstandarte's* commander, Sepp Dietrich, while recovering in hospital.

239

Officers of the *Leibstandarte* during a visit by the *Reichsführer-SS*, Heinrich Himmler. On the left is Heinrich Springer, followed by Sepp Dietrich, Joachim Peiper and Max Wünsche.

Springer returned to the front once he had recovered, and commanded *1 Kompanie, SS-Panzergrenadier Regiment 1* during the fighting at Taganrog. During the battle for Kharkov in March 1943 he received a serious head wound and was once again evacuated for hospital treatment. He was promoted to *SS-Sturmbannführer* and on his recovery was posted to the divisional staff of the new *12 SS-Panzer Division Hitlerjugend.*

In August 1944, Springer was posted as orderly officer to *Generalfeldmarschall* Walter Model, and was with Model's staff during the Allied airborne offensive at Arnhem. He remained a staff officer until the end of the war, when he was taken into British captivity.

After the war he returned to his civilian career as an architect, living in his native Schleswig-Holstein. He is still alive.

SS-HAUPTSTURMFÜHRER MICHAEL WITTMANN

One of the most famous of all *Waffen-SS* soldiers, Michael Wittmann was born on 22 April 1914 in Vogelthal. His family were farmers and Wittmann himself worked on his father's farm for a spell after completing his schooling. He joined the German Army in 1934 and completed two years of military service, reaching the rank of *Gefreiter.*

In April 1937, he volunteered for the *SS-Verfügungstruppe,* being accepted into the *Leibstandarte SS Adolf Hitler.* An *SS-Unterscharführer* by the outbreak of war, Wittmann commanded one of the first *Sturmgeschützen* (self-propelled assault guns) allocated to this elite unit. He quickly developed a reputation for being cool headed in action, and earned himself the Iron Cross Second Class on the Russian Front in July 1941, followed by the First Class just two months later. Having proved himself

an excellent leader, he was selected for officer training, and having completed the course at the *SS-Junkerschule* at Bad Tölz, he was commissioned as an *SS-Untersturmführer.* Shortly after his return to the *Leibstandarte,* he was transferred from the *Sturmgeschütze* to the newly established heavy Tiger tank detachment.

With this awesome new weapon at his disposal, Wittmann began his rise to fame with a steadily increasing score of enemy tanks destroyed. In one single day at the start of the great armoured offensive at Kursk in 1943, Wittmann destroyed eight enemy tanks and seven artillery pieces. By the end of the battle for Kursk, Wittmann had destroyed thirty enemy tanks and twenty-eight artillery pieces. In the autumn of that same year, Wittmann had another

SS-Hauptstürmführer Michael Wittmann. This legendary panzer commander is the most successful tank ace in history. Killed when his tank was outnumbered and taken out by a Sherman Firefly, it is predominantly his exploits which resulted in the awesome reputation of the Tiger tank.

particularly successful day, destroying ten enemy tanks in a single engagement, bringing his total score to sixty-six enemy tanks destroyed. On 13 January 1944, he was decorated with the Knight's Cross of the Iron Cross.

The death rate in the German panzer corps was high during these ferocious battles on the Russian Front, and few tank crewmen lived long enough to amass the levels of success that Wittmann enjoyed. Even more astonishing, therefore, was his subsequent achievement in increasing his score to eighty-eight enemy tanks destroyed only three weeks later. This brought the addition of the Oakleaves to his Knight's Cross, along with the personal congratulations of Adolf Hitler and a promotion to *SS-Obersturmführer*.

It was during the battles for Normandy following the Allied invasion of France in June 1944 that Wittmann was to take part in an action that was to earn him a place in history as the most successful tank commander of all time. On 13 June 1944, lead elements of the British 7 Armoured Division were approaching the French village of Villers Bocage. Their progress came to an abrupt halt, however, with the appearance of Wittmann and his Tiger. Knocking out the lead and tail vehicles in the enemy column, he proceeded along its length, destroying enemy armoured vehicles at almost point-blank range. The enemy tank shells, even at this short range, merely bounced off the thick armour of his Tiger. A total of twenty-five enemy armoured vehicles fell victim to Wittmann in this single engagement. Wittmann was only forced to withdraw when an enemy anti-tank gun disabled his Tiger.

This great propaganda victory brought Wittmann the Swords to his Oakleaves on 22 June 1944, and further promotion to *SS-Hauptsturmführer*. Wittmann's score had now risen to 138 enemy tanks and 132 artillery pieces destroyed.

Wittmann was then offered a posting as an instructor at a tank training school, where his undisputed skills could be put to good use training future tank crews. Wittmann refused to be parted from his comrades, however, and remained at the front.

On 8 August, Wittmann was ordered into action near Cintheaux in a mission to protect the flanks of *12 SS-Panzer Division Hitlerjugend*. The German tanks were intercepted by a squadron of Canadian Sherman tanks. Normally, the M4 Sherman would be no match for the Tiger. However, some of the Canadian tanks were the so-called Firefly variants mounting the superb 17-pounder gun, which was capable of eliminating even the formidable Tiger. The combined fire of up to five Shermans was too much even for Wittmann's Tiger, which took several direct hits and blew up, killing all the crew instantly.

Wittmann's remains were not discovered until 1983 during road-widening operations in the area. He is now interred in the cemetery at La Cambe.

SS-OBERSCHARFÜHRER ERNST BARKMANN

Another of the great panzer aces of the *Waffen-SS*, Ernst Barkmann, was born in Kisdorf, Holstein, in August 1919, and like his fellow ace Wittmann came from farming stock and worked on the family farm until he enlisted into the *SS-Verfügungstruppe* in April 1939. Barkmann joined the *SS-Standarte Germania* in Hamburg, eventually being posted to the *III Bataillon* in Radolfszell.

Barkmann began his career as an infantryman, serving as a machine-gunner during the Campaigns in Poland and

France. He was wounded in action during the early part of Operation Barbarossa, the invasion of the Soviet Union, and was decorated with the Iron Cross Second Class. On recovering from his wounds, he served for a time as an instructor before volunteering for transfer to the armoured regiment of the *Das Reich Division*. Barkmann earned the Iron Cross First Class during the battle for Kharkov. Promoted to *SS-Unterscharführer*, he was given command of one of the new PzKpfw V Panther medium tanks with which his battalion was being re-equipped.

In early 1944 the division was moved to the south of France for a period of rest and refitting, and was still there when the Allies landed in Normandy on 6 June. The division made the long march north, and by July was in action against US forces around Saint Lô. After so long on the Russian Front, on 8 July 1944 Barkmann knocked out his first US M4 Sherman tank. Over the days that followed Barkmann added several more enemy tanks to his score. On 26 July, nearby infantry warned Barkmann of the approach of an enemy armoured column. Manoeuvring his Panther into the shade of a large tree at a crossroads near the village of Le Lorey, Barkmann awaited the approaching enemy. As soon as the enemy came within sight, Barkmann opened fire, and soon the road was littered with blazing American vehicles, including tanks, half-tracks, trucks, petrol tankers and jeeps. The enemy called up a fighter-bomber strike to eliminate this lone Panther. A track was blown off, and the driver and radio operator's hatches jammed, trapping them inside. Despite the missing track, Barkmann's superb driver managed to manoeuvre the stricken Panther away, leaving at least nine enemy tanks among the numerous victims of this powerful armoured battlewagon. Barkmann and his

SS-Oberscharführer Ernst Barkmann is to the Panther tank what Wittmann was to the Tiger. Cool and calm under pressure, Barkmann and his Panther wrought havoc among enemy armour during the Normandy and Ardennes battles. He is still alive.

crew took eight days to reach the safety of their own lines. One month later, he was decorated with the Knight's Cross for his achievements.

Barkmann continued to serve with great distinction, adding significantly to his score of enemy tanks destroyed during the Ardennes Offensive. At one point, on 25 December, he suffered a head wound from shrapnel splinters. As soon as he had been treated for his wounds, he simply discharged himself from hospital and made his own way back to his unit.

SS-Oberscharführer Balthasar 'Bobbi' Woll. Panzer ace Michael Wittmann ensured that the credit for his many kills was shared with his gunner Bobbi Woll, and on his insistence Woll also received the Knight's Cross on 16 January 1944. He is seen here with tank crew comrades from the *Leibstandarte*.

By the final days of the war, Barkmann was in action around the town of Stuhlweissenburg, where he added four Soviet T-34 tanks to his score. By late March, Barkmann's unit had but six serviceable tanks remaining and was merged with the remnants of *SS-Panzer Regiment 1* under the command of Joachim Peiper.

By April 1945 Barkmann was involved in the defence of Vienna when his tank was mistaken for a Russian vehicle by a German soldier and hit by a *Panzerfaust* anti-tank projectile. Barkmann was seriously wounded.

Nevertheless, he attempted to continue, only to have his Panther slide into a massive bomb crater, where it was destroyed to prevent it falling into enemy hands. Barkmann and many of his comrades succeeded in making their way westwards to avoid Soviet captivity, and surrendered to British forces.

After the war, he returned to his native Schleswig-Holstein, where he became the *Burgermeister* of his home town. He is still alive. His final tally was an incredible 108 enemy tanks, 136 miscellaneous other vehicles and 43 enemy anti-tank guns.

SS-OBERSCHARFÜHRER BALTHASAR 'BOBBI' WOLL

In general terms, the vast majority of Panzer personnel who were decorated with the Knight's Cross of the Iron Cross were tank commanders, though the award was usually seen as recognition of the achievements of the entire crew. No tank commander could be successful without a first-class crew, and comparison with the U-boat commander in this respect is an apposite one, for in their case also the crew shared the hardships and suffering, and also had their achievements recognised by the award of the Knight's Cross to their commander as the figurehead representing the entire crew.

On rare occasions, however, one or more additional members might have played such an important part in the overall success of the crew that not only the commander, but they too, would be decorated with the Knight's Cross. Balthasar 'Bobbi' Woll was such a soldier.

Bobbi Woll was born on 1 September 1922 in Wemmetsweiler. He served originally in the elite *Leibstandarte*, and subsequently in *Schwere SS-Panzer Abteilung* *501*, the heavy-tank battalion of *1 SS-Panzerkorps*, of which the *Leibstandarte* was a key part.

He joined the crew of Michael Wittmann, and his innate accuracy in gunnery, as well as what appeared almost to be an ability to read Wittmann's mind, so well did he anticipate his commander's orders, contributed in no small part to the high rate of fire Wittmann's Tiger was able to sustain and consequent the ability to knock out enemy tanks before they could get their own shot in.

On 16 January 1944, on Wittmann's insistence, Woll was decorated with the Knight's Cross just two days after his commander for his part in Wittmann's sixty-six victories.

Woll was wounded in action during the fighting in Normandy, and it was while he was recovering in hospital that his commander and crew-comrades met their fate. Promoted to *SS-Unterscharführer*, Woll returned to combat service in early 1945, and was able to survive the last few hectic weeks of combat.

After the war, he lived quietly, working as an electrician, many assuming that he had died along with the rest of Wittmann's crew.

APPENDIX I

WAFFEN-SS RANKS

Rank	German Army Equivalent	Allied Equivalent
SS-Schütze	*Schütze*	Private
SS-Oberschütze	*Oberschütze*	Private First Class
SS-Sturmmann	*Gefreiter*	Lance-Corporal
SS-Rottenführer	*Obergefreiter*	Corporal
SS-Unterscharführer	*Unteroffizier*	Sergeant
SS-Scharführer	*Unterfeldwebel*	Staff Sergeant
SS-Oberscharführer	*Feldwebel*	QM Sergeant
SS-Hauptscharführer	*Oberfeldwebel*	Warrant Officer 2
SS-Stabsscharführer	*Stabsfeldwebel*	Warrant Officer 1
SS-Untersturmführer	*Leutnant*	2nd Lieutenant
SS-Obersturmführer	*Oberleutnant*	1st Lieutenant
SS-Hauptsturmführer	*Hauptmann*	Captain
SS-Sturmbannführer	*Major*	Major
SS-Obersturmbannführer	*Oberstleutnant*	Lieutenant-Colonel
SS-Standartenführer	*Oberst*	Colonel
SS-Oberführer		
SS-Brigadeführer	*Generalmajor*	Brigadier-General
SS-Gruppenführer	*Generalleutnant*	Major-General
SS-Obergruppenführer	*General*	Lieutenant-General
SS-Oberstgruppenführer	*Generaloberst*	General

It should be noted that while some basic ranks had direct equivalents, e.g. *Hauptsturmführer* to *Hauptmann*, some, like *SS-Oberführer*, had no direct equivalents, and others, such as some of the general ranks, had only approximate equivalents.

Waffen-SS ranks retained the 'SS-' prefix which was originally intended to differentiate between political organisations, SA, SS, NSKK, etc., which used the same rank titles. In order to emphasise their military status, general ranks also used a prefix linking their

SS rank to the Army equivalent, thus '*SS-Brigadeführer und Generalmajor der Waffen-SS*'. The rank of *Reichsführer-SS* had no direct military equivalent.

Officer candidates had specific rank titles, junior cadets being referred to as *SS-Standartenjunker* and senior cadets as *SS-Standartenoberjunker*. These personnel wore NCO insignia but with certain officer attributes, such as officer cap cords and officer piping to the collar patches.

APPENDIX II

CHRONOLOGY

March 1923	Formation of the *Stabswache*
May 1923	Formation of the *Stosstrupp Adolf Hitler*
9 November 1923	Abortive Putsch in Munich
20 December 1924	Hitler released from Landsberg Prison
April 1925	Hitler orders re-forming of his bodyguard unit
9 November 1925	Bodyguard renamed as the *'Schutz Staffel'*
6 January 1929	Heinrich Himmler appointed *Reichsführer-SS*
30 January 1933	Adolf Hitler becomes Chancellor after the Nazi Party achieves substantial victory in national elections
March 1933	First concentration camp opened at Dachau
17 March 1933	Formation of *Stabswache Berlin*
May 1933	Creation of *Sonderkommando Zossen*
September 1933	Bodyguard renamed as *Adolf Hitler Standarte*
9 November 1933	Birth of the *Leibstandarte SS Adolf Hitler*
30 June 1934	SA leadership eliminated by the SS in the 'Night of the Long Knives'
20 July 1934	SS declared a fully independent formation of the Nazi Party
24 September 1934	Creation of the *SS-Verfügungstruppe*
October 1934	Formation of the first officer training academy, *SS-Junkerschule Tölz*
1935	Establishment of *SS-Standarte 1 Deutschland*
29 March 1936	Creation of the *SS-Totenkopfverbände*
1936	Establishment of *SS-Standarte 2 Germania*
1938	Establishment of *SS-Standarte 3 Der Führer*
October 1938	SS-VT units take part in occupation of the Sudetenland
1 September 1939	*Leibstandarte SS Adolf Hitler*, *Deutschland* and *Germania* take part in the Polish Campaign on the outbreak of the Second World War
October 1939	First use of the term *'Waffen-SS'*
1939	SS-VT Regiments combined to form the *SS-Verfügungs Division*

1940	Formation of the *SS-Totenkopf Division*
	Creation of the first *Waffen-SS* unit to include substantial numbers of foreign volunteers, the *Wiking Division*
	Waffen-SS units play a major role in the attack through the Balkans, with *Leibstandarte* accepting the surrender of Greece
July 1941	Operation Barbarossa, the invasion of the Soviet Union, begins, with *Waffen-SS* units actively involved in the northern, central and southern sectors of the front
1942	The *Totenkopf Division* is instrumental in holding the Demjansk pocket against overwhelming odds
November 1942	The *Leibstandarte* captures Rostov
March 1943	The *SS-Panzerkorps* is driven out of Kharkov
	Paul Hausser's *SS-Panzerkorps* recaptures Kharkov
June 1943	*I* and *II SS-Panzerkorps* make greatest inroads into enemy territory during the ill-fated offensive at Kursk. World's greatest ever tank battle at Prokhorovka
June 1944	*SS-Panzer* Divisions holding area around Caen hold off Allied invasion forces for thirty-three days
July 1944	*SS-Hauptsturmführer* Michael Wittmann becomes highest-scoring tank ace in history after engagement against British units at Villers Bocage
	Single-handed defence of crossroads on the Saint Lô–Coutances road (Barkmann Corner) by tank ace *SS-Oberscharführer* Ernst Barkmann
September 1944	Successful defence of Arnhem against Allied airborne assault primarily by *SS-Panzer* troops from *Hohenstaufen* and *Frundsberg* Divisions commanded by Willi Bittrich
December 1944	SS heavy tank units commanded by *SS-Standartenführer* Jochen Peiper spearhead the German attack during the Ardennes Offensive
1945	Final major armoured assault on the Eastern Front around Lake Balaton in Hungary, led by *I SS-Panzerkorps*

GLOSSARY

Allgemeine-SS	The 'general' SS, as opposed to the *Waffen-SS*, originally a part-time volunteer force. These are the personnel who predominantly wore the black service uniform with swastika armband
Geheime Staatspolizei	*Gestapo*, or Secret State Police, controlled by the SS
Gesamt-SS	The 'whole' SS, comprising both *Allgemeine* and *Waffen-SS*
Heer	Army
Heeresgruppe	Army Group
Höhere SS und Polizei Führer	Higher SS and Police Leader, commander of SS Security Forces in the occupied territories
Oberabschnitt	An SS organisational area equivalent to the *Wehrkreis*, or Military District, of the *Wehrmacht*
Ordnungspolizei	Order Police, from which the *SS-Polizei Division* and the *SS-Feldgendarmerie* were initially recruited
Reichsdeutsche	German citizens born within the Reich
Reichsführer-SS	Commander-in-Chief of the entire SS
Reichssicherheitshauptamt	State Security Headquarters, which controlled the SD and *Gestapo*
Schutz Staffel	The SS. The term was first coined by Hermann Göring during the First World War to describe aircraft flying escort missions
Sicherheitsdienst	SS Security and intelligence service
SS-Hauptamt	SS Main Office, responsible for recruitment into the *Waffen-SS*
Standarte	SS unit equivalent to a Regiment
Sturm	SS unit equivalent to a Company
Sturmbann	SS unit equivalent to a Battalion
Totenkopfstandarte	Regimental-sized SS Deathshead units originally formed to staff the concentration camps
Totenkopfverbände	Collective name for the various Deathshead units
Verfügungstruppe	Armed SS troops at the disposal of the regime
Volksdeutsche	Person born outside Germany to parents with German blood, i.e. an 'ethnic' German

Waffen-SS	Armed SS
Wehrkreis	Military District
Wehrmacht	Armed Forces
Wirtschafts und	Economics and Administration Main Office
Verwaltungshauptamt	

BIBLIOGRAPHY

Angolia, John R., *Cloth Insignia of the SS*, R. James Bender Publishing, San Jose, 1983

Buss, P.H. and Mollo A., *Hitler's Germanic Legions*, McDonald & Janes, London, 1978

Beaver, Michael D., *Uniforms of the Waffen-SS*, Vols 1–3, Schiffer Military History, Atglen, 2002

Krawczyk, Wade and von Lukacs, Peter, *Waffen-SS Uniforms & Insignia*, Crowood Press, Marlborough, 2001

Krätschmer, E.G., *Die Ritterkreuzträger der Waffen-SS*, 3rd Edition, Verlag K.W. Schütz KG, Preussisch Oldendorf, 1982

Littlejohn, David, *Foreign Legions of the Third Reich*, Vols 1–4, R. James Bender Publishing, San Jose, 1979–87

Mann, Dr Chris, *SS-Totenkopf*, Spellmount, Staplehurst, 2001

Mattson, Gregory L., *SS-Das Reich*, Spellmount, Staplehurst, 2002

Messenger, Charles, *Hitler's Gladiator*, Brasseys, London, 1988

von Preradovich, Nikolaus, *Die Generale der Waffen-SS*, Kurt Vowinkel Verlag KG, Berg am See, 1985

Stein, George H., *Waffen-SS, Hitler's Elite Guard at War*, Cornell, New York, 1966/Cerberus, Bristol, 2002

Sydnor, Charles, *Soldiers of Destruction*, Princeton University Press, Princeton, 1977

Wegner, Bernd, *The Waffen-SS*, Basil Blackwell, Oxford, 1990

INDEX

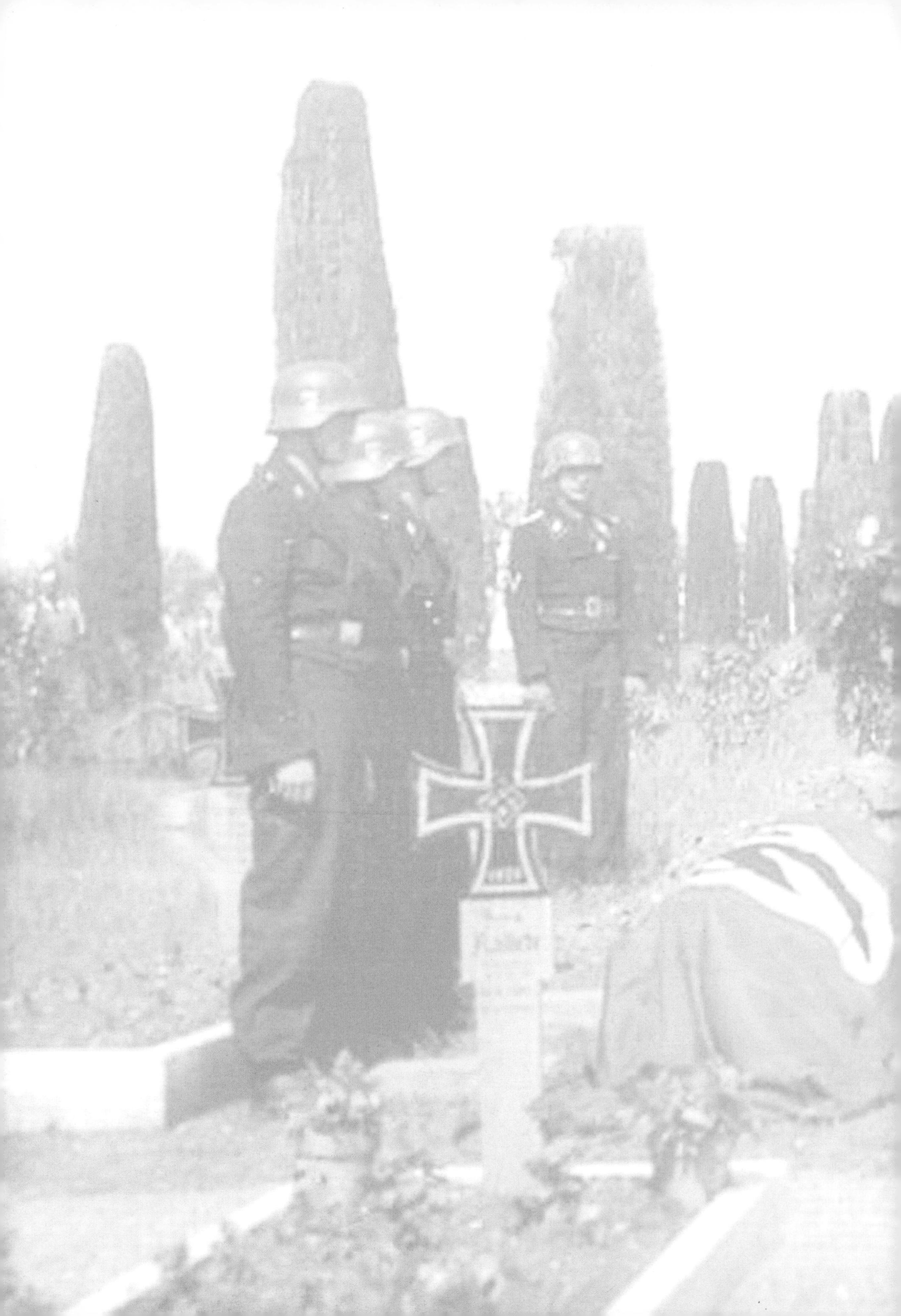

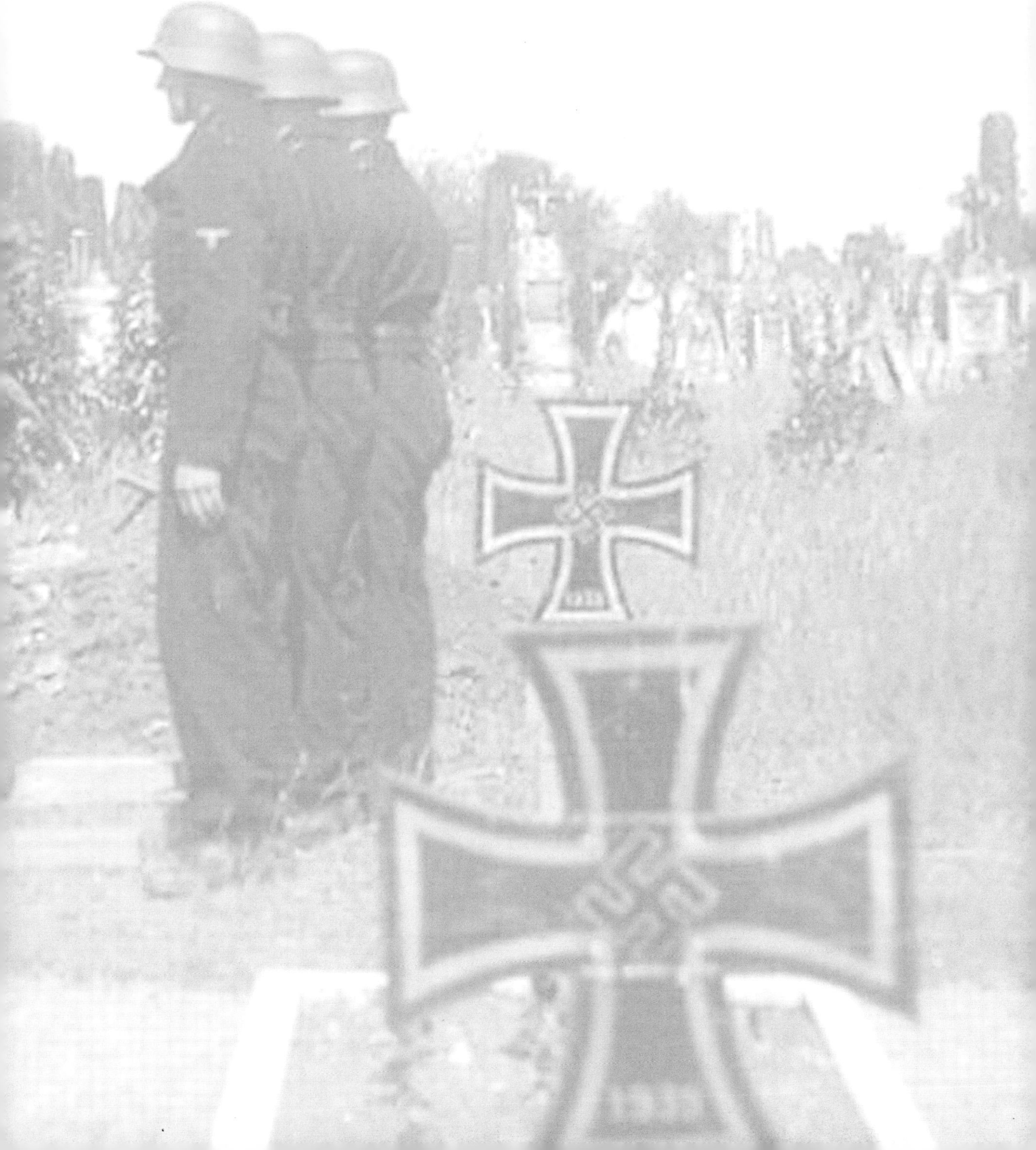

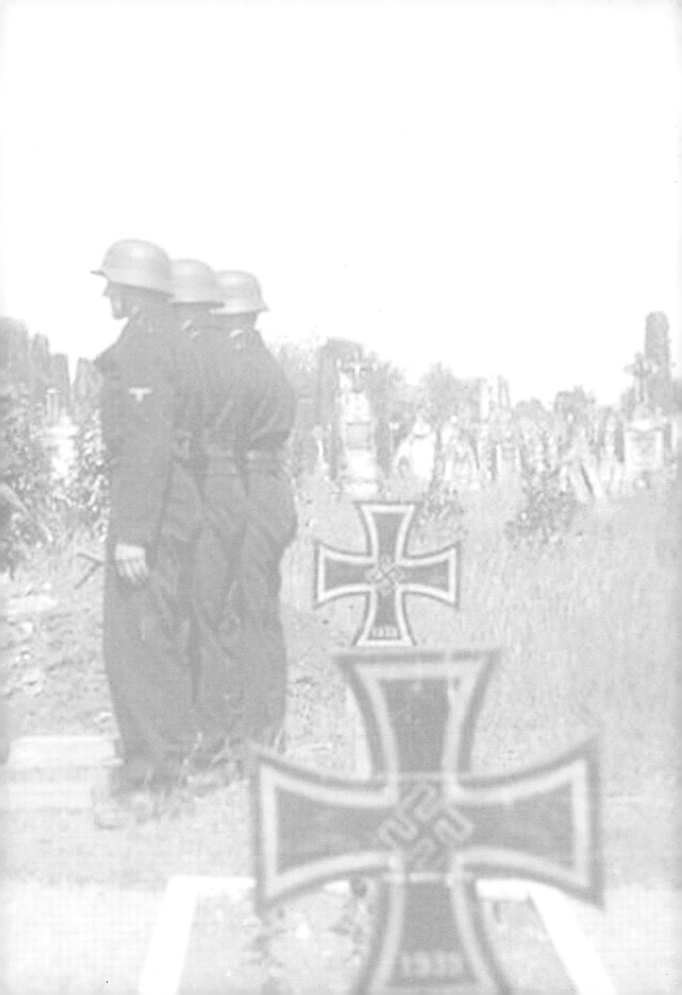